Lecture Notes in Computer Science   8490

Commenced Publication in 1973
Founding and Former Series Editors:
Gerhard Goos, Juris Hartmanis, and Jan van Leeuwen

Marina L. Gavrilova   C.J. Kenneth Tan
Xiaoyang Mao   Lichan Hong (Eds.)

Transactions on Computational Science XXIII

Special Issue on Cyberworlds

 Springer

Editors-in-Chief

Marina L. Gavrilova
University of Calgary, AB, Canada
E-mail: mgavrilo@ucalgary.ca

C.J. Kenneth Tan
CloudFabriQ Ltd., London, UK
E-mail: cjtan@CloudFabriQ.com

Guest Editors

Xiaoyang Mao
University of Yamanashi, Japan
E-mail: mao@yamanashi.ac.jp

Lichan Hong
Google Research, Palo Alto, CA, USA
E-mail: lichan.hong@gmail.com

ISSN 0302-9743 (LNCS)   e-ISSN 1611-3349 (LNCS)
ISSN 1866-4733 (TCOMPSCIE)   e-ISSN 1866-4741 (TCOMPSCIE)
ISBN 978-3-662-43789-6   e-ISBN 978-3-662-43790-2
DOI 10.1007/978-3-662-43790-2
Springer Heidelberg New York Dordrecht London

Typesetting: Camera-ready by author, data conversion by Scientific Publishing Services, Chennai, India

Printed on acid-free paper

Springer is part of Springer Science+Business Media (www.springer.com)

LNCS Transactions on Computational Science

Computational science, an emerging and increasingly vital field, is now widely recognized as an integral part of scientific and technical investigations, affecting researchers and practitioners in areas ranging from aerospace and automotive research to biochemistry, electronics, geosciences, mathematics, and physics. Computer systems research and the exploitation of applied research naturally complement each other. The increased complexity of many challenges in computational science demands the use of supercomputing, parallel processing, sophisticated algorithms, and advanced system software and architecture. It is therefore invaluable to have input by systems research experts in applied computational science research.

Transactions on Computational Science focuses on original high-quality research in the realm of computational science in parallel and distributed environments, also encompassing the underlying theoretical foundations and the applications of large-scale computation.

The journal offers practitioners and researchers the opportunity to share computational techniques and solutions in this area, to identify new issues, and to shape future directions for research, and it enables industrial users to apply leading-edge, large-scale, high-performance computational methods.

In addition to addressing various research and application issues, the journal aims to present material that is validated – crucial to the application and advancement of the research conducted in academic and industrial settings. In this spirit, the journal focuses on publications that present results and computational techniques that are verifiable.

Scope

The scope of the journal includes, but is not limited to, the following computational methods and applications:

- Aeronautics and Aerospace
- Astrophysics
- Big Data Analytics
- Bioinformatics
- Biometric Technologies
- Climate and Weather Modeling
- Communication and Data Networks
- Compilers and Operating Systems
- Computer Graphics
- Computational Biology
- Computational Chemistry

- Computational Finance and Econometrics
- Computational Fluid Dynamics
- Computational Geometry
- Computational Number Theory
- Data Representation and Storage
- Data Mining and Data Warehousing
- Information and Online Security
- Grid Computing
- Hardware/Software Co-design
- High-Performance Computing
- Image and Video Processing
- Information Systems
- Information Retrieval
- Modeling and Simulations
- Mobile Computing
- Numerical and Scientific Computing
- Parallel and Distributed Computing
- Robotics and Navigation
- Supercomputing
- System-on-Chip Design and Engineering
- Virtual Reality and Cyberworlds
- Visualization

Editorial

The Transactions on Computational Science journal is part of the Springer series *Lecture Notes in Computer Science*, and is devoted to the gamut of computational science issues, from theoretical aspects to application-dependent studies and the validation of emerging technologies.

The journal focuses on original high-quality research in the realm of computational science in parallel and distributed environments, encompassing the facilitating theoretical foundations and the applications of large-scale computations and massive data processing. Practitioners and researchers share computational techniques and solutions in the area, identify new issues, and shape future directions for research, as well as enabling industrial users to apply the techniques presented.

The current volume, edited by Xiaoyang Mao and Lichan Hong, is devoted to the topic of security in virtual worlds. It is comprised of the 11 best papers selected from numerous submissions to The International Conference on Cyberworlds 2013, held at Keio University, Yokohama, Japan, October 21–23, 2013.

We would like to extend our sincere appreciation to the special issue guest editors for their diligent work in preparing this special issue. We would also like to thank all of the authors for submitting their papers to the special issue and the associate editors and referees for their valuable work.

It is our hope that the fine collection of papers presented in this special issue will be a valuable resource for Transactions on Computational Science readers and will stimulate further research into the vibrant area of computer security.

March 2014

Marina L. Gavrilova
C.J. Kenneth Tan

Guest Editors' Preface
Special Issue on Cyberworlds

Cyberworlds are information worlds or communities created in cyberspace by participants collaborating, either intentionally or spontaneously. As information worlds, they accumulate information regardless of whether or not anyone is in, and they can be with or without 2D or 3D visual graphics appearance. Examples of such cyberworlds are communities created in different social networking services, 3D shared virtual environments, and multiplayer online games. Cyberworlds are closely related to the real world and have a serious impact on it, augmenting and sometimes replacing real life.

The present issue is devoted to the state-of-the-art computational technologies of cyberworlds. It contains the extended versions of 11 articles presented at the 2013 International Conference on Cyberworlds, Yokohama, Japan, covering the following 5 most fundamental topics of cyberworlds.

1. Modeling (2 papers)

The first paper, entitled "Incrementally Modular Abstraction Hierarchy Using Algebraic Topology", by Kenji Ohmori and Tosiyasu L. Kunii, introduces a new design method called incrementally modular abstraction hierarchy (IMAH) for modeling cyberworlds with seven levels of abstraction hierarchy. This design method, which is generally applicable to different applications, contributes to the theoretical fundamentals of cyberworlds. The second paper, entitled "Fast and Stable Deformations Using the Mesh Intersection Algorithm", by Luis F. Gutiérrez, Sergio Vargas, and Félix Ramos, addresses the deformation of objects. The paper proposes a new method for solving the stability problem of explicit integration schemes in simulating deformable objects and makes it possible to simulate a volumetric mesh using limited time step by employing another optimal surface.

2. Rendering

Perceptually enhanced rendering is becoming more and more important for effective and smooth communication in cyberwords. "Gaussian Curvature Based Localized Stylization Method for View-Dependent Lines Extracted from 3D Models", by Luis Cardona and Suguru Saito, introduces a new expressive rendering technique, which can stylize individual lines of 3D models while preserving their properties when the viewpoint is changed. "Image-Driven Haptic Rendering", by Shahzad Rasool and Alexei Sourin, proposes a new image-driven haptic rendering where a displayed image is used as a source of the force-feedback calculations at any pixel touched by the haptic device. While traditional haptic interaction requires the content creators to make haptic models of the virtual objects, the proposed technique makes it possible to use image and video for haptic communication.

3. Motion

Motion is another fundamental topic related to the modeling of the dynamics of cyberworlds.

"Multi-touch Interface and Motion Control Model for Interactive Character Animation", by Masaki Oshita, proposes a novel method for interactive motion control with a multi-touch interface. With the new system, a user can create various natural-looking motions simply by touching and dragging a character's body parts. "Audio-Visual Art Performance System Using Computer Video Output Based on Component Video to Audio Signal Conversion", by Yuichi Ito, Carl Stone, Masashi Yamada, and Shinya Miyazaki, presents a new method for controlling video images during a performance using video signals in the audio domain. The proposed method seeks to create a unique relationship between video and audio signals, and shows a new perspective regarding the use of computational devices.

4. Virtual Environments

Three papers on virtual environments are included in this special issue demonstrating the applications of cyberworld technologies to virtual travel, sports, and medicine. The first paper, entitled "Collision-Free Navigation with Extended Terrain Maps", by Andrei Sherstyuk and Kiyoshi Kiyokawa, shows how the problem of collision detection can be reduced from 3D to 2D when navigation is constrained to moving on a terrain surface. A new improved system is presented which is capable of processing collisions for various types of virtual travelers, ranging from immersed VR users to autonomous virtual agents, in dynamically changing environments with moving obstacles. The second paper, entitled "Efficacy of a Virtual Environment for Training Ball Passing Skills in Rugby", by Helen C. Miles, Serban R. Pop, Simon J. Watt, Gavin P. Lawrence, Nigel W. John, Vincent Perrot, Pierre Mallet, Daniel R. Mestre, and Kenton Morgan, presents a configurable virtual environment to train rugby ball passing skills. Two experiments were performed to validate the system's ability to correctly aid training. The third paper, "Preparing for International Operations and Developing Scenarios for Inter-cultural Communication in a Cyberworld: A Norwegian Army Example", by Ekaterina Prasolova-Førland, Mikhail Fominykh, Ramin Darisiro, Anders I. Mørch, and David Hansen, addresses the challenge of using virtual space for cultural awareness training. Methodology and training scenarios, performed with the cadets of the Norwegian Academy, in which participants were expected to face different cultural challenges, are presented.

5. Affective Computing

Affective computing is a relatively new and challenging topic of cyberworlds. This special issue includes two interesting papers addressing the problem of how

to predict the emotion of users from biological sensor data. The first paper, entitled "Experiments for Emotion Estimation from Biological Signals and Its Application", by Masaki Omata, Daisuke Kanuka, and Xiaoyang Mao, takes a model-based approach and describes elementary experiments for training multiple regression systems to estimate the emotion of a user from the biological signals of the user's central nervous system, such as cerebral blood flow and brain wave. To demonstrate the effectiveness of the proposed emotion estimation technique in emotion-based interaction, an emotional painting tool that dynamically adapts the colors of brush and the outline of canvas to the estimated emotion of the user is also presented. The second paper, entitled "Real-Time Subject-Dependent EEG-Based Emotion Recognition Algorithm", by Yisi Liu and Olga Sourina, takes an example-based approach for estimating a subject's emotion based on EEG. The proposed algorithm covers two parts: feature extraction and data classification with Support Vector Machine (SVM), and can recognize up to 8 emotions in real time.

The guest editors hope that readers of the *Transactions on Computational Science* (TCS) will benefit from the papers presented in this special issue on the latest advances in cyberworld technologies. We are deeply grateful to the TCS Editor-in-Chief Professor Marina L. Gavrilova and all of the editorial staff for their continuing support and assistance during the whole process.

March 2014   Xiaoyang Mao
                                                              Lichan Hong

LNCS Transactions on Computational Science – Editorial Board

Table of Contents

Incrementally Modular Abstraction Hierarchy Using Algebraic Topology

Kenji Ohmori[1] and Tosiyasu L. Kunii[2]

[1] Hosei University, Computer and Information Sciences
3-7-2 Kajino-cho, Koganei-shi 184-8584, Japan
`ohmori@hosei.ac.jp`
[2] Morpho Inc
Iidabashi First Tower 31F
2-6-1 Koraku, Bunkyo-ku, Tokyo 112-0004, Japan
`kunii@ieee.org`

Abstract. We have introduced a new design method called incrementally modular abstraction hierarchy (IMAH). IMAH is based on algebraic topology and it provides seven levels of abstraction hierarchy. Using IMAH, designers can begin their development at any level of the abstraction hierarchy. By ascending the hierarchy, they can generalize their design. By descending it, they can specialize their development. When complete, they are able to consider the entire conceptual and physical view of what they have achieved through their work. Though IMAH is a powerful tool, it requires only a simple explanation to be accepted by most researchers and developers. In this paper, we will use basic mathematical concepts, pushouts and pullbacks, to show how systems can be designed in both bottom-up and top-down fashions.

Keywords: design method, abstraction hierarchy, homotopy, pushout, pullback.

1 Introduction

There are few design methods and methodologies that are able to address the design requirements of two different application fields using the same tools and methods. Incrementally modular abstraction hierarchy (IMAH) [5] is exceptional in such circumstances. IMAH provides a general paradigm for designing systems in different application fields such as computer science, information technology, software engineering, and cyberworlds. IMAH is based on algebraic topology that combines geometry and algebra to provide additional general concepts in the field of mathematics. The mathematical combination of geometry and algebra is extended to provide a general paradigm in the field of design for many application areas. To verify the generality of IMAH, we have already applied IMAH to Kaleidoscope analysis [4], a logical thinking method [12], Japanese house architecture [11], a 3D sketchbook development [14], and an accounting system design [10].

M.L. Gavrilova et al. (Eds.): Trans. on Comput. Sci. XXIII, LNCS 8490, pp. 1–20, 2014.

IMAH is characterized by a hierarchical abstraction structure. Design is generalized by ascending the abstraction hierarchy and specialized by descending it. When designing a system, an abstraction model or concrete model of the system can be proposed by ascending or descending it, respectively. The properties that are proposed at an upper abstraction level are retained in the lower levels as invariants. A model in a lower abstraction level not only inherits the properties defined at the upper abstraction levels but also adds its own properties.

Previous papers explained how IMAH can be utilized as a design method and methodology in a formal manner using the modern mathematics of homotopy lifting and extension properties (HLP and HEP) [1]. However, because the mathematical concepts of HLP and HEP are difficult to comprehend without an understanding of algebraic topology, homotopy in particular, utilization of IMAH has been limited to only a few researchers. This paper is an extended version of the paper [13] that proposed more understandable utilization of IMAH using pushouts and pullbacks [8]. These are general concepts that cover set theory, homotopy theory, and category theory. In this paper, additional practical examples are included.

A complicated system is generally designed by dividing it into simple subsystems. These are further divided into sub-subsystems[6]. The design method of dividing a complicated system into simple subsystems on a systematic basis is generalized to a method that divides the system into two subsystems. This is called the divide-and-conquer method. This paper describes an IMAH utilization method for system design that also involves dividing the system into two subsystems.

The IMAH design method is separated into two parts. One part is application independent and general and is carried out at the upper abstraction levels. The other part is domain specific and is implemented at the lower, concrete levels. In this paper, we primarily describe the design method effectuated at the upper abstraction levels. The basic idea follows. A system is divided into two subsystems using a pushout and the two subsystems are combined into a system using a pullback. A pushout or pullback is utilized to ascend or descend the abstraction hierarchy. An abstract model or concrete model is proposed in the design process.

IMAH uses seven levels in its abstraction hierarchy: (1) the homotopy level that gives a designer the fundamental structure of a designed system; (2) the set-theoretical level that defines the elements of the system; (3) the topological space level that provides geometric relationships of the elements; (4) the adjunction space level that describes how the subsystems composing the system are connected; (5) the cellular space level that defines the physical dimension of the system; (6) the presentation level that describes how the system is modeled; and (7) the view (code) level that describes the implementation of the system. The first five levels are general and are independent of the application field. The remaining two levels are domain-specific. The conceptual (domain independent) design is carried out mainly from the homotopy level to the cellular space level. The physical (domain dependent) design is performed in the remaining levels.

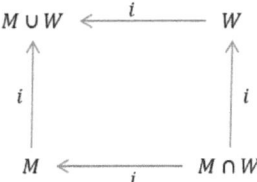

Fig. 1. The structure of the community is represented by a pushout and a pullback

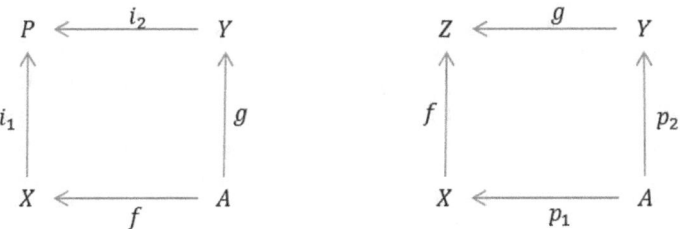

Fig. 2. The commutative diagrams of a pushout (left) and pullback (right)

2 Examples of Pushouts and Pullbacks

Before explaining the mathematical concepts of pushouts and pullbacks, let us look at a simple example that demonstrates their usefulness. Suppose that we are interested in the human relationships of a community and consider representing its structure. The community is somewhat peculiar. It is composed of a set of houses in each of which only one man lives, only one woman lives, or a man and a woman live together as a couple. Let the set of houses in which a man lives be represented by M (a house in which a couple lives is included in this set) and the set of houses in which a woman lives be represented by W.

The set of all the houses in the community can therefore be represented by $M \cup W$ and the set of houses in which a couple lives by $M \cap W$. A logical-OR $\cup$ gives a pushout and a logical-AND $\cap$ does a pullback. The structure of the community is shown in Fig. 1 where i is an inclusion.

A pushout is defined as follows. Given two morphisms $f : A \to X$ and $g : A \to Y$, the pushout of the morphisms f and g consists of an object P and two morphisms $i_1 : X \to P$ and $i_2 : Y \to P$ such that $i_1 \circ f = i_2 \circ g$. The diagram as shown in Fig. 2 (left) commutes.

In the above definition, a morphism refers to a structure-preserving mapping from one space to another. In set theory, a morphism is a function. In topology, it is a continuous function.

A pullback is defined as follows. Suppose that there are two morphisms $f : X \to Z$ and $g : Y \to Z$. The pullback of the morphisms f and g consists of an object P and two morphisms $p_1 : P \to X$ and $p_2 : P \to Y$ such that $f \circ p_1 = g \circ p_2$. The diagram as shown in Fig. 2 (right) commutes.

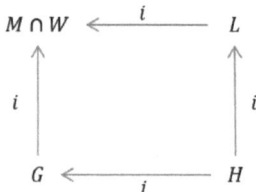

Fig. 3. The community is further specified by dividing it into a sub-community

From the commutative diagram in Fig. 1, it can be seen that $M \cap W$ is divided into$M$ and W by the two i's. These constitute a pushout $M \cup W$. From this example, it is shown that if there are two components constituting a system by sharing some part each other, the whole system is obtained by combining the two components. The pushout is interpreted as a process for composing a system from components in a bottom-up manner. It becomes clearer by explaining an attaching function in the next section.

It can also be seen that M and W are assembled into $M \cup W$ by the two i's. These constitute a pullback $M \cap W$. From this example, it is shown that if there is a system, the system may be separated into two individual components that share the same property or a common space. The pullback is explained as a process for decomposing a system into its components such as the divide-and-conquer method in a top-down fashion.

The community is further specified by dividing it into a sub-community. Suppose that we want to know what couples speak the same language. Let the couples who do so be represented by a set H. Also, let us represent couples whose age difference is more than five years by a set G and the others by L. In the commutative diagram of the pullback originating from $M \cap W$, it can be seen that the pullback of $i : G \to M \cap W$ and $i : L \to M \cap W$ is

$$(H, i : H \to G, i : H \to L), \tag{1}$$

as shown in Fig. 3.

3   Attaching Functions

The above solution to the couple problem is complicated. If sets of men M and women W are used instead of the sets of houses for men and houses for women, $M \cap W$ would no longer represent the set of couples. However, if an attaching function is used, the problem could be solved directly using the sets of men and women. The attaching map [16] is defined as follows.

Suppose that X is a topological space and is attached by another topological space Y, then:

$$Y_f = Y \sqcup_f X = Y \sqcup X / \sim \tag{2}$$

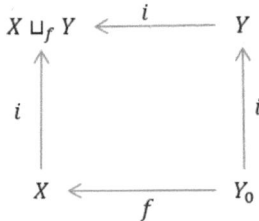

Fig. 4. The attaching map constitutes a pushout

is an attaching space obtained by attaching Y to X by an attaching map f (or by identifying each point $y \in Y_0|Y_0 \subseteq Y$ with its image $f(y) \in X$ by a continuous map f). $\sqcup$ denotes a disjoint union. The attaching map f is a continuous map such that $f : Y_0 \to X$, where $Y_0 \subseteq Y$. Thus, the attaching space $Y_f = Y \sqcup X/ \sim$ is a case of quotient spaces:

$$Y \sqcup X/ \sim = Y \sqcup_f X = Y \sqcup X/(y \sim f(y)|\forall y \in Y_0). \qquad (3)$$

The identification map g in this case is:

$$g : Y \sqcup X \to Y \sqcup_f X = Y_f = Y \sqcup X/ \sim = (Y \sqcup X - Y_0) \sqcup Y_0. \qquad (4)$$

The commutative diagram of the attaching map is depicted in Fig. 4.

The couple problem is resolved by representing the set of men by X, the set of women by Y, the set of women who are part of a couple by Y_0, and providing an attaching map f that gives the woman constituting a couple her partner.

Comparing Figs. 1 and 4 shows that the common area of the two spaces in Fig. 1 is replaced by the common area of one space that is attached to another space in Fig. 4. The union of the two spaces in Fig. 1 is replaced by the disjoint union of two spaces in Fig. 4. From the commutative diagrams, it can be seen that a rather complicated space consisting of two spaces is obtained by separating it into two spaces from the common area using a pushout and integrating them using a pullback.

4 Designing a Chair

Consider the design of a chair comprised of a seat and stand. IMAH allows the design to start at any level of the abstraction hierarchy. As the chair has two components, we can start the design from the adjunction space level, where the two components are attached. Let the seat and stand be topological spaces X and Y and the attaching space of the stand be a topological space $Y_0 \subseteq Y$. Using an attaching map f, the commutative diagram obtained is shown in Fig. 5.

By ascending IMAH, the design of the chair progresses towards more abstract models as shown in Fig. 6. At the topological space level, the topological spaces X and Y are defined. At the set-theoretical level, the chair is defined as a set C that

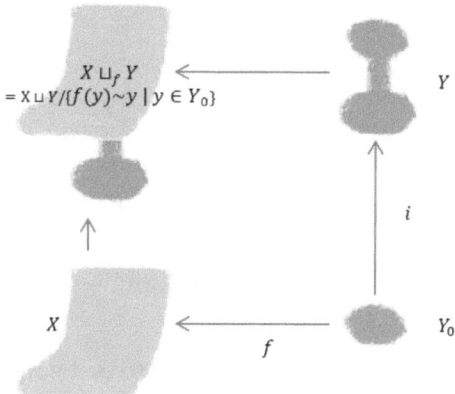

Fig. 5. Design of the chair starts from the adjunction space level using components

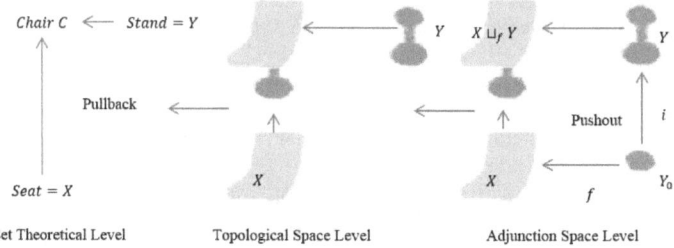

Fig. 6. Design of the chair progresses towards the abstract levels by ascending IMAH

has the seat X and the stand Y as its components, that is, $C = \{X, Y\}$. On this level, set C is divided into subsets X and Y, from which a pullback is constructed. As the chair is a single entity without holes, it is homotopically equivalent to a disk at the homotopy level or belongs to the fundamental group 0.

By descending IMAH, the design of the chair progresses towards more concrete models, as shown in Fig. 7. At the cellular space level, the topological spaces X and Y are transformed into closure-finite weak topology (CW) complexes by keeping the mathematical structure defined at the topological space level or at levels that are more abstract. In Fig. 7, two cells, e_0^2 and e_0^3, are provided for the surface of the stand. Another two cells, e_1^2 and e_1^3, are provided for the surface of the seat. e_0^2 and e_1^2, which are two-dimensional, are the attaching spaces. e_0^3 and e_1^3, which are three-dimensional, represent the rest of the bodies excluding the attaching space. At the presentation level, the chair is represented as CAD data. At the view level, a mock-up of the seat is displayed.

In summary, the chair was designed starting from the middle of the abstraction level. From the adjunction space level, the design was carried out by ascending the abstraction hierarchy. The attached space, represented by Y_0, was

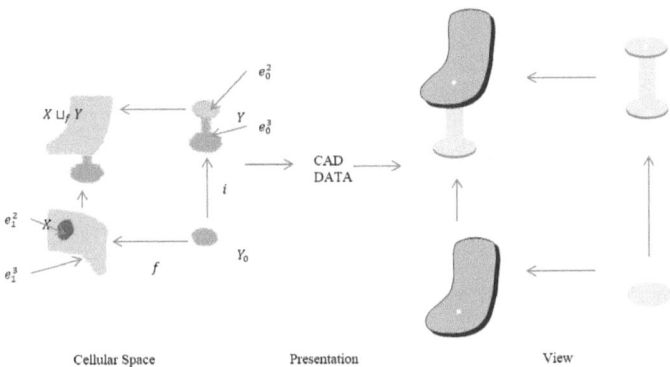

Cellular Space   Presentation   View

Fig. 7. Design of the chair progresses towards the concrete levels by descending IMAH

divided into the two spaces Y and X. The disjoint union of X and Y was then constructed.

Alternatively, the chair can be designed from the most abstract level to the most concrete level. In this case, at the homotopy level, the chair is represented as an entity belonging to the fundamental group 0 (or a disk). At the set-theoretical level, the chair is represented by set C. Set C consists of two elements, X and Y, which represent the seat and the stand, respectively. At this level, the chair is constructed as the disjoint union of X and Y and the pullback of $i : X \rightarrow C$ and $i : Y \rightarrow C$ and is ready for descending the abstraction hierarchy. The set-theoretical level inherits the property from the homotopy level.

At the topological space level, the topological spaces are introduced to X and Y. The topological space level also inherits the properties of the set-theoretical level. At the adjunction space level, the attaching function is introduced to attach Y to X. This level again inherits the properties of the topological space level.

At the cellular space level, the cells are introduced to explain how X and Y are constructed by the cells e_0^2, e_1^2, e_0^3, and e_1^3. The cellular space level also inherits the properties of the adjunction space level. Then, by keeping the properties of the cellular space level, the presentation and view levels, which are domain specific, are designed.

5   Designing a Concurrent System

There is an interesting example of a concurrent system on page 50 in the book *Communicating Sequential Processes* [3]. The example, which we slightly modify in this paper, is used to show the design process for a concurrent system by describing the behavior of a counter that starts at the center square on a board, and may move within the board *up*, *down*, *left* or *right*. Figure 8 shows the board and the initial position of the counter. (The original example consists of two columns and three rows and shows that the counter movement can be described using the concurrency of vertical and horizontal movements.)

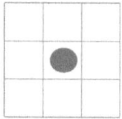

Fig. 8. The counter moves around the board

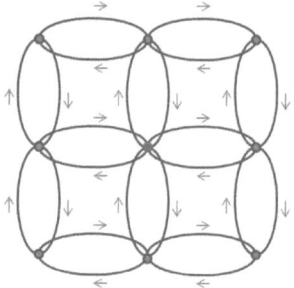

Fig. 9. Movements of the counter are described by paths

Let us start our design of the concurrent system from the homotopy level and continue by descending the abstraction hierarchy and presenting a model at each level that assists in showing how properties defined at an abstract level are preserved at a concrete level.

The homotopy level, as shown in Fig. 9, provides independent paths (movements) that start from the initial point and end at the initial point. (A multiple circle that visits the initial point multiple times is also allowed.)

When descending the abstraction hierarchy to the set-theoretical level, paths are divided into vertical and horizontal movements. For each movement, sets H and V are provided as shown in Fig. 10.

H consists of three positions: the initial point H_1, the right corner H_0, and the left corner H_2; and two movements: $right$ and $left$. V is also prepared in the same way. H and V are later used to construct a pullback.

$$H = \{Sq = \{H_0, H_1, H_2\}, Act = \{right, left\}\},$$
$$V = \{Sq = \{V_0, V_1, V_2\}, Act = \{up, down\}\}. \tag{5}$$

At the topological space level, a topological space is induced to each set. At the adjunction space level, the original point of both H and V are attached, as shown in Fig. 11. At this level, the pullback is complete.

At the cellular space level, H and V become state transition diagrams in which a square and an action become zero-dimensional and one-dimensional cells, respectively.

At the presentation level, concurrent processes are obtained from the cellular space level as shown in Fig. 12.

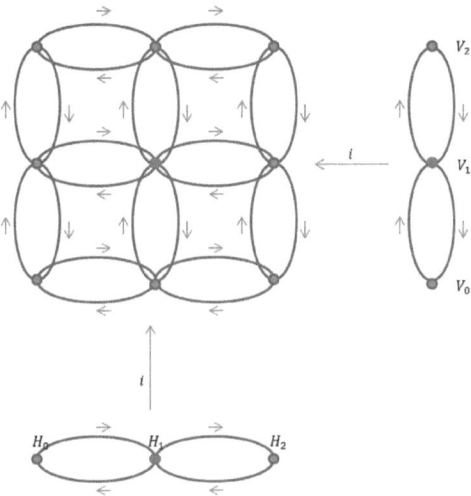

Fig. 10. Counter movements are separated into two sets

The above solution is slightly modified if the counter can move diagonally, *up-left*, *up-right*, *down-left*, or *down-right*, which is a simultaneous movement in the horizontal and vertical direction. These movements are added in *Acts* of H and V at the set-theoretical level and the following concrete levels are slightly modified by adding these properties. The state transition diagrams that are obtained by the cellular space level are similar to the previous one. Only the diagonal movements are added to the previous one.

At the presentation level, H is changed to

$$\begin{aligned} H = ((\ right|up\text{-}right|down\text{-}right \to \\ left|up\text{-}left|down\text{-}left \to H)| \\ (\ left|up\text{-}left|down\text{-}left \to \\ right|up\text{-}right|down\text{-}right \to H)). \end{aligned} \qquad (6)$$

V is similarly changed. If a diagonal movement such as *up-left*, *up-right*, *down-left*, or *down-right* is received by this system, horizontal and vertical movements are simultaneously performed.

In summary, when we design an object that is composed of two parts by descending IMAH, the object is categorized at the homotopy level. Then, at the set-theoretical level, it is composed of two elements representing the parts. This process is in preparation for a pullback. Then, the object and parts are represented as topological spaces that give them geometrical presentation. At the adjunction space level, the pullback that has been prepared at the set-theoretical level is completed by providing the attaching function and attached space. The following two examples are designed in this manner.

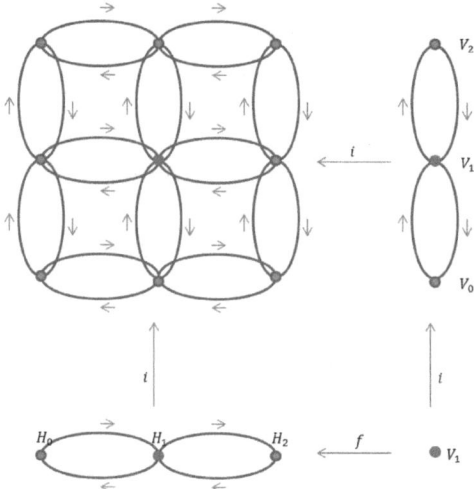

Fig. 11. The attaching function is used to join the two topological spaces

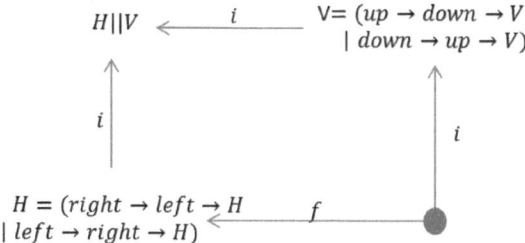

Fig. 12. Concurrent processes for the counter are obtained from the cellular space level

6   Designing an Embedded System

An embedded system that realizes its tasks with both hardware and software is a challenging technology. The embedded system is equipped with motors and sensors that receive environmental information and are activated or inactivated by the received information. When designing an embedded system, services that the embedded system provides for its user are defined. Each service is divided into several tasks. Each task is performed by hardware, software, or their combination.

The design of a line-tracing car is shown as a simple example of an embedded system. The line-tracing car runs along a black line while avoiding barriers. When the car encounters a barrier, it turns around and goes the other way. In addition, the black line has branches. The car has to choose one of them when it encounters a branch. Furthermore, we assume that the car is equipped with four devices: a line-sensor array that detects a line, an ultra-sonic sensor that detects

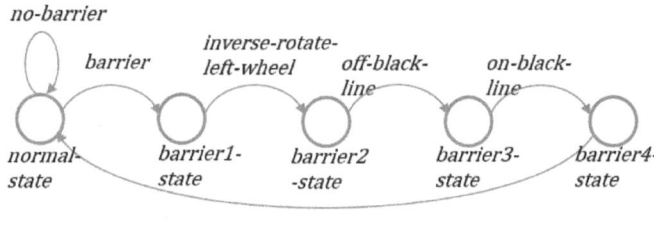

Fig. 13. The task of avoiding a barrier is a sequence of events that constitutes a topological graph

a barrier, and two motors that rotate the right and left wheels. The line-tracing car is implemented using LEGO blocks [2] with an event-driven and multi-thread processor [7], the motors, and the sensors.

Moreover, we assume the software system provides five services: controlling the car, detecting the black line, detecting barriers, rotating the left wheel, and rotating the right wheel.

After assembling LEGO blocks and designing the hardware system, the software system must be designed. The development of the software system is carried out using Agile software development where the most risky and important service is designed first. After completing the design and implementation, the next riskiest and important service is designed. In Agile software development, this process is repeated until the entire system is completed.

Among the software services that are provided with the line-tracing car, controlling the car is considered as the most risky and important. It is further divided into three tasks: running the car, avoiding a barrier, and selecting a path when encountering a branch. Let us try to design the task of avoiding a barrier.

Using IMAH, the task of avoiding a barrier is designed as follows.

At the homotopy level, it belongs to the fundamental group 0 since it consists of only one entity.

At the set-theoretical level, the following set is obtained:

$$
\begin{aligned}
TB = \{ &normal\text{-}state, barrier\text{-}state, on\text{-}black\text{-}line, off\text{-}black\text{-}line, \\
&barrier, non\text{-}barrier, rotate\text{-}right\text{-}wheel, \\
&inverse\text{-}rotate\text{-}right\text{-}wheel, rotate\text{-}left\text{-}wheel, \\
&inverse\text{-}rotate\text{-}left\text{-}wheel \}.
\end{aligned} \tag{7}
$$

In the above set, necessary states and events are included. At the topological space level, the sequence of events that constitutes a topological graph is determined. The task of avoiding a barrier is depicted in Fig. 13.

Similarly, the task of operating the car is obtained, as shown in Fig. 14.

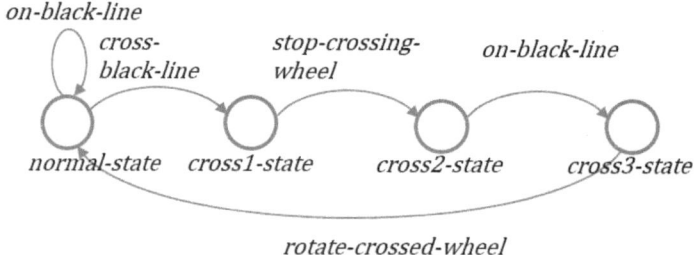

Fig. 14. The task of operating the car is represented by a sequence of events

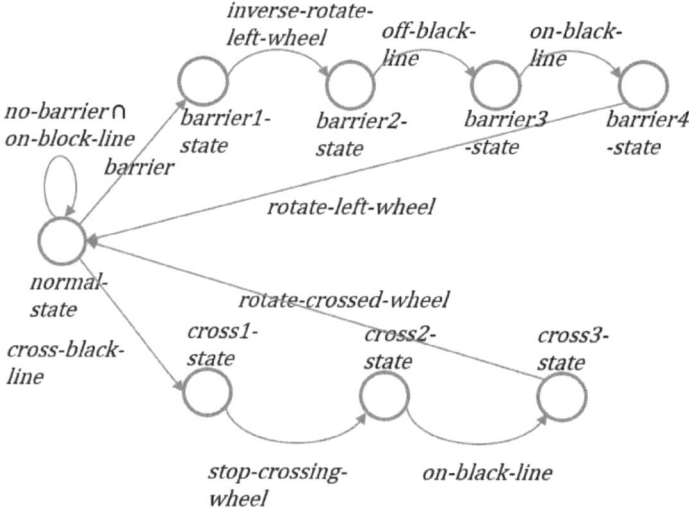

Fig. 15. Two tasks are joined by the attaching function

At the adjunction space level, the two tasks are attached using the attaching function shown in Fig. 15. The two tasks share the states *normal-state* that are combined into one space. At the states *normal-state*, one task has a cyclic event *no-barrier* and the other task has *on-black-line*; these events are combined as an event

$$no\text{-}barrier \cap on\text{-}black\text{-}line. \tag{8}$$

The service of controlling the car is completed by adding the task of selecting a path when encountering a branch. A Mealy machine for this service that is transformed from the sequence of events is obtained as shown in Fig. 16. The Mealy machine, which is a state transition diagram, belongs to the cellular space level. As the cellular space has dimensions, the nodes and links are represented as 0-dimensional and 1-dimensional entities, respectively.

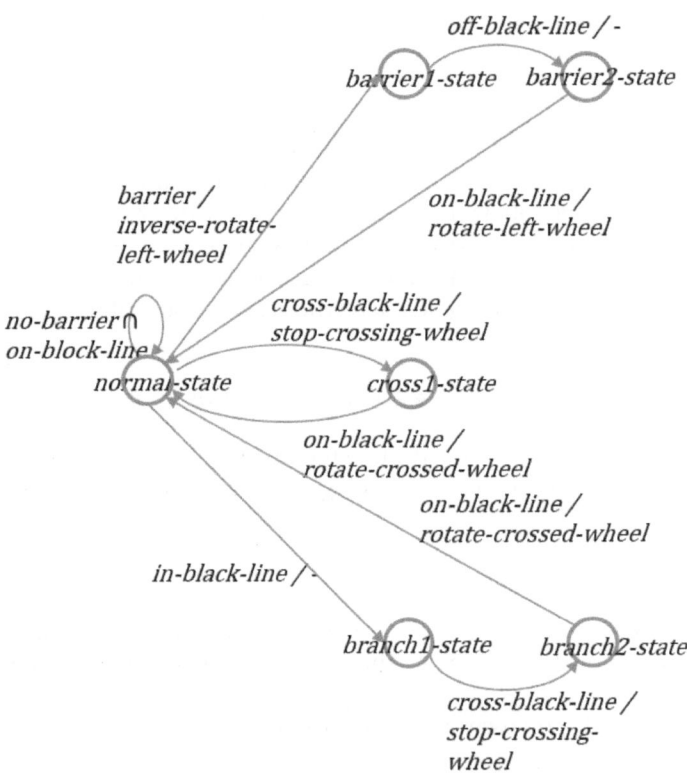

Fig. 16. A Mealy machine for the service of controlling the car is obtained at the cellular space level. The Mealy machine can be implemented by sequential logical circuits or CSP.

Four other services are designed similarly. These services are represented as independent state transition diagrams.

At the cellular space level, each service is represented by a Mealy machine so that it is possible to implement the service not only by means of hardware but also by means of software. In the case of hardware, each service becomes an individual sequential logical circuit. As services interact with each other, their sequential logical circuits also communicate with each other. In the case of software, the services become processes (or threads) that communicate with each other.

At the presentation level, processes are obtained from the state transition diagrams. The following process C is obtained for the service of controlling the car, whose state transition diagram is shown in Fig. 16:

$$C = (no\text{-}barrier \cap on\text{-}black\text{-}line \rightarrow C)$$
$$\Box(barrier \rightarrow inverse\text{-}rotate\text{-}left\text{-}wheel \rightarrow ... \rightarrow C)$$

$$\Box(\textit{cross-black-line} \to \textit{stop-crossing-wheel} \to \ldots \to C)$$
$$\Box(\textit{in-black-line} \to \textit{cross-black-line} \to \ldots \to C). \qquad (9)$$

In the above expression, $\Box$ is an external choice operator that allows the future evolution of a process to be defined as a choice between the two component-processes located on the sides of $\Box$. In the above expression, when an event *barrier* is received, the following process *inverse-rotate-left-wheel* is processed.

The service of detecting barriers is described by the following process B. The ultrasonic sensor sends a message indicating whether a sound is reflected or not. Upon receiving it, the sensor sends it to the service controlling the car.

$$B = (\textit{reflection} \to \textit{barrier} \to B)\Box(\textit{no-reflection} \to \textit{barrier} \to B). \qquad (10)$$

The other services are obtained in a similar manner.

The software system of the line-tracing car is represented as concurrent processes:

$$SoftwareSystem = C \parallel B \parallel \ldots \qquad (11)$$

In the above expression, $\parallel$ is a concurrency operator that allows the two processes located on both sides of the $\parallel$ to run concurrently in lock-step synchronization.

At the view level, processes are transformed into programming codes.

7   Designing Google Maps

In this section, we use our method to design Google maps. Google maps show the location of organizations operating in a given business category in a state. Our example uses the homotopy lifting property (HLP) defined in Fig. 17, where E, X, and B are topological spaces, I is an interval, and π, H, $\hat{H}$, and $\hat{h}_0$ are continuous functions. H and $\hat{H}$, in particular, are called homotopy functions since these functions change along an interval $[0, 1]$. HLP has a pushout and a pullback. The pullback of π and H is $(X, \hat{h}_0, X \times \{0\})$. The pushout of $\hat{h}_0$ and $X \times \{0\}$ is (B, π, H). Utilizing these properties, B is obtained by ascending the abstraction hierarchy from the adjunction space level to the homotopy level, and X is obtained by descending the abstraction hierarchy from the homotopy level to the adjunction space level. When I is not continuous, but discrete, I takes the form of an ordered set $I = \{i_0, i_1, \ldots, i_n\}$.

HLP has a more important property in which $\hat{H}$ lifts H so that $H = \pi\hat{H}$. Using this property, E is constructed from a set of $\{X \times i_0, X \times i_1, \ldots, X \times i_n\}$ in a bottom-up fashion. If π is a projection map, the inverse map π^{-1} can be defined. As shown in Fig. 18, we can obtain a commutative diagram in which $(E, \hat{H}, \pi^{-1})$ is a pushout of H and i. Therefore, let us consider constructing Google map E from the components $X \times I$. Google maps consist of multiple layers. Each layer provides a map that shows the locations of organizations belonging to a

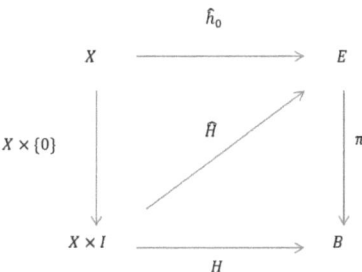

Fig. 17. The homotopy lifting property

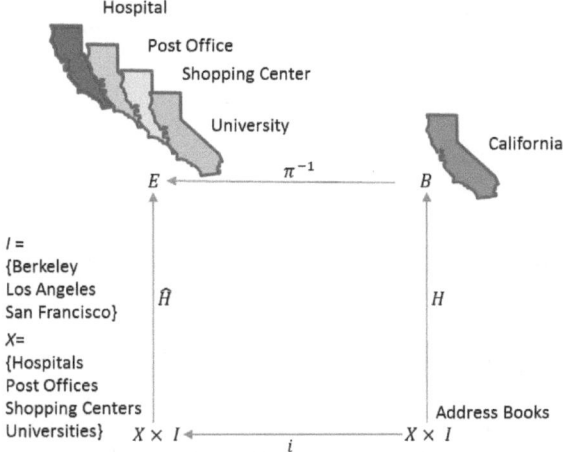

Fig. 18. Google maps at the adjunction space level

given business category. The components are address books. Each address book, which records information about a given city, provides institution lists that are categorized according to their business.

In this figure, B is the state map, where a topological space, such as a distance space, is induced. A topological space is also induced to E in the same manner. π^{-1} is the inverse map of π. This is a projection map from E to B such that a point on each Google map is mapped to the same point on the state map. X is the template of an address book that is categorized by business type such that $x_j \in X$ is a business category such as Hospitals, Post Offices, Shopping Centers, or Universities. I is an ordered set of cities in the state where i_k is an element of I and represents a city. $(x_j, i_k) \in X \times I$ indicates a list of the organizations operating business type x_j in city i_k that is obtained from the address book of i_k.

$\hat{H}(x_j, i_k)$ maps the list of the organizations to their locations on the layer provided for the business type x_j. $H(x_j, i_k)$ maps the list of the organizations to

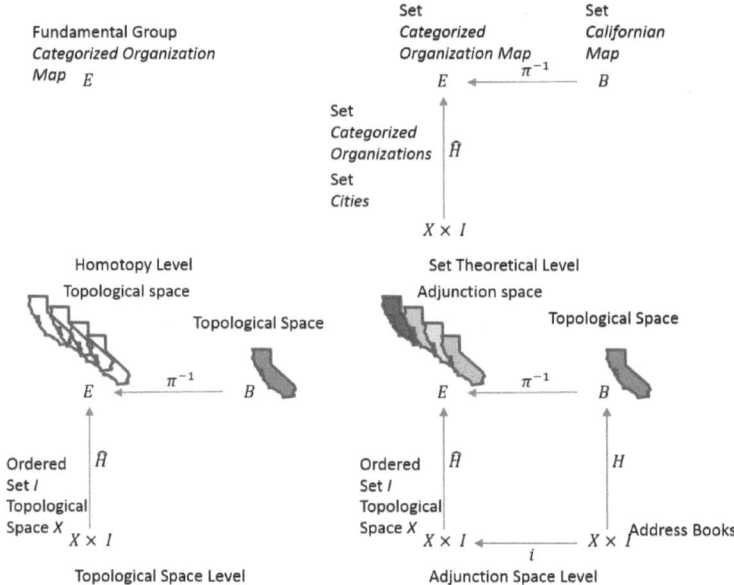

Fig. 19. The abstract levels of Google maps are designed by ascending IMAH

the state map. Using $\hat{H}$, Google maps can be designed at the adjunction space level.

By ascending IMAH, the abstract levels are obtained as shown in Fig. 19. In a similar fashion, the concrete levels are obtained by descending IMAH.

8   Applying IMAH to Deductive Reasoning

The homotopy extension property (HEP) is dual to the homotopy lifting property and is defined as follows. Given any commutative diagram of continuous maps as shown in Fig. 20 (left), there is a continuous map $\hat{K} : X \rightarrow Y^I$ such that $p_0 \times \hat{K} = k$ and $\hat{K} \times i = K$. The homotopy $\hat{K}$ thus extends K over i and lifts k through p_0 where $p_0(\lambda) = \lambda(0)$.

In the above definition, λ is called a path that is defined as follows. A continuous map $\lambda : I \rightarrow X$ yields a path. $\lambda(0) = x$ and $\lambda(1) = y$ are called the initial and terminal points. The path is denoted by $w = (W; \lambda)$ where $W = \lambda(I)$. Y^I is called a path space and is defined as follows. The path space on Y, denoted Y^I, is the space $\{\lambda : I \rightarrow Y | continuous\}$. In a later discussion, the interval I is modified to an ordered set so that the path is adaptable to a discrete system.

The pullback mechanism of the HEP is emphasized by Fig. 20 (right). In this figure, the pullback of $\hat{K} : X \rightarrow Y^I$ and $p_0^{-1} : Y \rightarrow Y^I$ is

$$(A, i : A \rightarrow X, i : A \rightarrow Y). \tag{12}$$

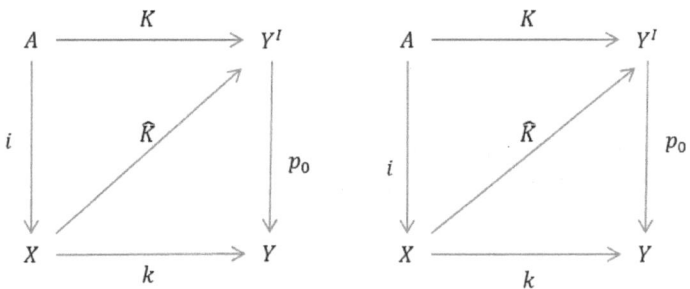

Fig. 20. The homotopy extension property (left) and its pullback diagram (right)

The mechanism of a divide-and-conquer algorithm is explained using Fig. 20. The divide-and-conquer method solves a complicated problem by dividing it into a simple, smaller problem of the same type as the original. As an example, if $f(n)$ depicts a factorial n, then using the divide-and-conquer algorithm, it is described as $f(n) = n \times f(n-1)$, where $f(0) = 1$.

In Fig. 20, Y^I is assumed to be a solution of the complicated problem. X is a divide-and-conquer algorithm to solve the complicated problem. A is the part of the divide-and-conquer algorithm that gives the same type of problem as the original problem. The solution Y^I is split into X and Y. The divide-and-conquer algorithm X gives a series of problems to be solved. Y is the original problem. Y^I explains how the problem is solved along I. Therefore, Y^I starts at the original problem Y, follows the first deductive solution that is obtained by applying the algorithm X and follows the second deductive solution. This is repeated until the final deduction is performed. Therefore, Y^I is supposed to be generated by attaching Y and X, where I is an ordered set of $\{0,1,..,10\}$. For factorial 10, $Y^{0 \in I}$ is 10!. $Y^{[0,1] \in I}$, which is the result of the first application of the divide-and-conquer algorithm, is $10 \times 9!$, and $Y^{[0,2] \in I}$, which is the result of second reduction, is $10 \times 9 \times 8!$. Finally, we will get $Y^{[0,10] \in I}$ as $10 \times 9 \times ... \times 1 \times 1$.

Using the divide-and-conquer algorithm, we will solve the following puzzle.

Assume there is a chessboard with a dimension of 2^m (that is, it consists of 2^m squares) with a hole, that is, one arbitrary square is removed. There are a number of L-shaped tiles and your task is to cover the board with these tiles (the orientation of a tile is not important). How can you do it? Where should you start? (*Puzzle-Based Learning: An introduction to critical thinking, mathematics, and problem solving*, p68 [9]).

Suppose that the hole is provided as shown in Y of Fig. 21, where $m = 4$. Y^I shows how the L-shaped tiles are placed on the board, step-by-step, along I. A is the same type of problem. If we can define it as a topological space with a reserved square, that is the hole or a square of an L-shaped tile that has already been placed on the board, then A is topologically equal to the original problem Y. In this figure, A is described as a quarter-circle for explanatory convenience. X is described as a circle for the same reason.

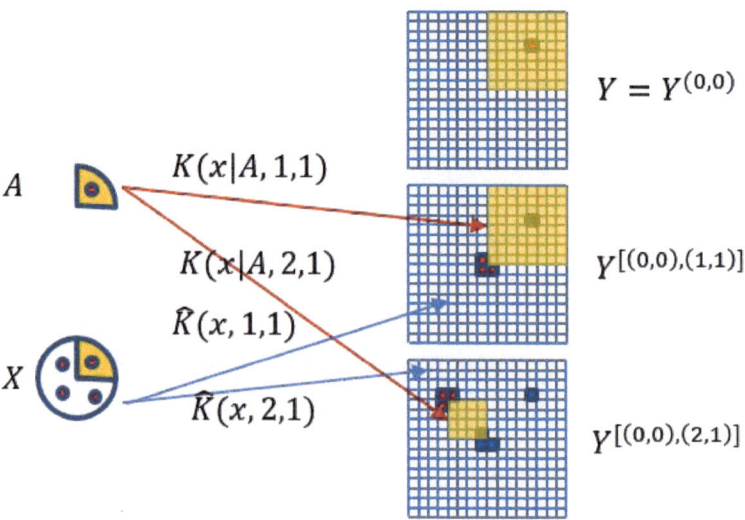

Fig. 21. The chess board puzzle is solved using the divide-and-conquer algorithm

A new L-shaped tile is placed on $(X - A)$. This is a three-quarter circle representing the simple solution of the algorithm. We will divide the three-quarter circle into three parts, each of which is a quarter circle. Each quarter circle has a reserved square that is a square of the new L-shaped tile. Since each divided quarter circle is topologically equal to the original solution, it is also solved using the divide-and-conquer algorithm.

Now that we have finished preparing for the problem solution, we will show how the puzzle is solved. The length and width of the board are divided equally, lengthwise and crosswise, as the divide-and-conquer algorithm proceeds. The steps for solving the problem are described by $I = J \times K$. $j \in J$ is a divided number and $j = 1, 2, 3, 4$. K is an indexed number of a block that is obtained by dividing the board equally and $k = 1, .., 2^{2 \times (j-1)}$.

The first deduction is obtained as follows. The board is divided into four equal parts as shown in Fig. 21. The upper-right part of the board corresponds to A. Therefore, A is mapped to this part. The rest of the board corresponds to $(X-A)$. $(X - A)$ is mapped to this part. However, the three reserved squares of X are mapped to configure an L-shaped tile. Therefore, we will obtain $Y^{[(0,0),(1,1)] \in I}$ as shown in Fig. 21. By applying the second deduction to the upper-left part of the board, we get $Y^{[(0,0),(1,1)] \in I}$ as shown in Fig. 21. By repeating this algorithm, we can obtain a solution of this puzzle.

In summary, the puzzle is solved successfully by repeatedly utilizing the pullbacks that give a basic framework of the divide-and-conquer algorithm.

9   Conclusion

The paper has shown that IMAH is a general method applicable to various application fields. Design using IMAH is performed by continuous processes of generalization and specification. Abstraction hierarchy is introduced in IMAH so that IMAH provides a logical framework for the generalization and specification processes. The five examples in this paper successfully explain how IMAH is a useful and powerful tool for logical system design. In particular, when a designer wishes to design a new system, IMAH allows the designer to start with a level with which he is most familiar and comfortable. Then, by ascending or descending the abstraction hierarchy, he can effectively generalize or solidify his design, respectively. The advantage of starting at any level and generalizing and solidifying his design by ascending and descending the abstraction hierarchy are explicitly described in the examples provided in this paper. Upon completing his design, the designer is able to view the entire scope of his design from general levels to specific levels. This is another advantage of IMAH that allows the user to understand the entire design and to easily advance with further enhancements and modifications.

In the design process, composition and decomposition are additional issues. Decomposition is a bottom-up approach in which a system is composed from components. Decomposition is a top-down approach in which a system is decomposed. This paper provides mathematical backgrounds for composition and decomposition using the mathematical concepts of pushouts and pullbacks. As useful mathematical theories for pushouts, the attaching function and homotopy lifting property are used to design the systems. As effective mathematical theories for pullbacks, the divide-and-conquer method and homotopy extension property are employed. Logical design for composition and decomposition using these mathematical tools has been successfully demonstrated in the examples.

Reusability, which is not shown in this paper, is another advantage of IMAH. As the upper abstraction levels are conceptual, applications for different fields can be represented in the same manner and we can reuse previous applications when designing a new application with the same properties in the upper abstraction level.

In this paper, IMAH was applied to applications in computer science and information engineering. As IMAH is a general design method, we would like to apply it to very different fields such as art, literature, and social science. In particular, visualization of the dynamism of Meiji Restoration, through which Japan succeeded in modernization, is a possible next candidate for an IMAH application. As the dynamism of Meiji Restoration is similar to the rapid changes of cyberworlds, characterized by the world of current Internet connections, this application is worthy of study.

References

1. Dodson, C., Parker, P.E.: A User's Guide to Algebraic Topology. Kluwer Academic Pub., Boston (1997)
2. Ferrari, M., Ferrari, G.: Building Robots with LEGO Mindstorms NXT. Syngress, Burlington (2007)
3. Hoare, C.A.R.: Communicating Sequential Processes. Prentice Hall, Upper Saddle River (1985)
4. Kunii, T.L., Ohmori, K.: Cyberworlds: A kaleidoscope as a cyberworld and its animation: Linear architecture and modeling based on an incrementally modular abstraction hierarchy. Computer Animation and Virtual Worlds 17, 145–153 (2006)
5. Kunii, T.L., Ohmori, K.: Cyberworlds: Architecture and modeling by an incrementally modular abstraction hierarchy. The Visual Computer 22(12), 949–964 (2006)
6. Martin, R.C.: Agile Software Development, Principles, Patterns, and Practices. Prentice Hall, Upper Saddle River (2002)
7. May, D.: Communicating process architecture for multicores. In: The 30th Communicating Process Architectures Conference, pp. 21–32 (July 2007)
8. May, J.P.: A concise course in algebraic topology. University of Chicago Press, Chicago (1999)
9. Michalewicz, Z., Michalewicz, M.: Puzzle-based Learning: Introduction to critical thinking, mathematics, and problem solving. Hybrid Publishers, Melbourne (2008)
10. Ohmori, K.: Design and implementation of enterprise systems in fine-grained concurrent computation. Procedia Technology 5, 344–353 (2012); 4th Conference of ENTERprise Information Systems - aligning technology, organizations and people (CENTERIS 2012)
11. Ohmori, K., Kunii, T.L.: Visualized deformation of joinery to understand jointing process by homotopy theory and attaching maps. In: Proc. Int. Conference on Cyberworlds 2011, Calgary, Canada, pp. 203–210 (October 2011)
12. Ohmori, K., Kunii, T.L.: Visualizing logical thinking using homotopy: A new learning method to survive in dynamically changing cyberworlds. In: Proc. 2011 Int. Conf. on Frontiers in Education: Computer Science and Computer Engineering, Las Vegas, USA, pp. 186–191 (July 2011)
13. Ohmori, K., Kunii, T.L.: A general design method based on algebraic topology - a divide and conquer method. In: Int. Conf. on Cyberworlds 2013, Yokohama, Japan, pp. 267–273 (October 2013)
14. Ohmori, K., Kunii, T.L.: Mathematical foundations for designing a 3-dimensional sketch book. In: Gavrilova, M.L., Tan, C.J.K., Kuijper, A. (eds.) Transactions on Computational Science XVIII. LNCS, vol. 7848, pp. 41–60. Springer, Heidelberg (2013)
15. Sieradski, A.J.: An introduction to topology and homotopy. PWS-Kent Publishing Company, Boston (1992)
16. Whitehead, J.H.C.: Algebraic homotopy theory. In: Proc. International Conference of Mathematics II, pp. 354–357 (1950)

Fast and Stable Deformations
Using the Mesh Intersection Algorithm

Luis F. Gutiérrez[2], Sergio Vargas[1], and Félix Ramos[1]

[1] CINVESTAV Campus Guadalajara
[2] Instituto Tecnológico y de Estudios Superiores de Occidente (ITESO)
`lgutierrez@iteso.mx`

Abstract. In this research, the stability problem of explicit integration schemes in simulations of deformable objects is addressed. We present a method that makes it possible to simulate a volumetric mesh using the magnitude order of the limit time step provided by another optimal mesh. The volumetric object to simulate, represented by a surface mesh (made up of triangles), is extracted from an optimal volumetric mesh (e.g. a tetrahedralized cube). The optimal mesh is easily tetrahedralized and thus the overall quality can rarely be surpassed. The simulation of the intersection can be performed in a stable manner using the eXtended Finite Element Method (XFEM) which introduces discontinuities (e.g. cutting and dissection) while it maintains the original mesh configuration. The elements (tetrahedra) are classified and those that lie outside the surface mesh are fixed and neglected in the simulation. Interface elements (those that lie inside and outside the surface mesh) are dissected and only the volume part lying inside the surface mesh is simulated. The intersection is performed only once before starting the simulation. Using our approach, the meshing methods and mesh optimization strategies are avoided. Furthermore, our approach can be directly switched to implicit solvers. The proposed method is useful for designing simulations of deformable objects without meshing techniques.

1 Introduction

Physically-based simulations of deformable objects have been an important research field in recent decades. Several applications can be found for simulation and animation. Accurate simulations are commonly computed offline. On the other hand, there are a wide number of interactive applications that call for real-time soft body simulation, such as virtual surgery training simulations in the medical field, and in the videogames industry, the enhancement of realistic behaviors within games such as plant deformation, cloth simulation, and the representation of other materials like rubber, balls, rope etc. One key factor of the simulation performance is the time integration approach, which could be implicit or explicit. Even though implicit integration schemes require solving a system of equations, they have been a standard on most interactive applications. The main reason for this is their unconditional stability, i.e. implicit methods

M.L. Gavrilova et al. (Eds.): Trans. on Comput. Sci. XXIII, LNCS 8490, pp. 21–39, 2014.
© Springer-Verlag Berlin Heidelberg 2014

are stable for any time step. On the other hand explicit integration schemes are fast to compute because the computation is direct, i.e., there is no need to solve the system of equations. Unfortunately, they are not considered for interactive applications due to their conditional stability problem, which means that the simulation is limited to a very small time step and this forces the simulation to compute unnecessary iterations, leading to a very slow simulation. Nevertheless, explicit integrations seem to be better suited for applications that require high update rates, for instance, applications using haptic devices. The accuracy of these devices depends on the update rate that is achieved, which is directly related to the simulation time step.

The stability limit time step of explicit integration solvers relies on the material parameters and the mesh topology configuration [1]. This research focuses on determining the largest possible time step while avoiding mesh dependence as much as possible, i.e., without requiring mesh improvement approaches.

We focus on simulating linear elastic deformable models using explicit integration methods in a stable manner. With this aim, we employ the corotational formulation described in [2].

In this research, the mesh intersection algorithm (MI) is presented. This approach consists of computing an intersection of two meshes: a volumetric tetrahedralized mesh and a surface mesh. The volumetric mesh, which is bigger than the surface mesh (for instance a cubic mesh), has the largest possible time step for a particular refinement, because all of its elements are regular. The surface mesh is the object shape to be simulated. The intersection is obtained using the extended finite element method (XFEM), which handles the discontinuities in a stable manner. The volumetric nodes outside the surface mesh are ignored in the simulation; details of how it is performed are described in Sect. 4.

The main advantages of using the MI algorithm are:

Larger time steps: We use the time step obtained from the best quality mesh that can be easily tetrahedralized; in this way the obtained time step is virtually unsurpassable.

Stable simulations: The time step is maintained by the XFEM even for topological changes.

Avoiding meshing approaches: The input mesh is a surface mesh; our intersection algorithm handles the deformation without requiring meshing methods.

2   Related Work

Terzopoulos [3] has been a pioneer in this line of research that combines physics and computer graphics. Nowadays, there are numerous research articles related to deformable objects . Among the physics methods used for deformable objects we can find (to name a few) the finite element method (FEM), mass-spring models (MSM), and meshless methods. Accurate approaches such as [4–6] are computed in offline mode. These approaches are designed for animation and highly detailed simulations. Therefore, they can use implicit integration solvers without any problem aside from the cost of computation time. *Meshless methods* have been also used in the context of highly detailed deformations [7, 8].

Nealen et al. [9], provide an important survey of physically-based methods and applications.

On the other hand, interactive applications like [10] propose a shape-matching approach, which is physically plausible and capable of using explicit integration in a stable manner. Unfortunately, this kind of approach is not accurate enough, particularly for haptic rendering. A hybrid approach of FEM and shape matching has been proposed in [11]; this approach uses a threshold time step, and all the elements that are stable use FEM while the unstable elements are simulated by shape matching. This approach is dependent on the initial time step: if the time step threshold is very small, most of the elements will be simulated using shape matching. A similar disadvantage can be observed for methods that combine explicit and implicit approaches, since the explicit stability is limited by the initial time step that commonly is too small [12].

The problem of stability in explicit integration is a challenging task, and researchers try to find a way to avoid the high frequencies that go out through the body and cause instability; see for example [13, 14]. Such approaches are important to determine the elements that are unstable in order to apply frequency filters. Even though the simulation becomes more stable, it loses accuracy and is dependent on the initial time step.

Other approaches based on GPU computing increase the update rates using implicit methods [15]. This fact can also be an advantage for explicit schemes since it is independent of the method; hence, if the time step is larger (longer?) in explicit methods, these could simulate more elements in the same time as implicit solvers.

As we said before, stability is related to mesh topology. Commonly, tetrahedral elements are classified according to the magnitude of their dihedral angles. Elements with extreme dihedral angles, also known as ill-shaped elements (e.g. sliver element), interfere with the stability or accuracy of the simulation. In the context of the finite element method, the conditioning of the stiffness matrix depends on the mesh topology. Important references related to this are [1, 16]. Researchers have thus been looking into meshing methods in search of a way to overcome the instability issues. Different mesh enhancement strategies have been proposed, which generally are classified as: *smoothing methods*, which displace the mesh nodes to a position that improves the accuracy of all the adjacent elements to the reference node [17]; and *topological transformations*, which change the mesh connectivity but maintain the nodes' position [18]. These strategies work better when they are combined [19, 20]. Even though mesh improvement approaches can be used to adaptively optimize the mesh depending on the deformation [21], these approaches are not suitable for real-time applications when an explicit integration method is used. The main reasons are their expensive processing time and their inability to maintain the limit time step after a topological change [22].

Another option to enhance mesh quality is mesh refinement [23]. In the context of explicit integration, the limit time step is associated with the size and volume of the smallest element [1] and thus refining the mesh reduces the stable time step.

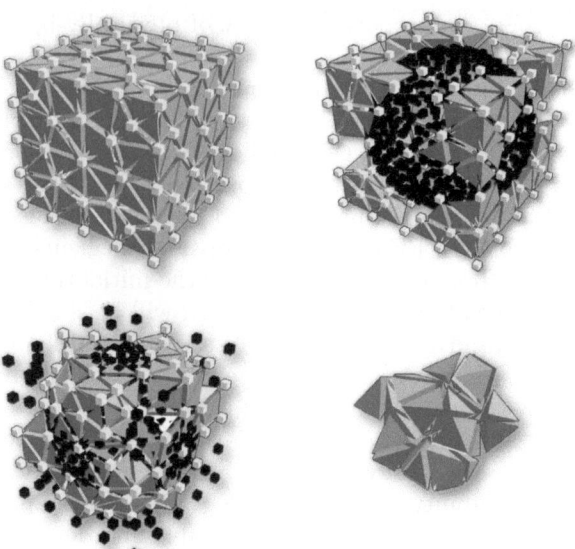

Fig. 1. Intersection of a tetrahedralized cube mesh (upper left) and a sphere mesh. The elements are classified into three types: inside elements (bottom right), interface elements (bottom left) and outside elements (upper right). Interface elements must share a node inside and outside the object mesh. Elements outside will be fixed and thus ignored in the simulation.

The XFEM has already been employed for simulations of deformable objects. This method introduces new control points, making it possible to simulate discontinuities in a mesh without remeshing. This method can be used to simulate heterogeneous materials, but also to simulate topological changes such as cutting and dissection [24, 25]. The XFEM maintains the magnitude order of the stability limit of explicit integration methods when a specific mass lumping technique and an enrichment function are employed, in this case the weighted diagonal and the shifted function respectively [26]. Even though the XFEM avoids instability, it has also been dependent on the mesh, and consequently on the initial limit time step.

A similar approach is the virtual node algorithm [27], which creates copies of nodes and elements associating the corresponding part of volume depending on the cut. However, this method has been used together with implicit methods for offline simulations.

3   Stability of Explicit Solvers

In a discrete model, a wave of pressure moves through the mesh across the elements; the stability is preserved as long as the time step is smaller than the time it takes the wave to go through the elements. This observation has been the basis for defining the Courant-Friedrichs-Lewy (CFL) condition [28] which is formulated as:

$$\Delta t_c = \frac{c}{\sqrt{\omega^2}},\tag{1}$$

where ω^2 are the squared modal frequencies and c is a constant that depends on the explicit solver, and Δt_c is the stable limit time step, also known as the *critical time step* . In the case of finite element simulation for undamped system, we have ω^2 corresponding to the maximal eigenvalue (λ_{max}) of $\mathbf{M}^{-1}\mathbf{K}$ where $\mathbf{M}$ and $\mathbf{K}$ are the global mass and stiffness matrix respectively. The constant can be $c = 2$ for some solvers, such as verlet, semi-implicit Euler, explicit Newmark, among others [13]. Finally, the critical time step is defined by:

$$\Delta t_c = \frac{2}{\sqrt{\lambda_{max}(\mathbf{M}^{-1}\mathbf{K})}},\tag{2}$$

An application, to be in real time, requires that the critical time step be large enough to compute a simulated second before a real second. However, a simulation may also consider the expensive processing time of collision detection and visualization methods. Moreover, using a larger time step means fewer iterations to reach a simulated second, thus the size of the time step is proportional to the performance.

4   Mesh Intersection Algorithm

So far, we have stated that the time step is limited by the mesh; this dependence is considered our main problem to overcome. We need to go beyond the mesh topology structure and try to find a larger time step. The underlying idea of this research is quite simple, but at the same time, it conceals an important contribution. The idea emerged from the thought that the largest possible time step would belong to a very simple mesh, for instance, a cubic mesh that can be optimally tetrahedralized by several mesh generators. In consequence, we observed that a way to maintain this time step stable after a mesh cutting can be by using the XFEM, which allows us to create discontinuities like dissections to the mesh without harming the stability. Even though other approaches have been working in the context of simulating topological changes using the XFEM, we do not directly focus on this. Instead, the XFEM is used to perform the mesh intersection between the volumetric and triangular meshes by handling the boundary dissections as discontinuities. We do not actually simulate how the mesh has been cut; rather we are concerned with maintaining the time step of the optimal mesh, in this case the cubic mesh.

In order to explain our method, we denote the optimal mesh or volumetric mesh as M_v, and the surface mesh (triangular mesh) that corresponds to the shape we want to simulate as M_s.

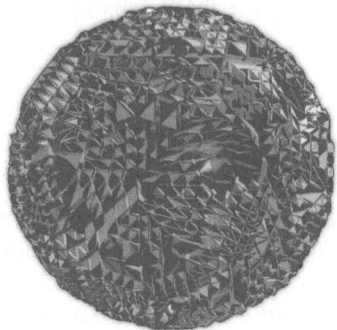

Fig. 2. Sphere refinement after 3 iterations. Only interface elements have been refined. The volume of each interface element is obtained by adding the refined elements that lie inside the surface mesh.

4.1   Node and Element Classification

Our mesh intersection algorithm (MI) consists of three main steps: element classification, volume computation and mesh deformation.

First, tetrahedral elements are classified into three types: internal, interface and external elements. With this aim, we need to classify the nodes first into outside, boundary and inside nodes; we denote the sets respectively as follows N_o, N_b and N_i. A node whose distance to the boundary is less than a specified threshold is considered boundary (see algorithm 1).

for *each n in M_v* **do**
> $F = M_s.hashMap(n)$;
>   **if** *($\forall f_i \in F$)areInside(M_s)* **then**
>   > $N_b = N_b \cup n$;
>
>   **else**
>   >   **if** *isOutside(n,M_s)* **then**
>   >   > $N_o = N_o \cup n$;
>   >
>   >   **else**
>   >   > $N_i = N_i \cup n$;
>   >
>   >   **end**
>
>   **end**

end

Algorithm 1. ClassifyNode(n): determine if a node $n \in M_v$ is outside, boundary or inside the object mesh M_s. The function $hashMap(node)$ returns a set of faces F that lie on the same grid as the input node (The function $isPointInside$ is detailed later in this work).

Once the nodes have been classified, we can proceed with the classification of the elements. External elements are those whose four nodes lie outside of M_s or at the boundary but not inside; interface or boundary elements are those with at least one of their nodes inside and another outside of M_s; finally, we define an element as internal when its nodes are either inside or boundary (or a combination) (see algorithm 2). The corresponding elements sets are denoted respectively as E_o, E_b and E_i (see Fig. 1).

```
for each e in M_v do
    F = M_s.hashMap(n);
    if ∀n∈N_e (n ∉N_O) then
    |   ε_i = ε_i ∪ e;
    else
        if ∀n∈N_e (n ∉N_i) then
        |   ε_o = ε_o ∪ e;
        else
        |   ε_b = ε_b ∪ e;
        end
    end
end
```

Algorithm 2. ClassifyElement(e): determine if an element $e \in M_v$ is outside, boundary or inside the object mesh. N_e is the set of element nodes.

The second step consists of computing the volume of all the interface elements. Instead of computing the volume through the intersection of each element and the surface, we decided to perform an iterative refinement of all interface elements; that way we can compute the element volume without caring about the way the element has been cut by the surface (see Fig. 2).

4.2   Object Deformation Using the XFEM

Finally, the third step of our method consists of creating the discontinuities with the XFEM. After splitting an element, the XFEM introduces new control points or degrees of freedom that maintain the partition of unity property of shape functions denoted as $\Phi_i(x)$; the property is defined by:

$$\sum_{i=1}^{n} \Phi_i(x) = 1 \tag{3}$$

This property makes it possible to construct basis functions through products of standard shape functions and a local enriched basis [29], meaning that a discontinuity is handled by enriching the element nodes with a global discontinuous enrichment function based on the product of shape functions and the local enriched basis. Therefore, the displacements can be computed as follows:

$$u(x) = \underbrace{\sum_{i=1}^{n} \Phi_i(x)\mathbf{u}_i}_{\text{standard}} + \underbrace{\sum_{j=1}^{n} \Phi_j(x)\psi_j(x)\mathbf{a}_j}_{\text{enrichment}} \tag{4}$$

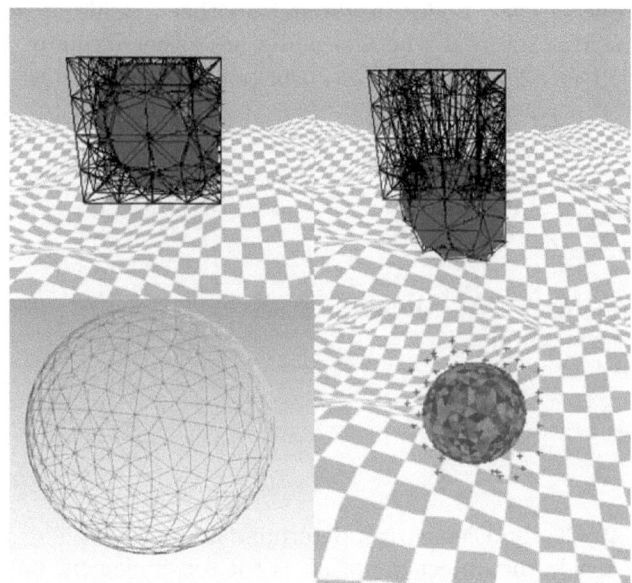

Fig. 3. Interface elements are divided into two new virtual elements. The simulation takes into account only the internal elements and the corresponding virtual elements that belong to the object shape. Other parts are fixed and ignored for the simulation. Finally, the object is simulated using an embedded mapping of the surface mesh and the volumetric mesh.

where $\mathbf{a}_j$ are the new DOFs (or control points) and the discontinuous enrichment functions are denoted by $\psi_j(x)$; in this work, we are using the shifted function [26].

This fact makes it possible to simulate discontinuities within an element without remeshing. It is easy to handle the cut of an element as two elements composed by the combination of old nodes and new control points, associating the corresponding part of volume. These elements are called *virtual elements* and use a similar structure proposed in [30], but with some modifications.

Each interface element on E_b must be subdivided into two virtual elements that are classified as inside or outside represented as E_i^v and E_o^v respectively. The virtual elements that lie outside the object mesh M_s are fixed, thus we only maintain the degrees of freedom that correspond to the nodes that lie inside of M_s.

In order to ease the intersection of both meshes we use the optimal mesh as a unitary cube positioned at the origin and we scale the input surface mesh M_s to lie inside the cube. Once the intersection is performed it is necessary to resize the meshes and volume values to match the initial size of M_s. It is important to observe that virtual elements that share a node are using the same control points after cutting, so the number of control points is less than four times the number of E_b.

1. scaleAndCenter(M_s, M_v)
2. M_s.createHash()
3. classifyNode($n|\forall n \in M_v$)
4. classifyElement($e|\forall e \in M_v$)
5. computeVolumeByRefinement($e|\forall e \in \epsilon_b$)
6. createVirtualElements($e|\forall e \in \epsilon_b$)
7. createSurfaceMapping(M_s, $\epsilon_i \cup \epsilon_i^v$)

Algorithm 3. MeshIntersection(M_v,M_s): performs the intersection between the volumetric mesh M_v and the surface mesh M_s

Our MI Algorithm is preprocessed off-line, and the intersection needs to be computed only once. However, it is better to use fast data structures to obtain the intersection in short time due to the number of nodes and elements that need to be checked. Therefore, we first hash the faces of M_s into boxes or cubes of equal size that subdivide the cubic mesh M_v. This structure allows us to query the faces lying on the same box of a vertex point of M_v and classify the nodes depending on their side.

In order to determine if a point lies inside or outside a complex manifold, we use the hash structure of the surface mesh; a point first is tested to see if it belongs to the boundary; if it does not, we test to see if a ray intersects the boundary as follows: we enlist all the boxes (used for the hash structure) that the ray crosses and obtain all those faces that belong to these boxes; then we test to see if the ray intersects these faces. If the number of intersections is even, then we determine that the point is outside; otherwise the point is inside. We perform this test using an even number of rays. The rays are created randomly, because this kind of method is prone to fail if the ray is aligned with the boundary. No intersections mean that the point is outside. We show this process for a single ray in the algorithm 4.

So far, we know how to compute the mesh intersection, but the visualization of the surface mesh M_s is missing. Hence, it is necessary to create an embedded mapping between the M_s and M_v, where each surface node is associated with the closest tetrahedron. However, this is not direct since fixed elements and virtual elements may be overlapping. The mapping must consider only the internal elements E_i plus internal virtual elements E_i^v, which is represented in line 7 of algorithm 3. We could also perform the MI algorithm using a coarse surface mesh and for the visualization it can be changed to a detailed surface mesh; this would reduce the processing time for computing the volume of interface elements. The MI algorithm of a volumetric cube and a sphere is presented in Fig. 3.

Table 1. Comparing the stability of our method (MI) against the standard meshing or subdivision strategies. A bar mesh has been employed for the test. The first column indicates the portion of mesh considered in the simulation. 100% means the original mesh without cuts.

	Remesh		Subdivision		MI	
	nodes / elements	Δt_c (ms)	nodes / elements	Δt_c (ms)	Nodes / Elements	Δt_c (ms)
100%	90 / 210	0.638	90 / 210	0.638	90 / 210	0.638
75%	72 / 158	0.387	302 / 904	0.172	87 / 210	0.683
50%	88 / 238	0.375	96 / 176	0.378	80 / 146	0.715
25%	119 / 400	0.094	268 / 786	0.160	80 / 46	0.843

```
M_s.createHash()
if isBoundary(p) then
|   return False
else
|   n_int = 0
|   r = createRandomRay(p)
|   β = M_s.getCrossedBoxes(r)
|   F = M_s.getFacesInBoxes(β)
|   for each f ∈ F do
|   |   if intersectRayFace(r, f) then
|   |   |   n_int + 1
|   |   end
|   end
|   if n_int  mod  2 = 0 then
|   |   return False
|   else
|   |   return True
|   end
end
```

Algorithm 4. isPointInside(p, M_s), where p is the point to test and n_{int} is the number of intersections of a ray and the boundary surface.

Fig. 4. The bar used for comparing the MI algorithm to meshing and mesh subdivision strategies. The bar is cut by a plane, and we only consider the top part for the simulation. For the testing, three types of cuts have been considered, removing 25%, 50% and 75% of the initial mesh.

5   Results

For the testing, we analyze the exact limit time step of our mesh cube and this value will be used to compare the contribution of our approach regarding the time step after cutting the mesh with a plane. Since we care about the performance we need to measure the nodes and elements used for the simulation. In addition, we would like to compare how our approach can offer advantages over other mesh improvement methods.

The time step is dependent on the mesh topology and the material parameters; therefore we set the Young's modulus to 30 kPa, the density to $1000kg/m^3$, and the Poisson ratio to 0.3. For computing the volume of the interface elements E_b, we refine the elements setting the number of iterations to 5.

We employ a simple bar mesh that can be easily tetrahedralized; it is used to compare the time step of a portion after cutting using a cutting plane (see Fig. 4). The bounding box of this bar is $min = (0,0,0)$ and $max = (1,1,10)$ We measure the time step in different displacements of the plane, considering three approaches: remeshing, subdivision, and the MI method (using the XFEM). Remeshing means to create the mesh from scratch. Subdivision only splits the edges of the original mesh; in this case we use snapping with 0.1 as threshold distance. And the MI method creates the discontinuities by introducing control points. These results are presented in the table 1 and Fig. 7. Note that for testing the MI algorithm we are ignoring the lower part in the simulation, so the upper part can overlap the mesh without problems, because during the simulation the lower part is hidden from the user. The number of elements for the MI method is computed by adding the internal elements and the virtual elements that belong to the surface.

Further, we compare our mesh intersection algorithm using a cubic mesh (made up of tetrahedra) as an initial volumetric mesh. From this mesh we extract different surface meshes as shown in Fig. 5. For each mesh we compute the intersection algorithm described in Sect. 4 and we compare their time steps with regard to meshing strategies. In order to compare the meshes, they must be of the same size, hence we have scaled the meshes to exactly fit a 10-cm cube. The information about the meshes and the results are shown in Tab. 2 and Fig. 8.

For the sake of completeness, we must not be restricted to some particular meshes; we would like to perform a test that will give us an idea of how the time step behaves using several random meshes. The test consists of the following: First we randomly choose an initial tetrahedron of our ideal mesh (the cube mesh) and a random value of iterations between 1 and 7. At each level we obtain a randomly connected mesh by including some of the adjacent elements for all the elements that have been previously selected to be on the random mesh. Finally, the elements that do not belong to the random mesh are treated as fixed elements. This procedure has been performed to create 100 meshes and the results are presented in Fig. 6.

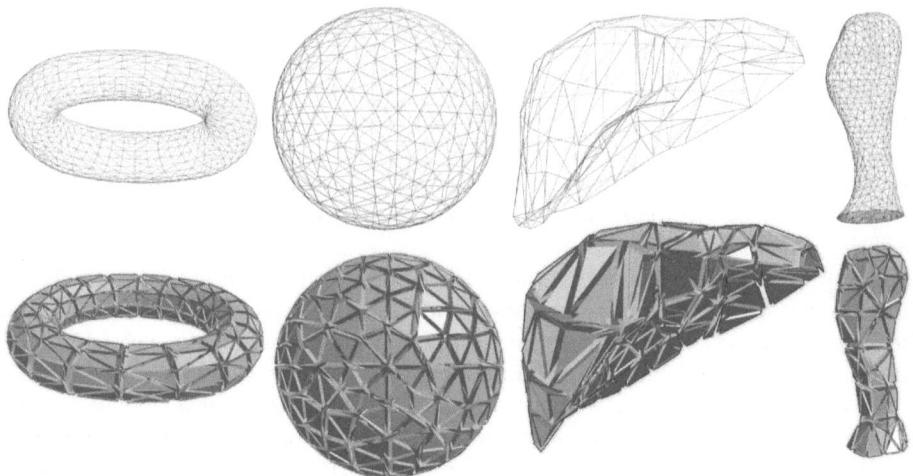

Fig. 5. The four meshes employed for the tests. From left to right: *torus*, *sphere*, *liver* and *polyp*. The upper meshes are surface meshes made up of triangles. The lower tetrahedral meshes are based on meshing strategies.

6   Discussion and Limitations

Our approach offers distinct advantages over meshing and subdivision approaches, particularly when the simulation part becomes thinner. Subdivision methods have the disadvantage of being based on the configuration of the original mesh: a topological change could produce badly-shaped elements at the boundary. Meshing approaches could result in a better shape while the number of elements and nodes may be smaller than with subdivision methods since meshing methods consider the whole space. Moreover, the average size of the elements is smaller, which harms the time step. The MI algorithm is superior to all other methods for thin models because the number of nodes and elements is smaller, and the time step is even larger than the initial one. Meshing approaches cannot ensure that the stability will be maintained [22].

We decided to use a bar mesh for the simulations because it is very easy to be tetrahedralized; it would not make sense to consider a complex mesh because we could easily obtain a better time step using any coarser mesh. Therefore, here we are comparing with a high quality mesh since its shape is quite simple.

The time step of our MI method is larger than the initial mesh because we are fixing the nodes that lie outside the surface mesh, i.e., we are considering a different volumetric mesh and not the whole bar. Even though the stable limit time step of our reference meshes (bar and cube) is slightly better, the magnitude order remains. Thus the simulation remains stable even after changing the topology. Observe that the number of simulated nodes and elements does not impact the simulation performance.

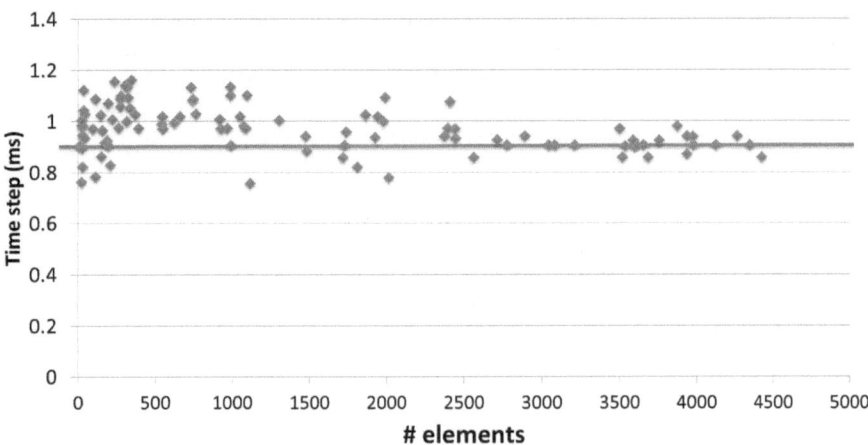

Fig. 6. Time step of random meshes extracted from the initial mesh. The initial time step is depicted as the red line.

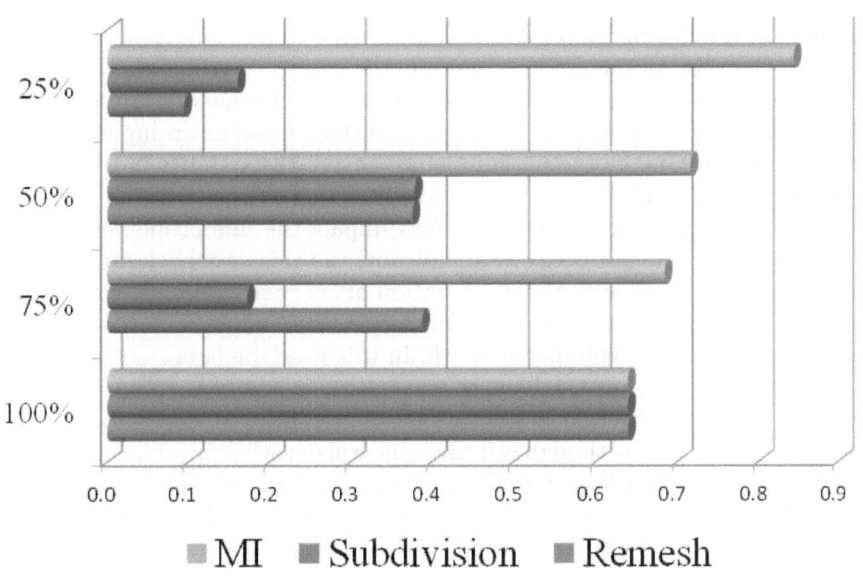

Fig. 7. The time step is improved no matter how the bar mesh is cut. 100% corresponds to the initial mesh.

We should probably prove that the critical time step will not deteriorate for all the possible intersections applied to the cube; however, our idea stems from the fact that elements in the volumetric mesh are well shaped and all the meshes have a similar quality. We therefore expect that every intersection will produce a new mesh with a stability similar to that of the initial mesh;

Table 2. Comparing the stability of our method (MI) to the standard meshing strategies. A cube mesh (made up of tetrahedra) has been employed as the initial volumetric mesh. For the MI algorithm the number of internal (E_i) and boundary (E_b) elements are shown. Our approach makes it possible to obtain time steps that are even larger (longer?) than those of the initial cubic mesh.

	Meshing			MI			
	nodes	elements	Δt_c (ms)	nodes	elements	E_i /E_b	Δt_c (ms)
Cube	1080	4830	0.862	-	-		-
Sphere	467	2115	0.696	859	1820/913		1.104
Liver	181	596	0.273	361	465/286		1.126
Polyp	138	290	0.3951	174	56/334		1.185
Torus	264	862	0.6165	302	73/616		1.540

this fact has been partially proven experimentally by generating several random intersection meshes. This test indicates that the magnitude order of the time step is maintained since this does not change widely from the initial one (the ideal mesh time step).

Furthermore, we compare the initial critical time step of four different meshes. We observe that, for all the meshes, our approach surpasses the meshing strategy and, in some cases, obtains a time step more than twice as large (long?) as the meshing ones. Our approach only requires a surface mesh as an input, and thus we avoid using meshing methods that cannot ensure the stability in a simulation [22]. However, our method sometimes introduces an overhead in the number of nodes an element can simulate; this fact may impact the simulation performance, but the overhead would not really be significant, and this drawback can disappear if GPUs are used to compute the deformation of every new virtual element. It is important to see that the number of nodes and elements to simulate is related to the refinement of our volumetric mesh, in this case the cube.

In this research we have used tetrahedral meshes; however, the proposed approach can be directly switched to other element types. We can state the same for implicit solvers: even though we are concerned with improving the performance of explicit approaches, our MI algorithm can be used with implicit solvers without difficulty, since the method is solver-independent. The MI algorithm can help to avoid the mesh generation and bad conditioning caused by topological changes.

However, our MI algorithm comes with some limitations. The volume of a virtual element computed through the mesh refinement is given to the virtual element without extra information about the shape, thus the virtual element treats the corresponding volume as a linear cut. Moreover, we are considering that an interface element is forced to have a node outside and inside the surface mesh if the mesh contains very thin portions that cross an element without touching at least one element node; these elements are considered to be outside and the thin portions are disregarded, i.e., a tetrahedron of the initial mesh is

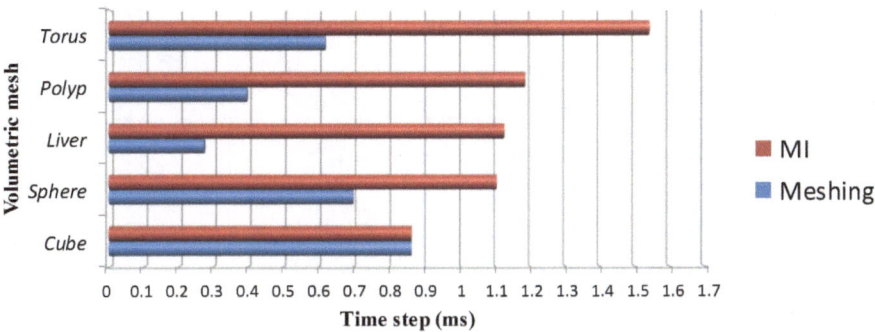

Fig. 8. Comparing the meshing strategy (meshing) and our Mesh Intersection approach (MI)

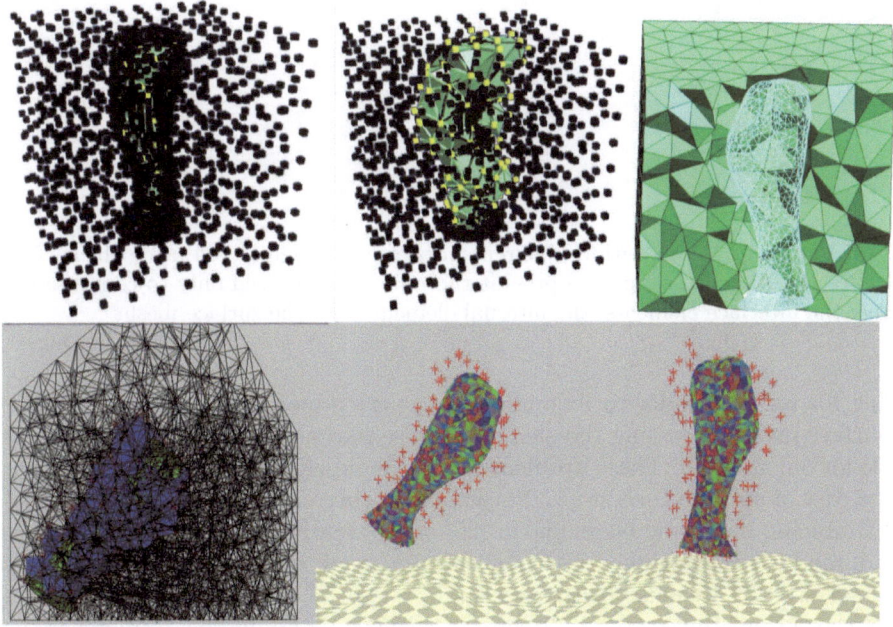

Fig. 9. Modeling a polyp (tumor) using the MI algorithm. Our approach can be used for surgery simulation. The mesh intersection algorithm produces the three meshes at the top. First, the internal elements of the polyp are presented; the black nodes are fixed in the simulation. The other two meshes are the boundary and fixed elements respectively. We simulate the polyp to be fixed in a single vertex from its upper part. The blue elements are interface elements; the new virtual nodes are shown as red crosses. Using this approach, the time steps are higher, thus making it possible to accurately update the forces for haptic rendering.

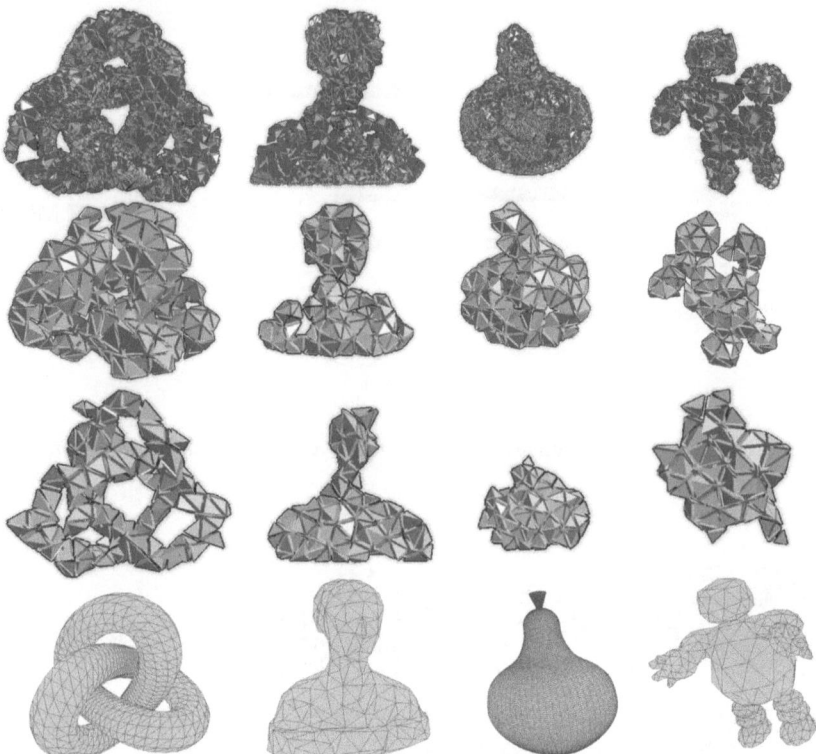

Fig. 10. Using our MI algorithm, different meshes can be simulated using the surface mesh directly. For each shape, we present the refined mesh used only to compute the volume, the interface elements, the internal elements and the surface mesh.

too big for its four nodes to lie outside the surface mesh but at the same time the surface mesh is crossing the element. These parts of the initial mesh are not visible for our method. These problems can be handled through mesh refinement with a cost of smaller time steps. Nevertheless, these limitations may be solved by introducing harmonic bases like in [25] or by treating these very thin models (or sub-models) as multiple dissections within a single element. All these changes are considered as areas for further research.

Another interesting research direction to follow is finding how to increase the explicit time step even more by exploiting the stability of implicit methods, with the aim of reaching the desired equilibrium between performance and stability.

Our MI algorithm can be important for different applications, for instance a virtual surgery simulation (see Fig. 9), but it can be used for other kinds of purposes since we only require the initial surface mesh (see Fig.fig:difMeshes).

7   Conclusion

The problem of stability of explicit integrations has been addressed in the context of a linear elastic FEM-based deformable objects simulation. The mesh intersection algorithm has been proposed, which consists of extracting the object surface mesh from a volumetric mesh using the XFEM. The XFEM makes it possible to extract a sub-mesh similar than performing dissections to the initial meshe. The original mesh remains intact and the magnitude order of the initial time step is maintained. The nodes lying outside the surface mesh are fixed and ignored in the simulation, thus the performance is not deteriorated. The results indicate that our approach is a better alternative than meshing approaches. In addition, the proposed method can be easily adapted to work with implicit solvers, other types of elements (not only tetrahedra) and topological changes such as cutting. Important limitations must still be overcome, for instance considering the very thin parts of a complex shape lying in an element without touching an internal element; in the current implementation these parts are ignored.

We think that improving the stability of explicit integration is an important research field in the context of deformable models. GPU computing and combination with implicit methods must be considered to reach real-time simulations using explicit integration.

The presented mesh intersection algorithm can be used to simulate meshes using explicit integration with larger time steps avoiding the expensive meshing methods. The MI algorithm seems to be particularly important for simulations that include haptic devices such as surgery training simulations. However, if the presented limitations are solved, this approach could also be employed for complex meshes and for different kinds of scenarios.

Acknowledgment. This research was supported by CONACYT grant no. 282131.

References

1. Shewchuk, J.R.: What is a good linear element? interpolation, conditioning, and quality measures. In: 11th International Meshing Roundtable, pp. 115–126. Springer (2002)
2. Müller, M., Gross, M.: Interactive virtual materials. In: Proceedings of Graphics Interface 2004, GI 2004, pp. 239–246 (2004)
3. Terzopoulos, D., Platt, J., Barr, A., Fleischer, K.: Elastically deformable models. SIGGRAPH Comput. Graph. 21(4), 205–214 (1987), http://doi.acm.org/10.1145/37402.37427
4. Irving, G., Teran, J., Fedkiw, R.: Tetrahedral and hexahedral invertible finite elements. Graph. Models 68(2), 66–89 (2006), http://dx.doi.org/10.1016/j.gmod.2005.03.007
5. Wicke, M., Botsch, M., Gross, M.: A Finite Element Method on Convex Polyhedra. Computer Graphics Forum 26(3), 355–364 (2007)

6. Martin, S., Kaufmann, P., Botsch, M., Wicke, M., Gross, M.: Polyhedral Finite Elements Using Harmonic Basis Functions. Computer Graphics Forum 27(5), 1521–
   1529 (2008)
7. Adams, B., Ovsjanikov, M., Wand, M., Seidel, H.-P., Guibas, L.J.: Meshless modeling of deformable shapes and their motion. In: Proceedings of the 2008 ACM
   SIGGRAPH/Eurographics Symposium on Computer Animation, SCA 2008, pp.
   77–86. Eurographics Association, Aire-la-Ville (2008), http://dl.acm.org/
   citation.cfm?id=1632592.1632605
8. Faure, F., Gilles, B., Bousquet, G., Pai, D.K.: Sparse meshless models of complex
   deformable solids. ACM Trans. Graph. 30(4), 73:1–73:10 (2011), http://doi.acm.
   org/10.1145/2010324.1964968
9. Nealen, A., Muller, M., Keiser, R., Boxerman, E., Carlson, M.: Physically Based
   Deformable Models in Computer Graphics. Computer Graphics Forum 25(4), 809–
   836 (2006)
10. Müller, M., Heidelberger, B., Teschner, M., Gross, M.: Meshless deformations based
    on shape matching. ACM Trans. Graph. 24(3), 471–478 (2005), http://doi.acm.
    org/10.1145/1073204.1073216
11. Fierz, B., Spillmann, J., Hoyos, I.A., Harders, M.: Maintaining large time steps
    in explicit finite element simulations using shape matching. IEEE Transactions on
    Visualization and Computer Graphics 18(5), 717–728 (2012)
12. Fierz, B., Spillmann, J., Harders, M.: Element-wise mixed implicit-explicit integra-
    tion for stable dynamic simulation of deformable objects. In: Proceedings of the
    2011 ACM SIGGRAPH/Eurographics Symposium on Computer Animation, SCA
    2001, pp. 257–266. ACM, New York (2011), http://doi.acm.org/10.1145/
    2019406.2019440
13. Aguinaga, I., Fierz, B., Spillmann, J., Harders, M.: Filtering of high modal frequen-
    cies for stable real-time explicit integration of deformable objects using the finite
    element method. Progress in Biophysics and Molecular Biology 103(2-3), 225–235
    (2010)
14. Fierz, B., Spillmann, J., Harders, M.: Stable explicit integration of deformable
    objects by filtering high modal frequencies. Journal of WSCG 18(1-3), 81–88 (2010)
15. Courtecuisse, H., Jung, H., Allard, J., Duriez, C., Lee, D.Y., Cotin, S.: GPU-based
    real-time soft tissue deformation with cutting and haptic feedback. Progress in
    Biophysics and Molecular Biology 103(2), 159–168 (2010)
16. Klingner, B.: Tetrahedral mesh improvement. Ph.D. dissertation, Department of
    Electrical Engineering and Computer Sciences, University of California at Berkeley,
    Berkeley, California (2008)
17. Steinemann, D., Harders, M., Gross, M., Szekely, G.: Hybrid cutting of deformable
    solids. In: IEEE Virtual Reality, pp. 35–42 (2006)
18. Shewchuk, J.R.: Two discrete optimization algorithms for the topological improve-
    ment of tetrahedral meshes. Unpublished manuscript (2002),
    http://citeseerx.ist.psu.edu/viewdoc/summary?doi=10.1.1.19.6990
19. Freitag, L.A., Ollivier-Gooch, C.: Tetrahedral mesh improvement using swap-
    ping and smoothing. International Journal for Numerical Methods in Engineer-
    ing 40(21), 3979–4002 (1997)
20. Klingner, B., Shewchuk, J.: Aggressive tetrahedral mesh improvement. In: Proc.
    of the 16th International Meshing Roundtable, pp. 3–23 (2007)
21. Wicke, M., Ritchie, D., Klingner, B.: Dynamic local remeshing for elastoplastic
    simulation. ACM Transactions on Graphics (TOG) 29(4), 1–11 (2010)

22. Gutiérrez, L.F., Aguinaga, I., Fierz, B., Ramos, F., Harders, M.: Pitting a new hybrid approach for maintaining simulation stability after mesh cutting against standard remeshing strategies. In: Proceedings of Computer Graphics International (June 2011)
23. Burkhart, D., Hamann, B., Umlauf, G.: Adaptive and Feature-Preserving Subdivision for High-Quality Tetrahedral Meshes. Computer Graphics Forum 29(1), 117–127 (2010)
24. Nesme, M., Kry, P.G., Jeřábková, L., Faure, F.: Preserving topology and elasticity for embedded deformable models. ACM Trans. Graph. 28(3), 52:1–52:9 (2009), http://doi.acm.org/10.1145/1531326.1531358
25. Kaufmann, P., Martin, S., Botsch, M., Grinspun, E., Gross, M.: Enrichment textures for detailed cutting of shells. ACM Trans. Graph. 28(3), 50:1–50:10 (2009), http://doi.acm.org/10.1145/1531326.1531356
26. Jeřábková, L., Kuhlen, T.: Stable cutting of deformable objects in virtual environments using xfem. IEEE Comput. Graph. Appl. 29(2), 61–71 (2009)
27. Molino, N., Bao, Z., Fedkiw, R.: A virtual node algorithm for changing mesh topology during simulation. ACM Trans. Graph (SIGGRAPH Proc.) 23, 385–392 (2004)
28. Courant, R., Friedrichs, K., Lewy, H.: Über die partiellen differenzengleichungen der mathematischen physik. Mathematische Annalen 100(1), 32–74 (1928)
29. Babuska, I., Melenk, J.M.: The partition of unity method. International Journal of Numerical Methods in Engineering 40, 727–758 (1997)
30. Gutiérrez, L.F., Ramos, F.: Xfem framework for cutting soft tissue - including topological changes in a surgery simulation. In: GRAPP 2010, pp. 275–283 (2010)

Gaussian Curvature Based Localized Stylization Method for View-Dependent Lines Extracted from 3D Models

Luis Cardona[1] and Suguru Saito[2]

[1] Tokyo Institute of Technology,
Tokyo, Japan
luis@img.cs.titech.ac.jp
[2] Ochanomizu University / Tokyo Institute of Technology,
Tokyo, Japan
suguru@is.ocha.ac.jp

Abstract. We propose a method to stylize individual lines and preserve their properties when the viewpoint is modified. As the camera position changes and view-dependent lines move across the surface, we track each line in order to generate the region of the surface in which they appear. We call this region the *tracked area* of the line. In our algorithm, we use the Gaussian Curvature for surface segmentation as well as to divide the contour lines at inflection points. Each line has an unique reference linked to its *tracked area*, that we use to check an indexed table from which we can recover its stylization after arbitrary camera movements. In this paper we show how each line only appears in a limited area of the surface corresponding to its *tracked area* and we also discuss and evaluate two different smoothing methods to deal with highly detailed models.

Keywords: NPR, line drawings, stylization, segmentation, tracking.

1 Introduction

1.1 Background and Purpose

Computer-generated 3D models have been extensively used in applications that try to replicate realistic imagery. However, there is another branch of computer graphics called NPR (Non-photorealistic rendering), that focuses on how to imitate the principles of abstraction used by artists. NPR research covers different topics like line extraction algorithms, stylization and animation coherence. Yet, there are still many problematics to solve in order to generate imagery with the same degree of abstraction and stylization as human-made drawings.

As stated in a recent study[1], most of the lines drawn by artist to convey 3D shape can be explained by some of the most commonly-known line extraction algorithms. However, artists often make global decisions such as the omission of implicit lines or stylistic decisions which tend to depart from realism. Therefore,

M.L. Gavrilova et al. (Eds.): Trans. on Comput. Sci. XXIII, LNCS 8490, pp. 40–57, 2014.
© Springer-Verlag Berlin Heidelberg 2014

there is a need for flexible user interfaces which enables designers to customize the appearance of drawings as well as to emphasize or omit some of its details.

Usually line drawings have a consistent style for the entire scene but artists also include subtle sytilization differences in each stroke. However, algorithms for extracting lines only provide local information like the location of lines or curvature data for each vertex of the mesh. Our system performs a segmentation of the extracted lines to differentiate individual continuous lines and divide them at inflection points.

We also provide an user interface to easily apply a wide range of stroke styles to the lines extracted from a given 3D model(Fig. 1). The user can choose from two input methods: directly draw over the contour lines to apply a previously defined brush style; select every line inside a *Gaussian curvature area* and use sliders to adjust the desired width and shape.

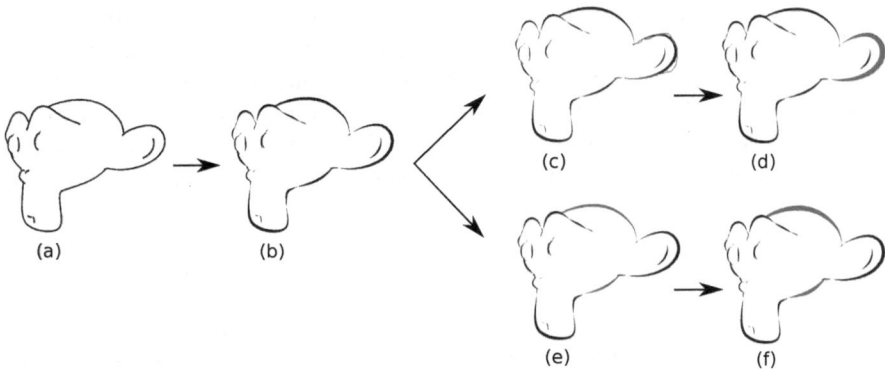

Fig. 1. The initial state without stylization (a) and the result obtained after defining a base style and applying it to all contour lines (b). The user can then change individual lines by drawing directly over them (c)(d) or click on the surface to select and modify at once all lines inside the same Gaussian curvature area (e)(f).

The main problem to solve in order to successfully achieve *localized stylization* of view-dependent lines is how to recognize each of them as the same entity as the viewpoint changes.

1.2   Related Work

Various methods have been proposed in order to extract lines from 3D models. Image-space algorithms focus on image processing methods such as edge detection to extract the lines at each pixel of the output image[2–5]. This type of algorithm generates quite convincing images but suffers from noise problems and are unsuitable for further stylization.

Object-space algorithms are based on the field of differential geometry which analyzes the properties of curves and surfaces. Previous research has successfully characterized different type of lines by making use of derivatives of different order. The main contributions in this category are occluding contours[6], suggestive contours[7, 8], ridges and valleys[9] and apparent ridges[10].

Recently, some researches have focused on how to propagate the parameters of the lines in order to maintain the coherence of stylized strokes as the viewpoint changes or the 3D model is animated[11–15].

Previous papers have stated the need for user interfaces to provide better control of the rendering styles[16, 17]. These systems are useful to quickly define the style of the whole scene but do not provide the means to customize individual details.

Additionally, 3D model segmentation algorithms have mainly focused on how to divide surfaces into meaningful parts consistent with how humans perceive the shape of objects[18] but as far a we know, no method has been used in order to customize view-dependent lines.

In contrast, we consider that the major contribution of this paper is that by introducing the concept of Localized Stylzation, we were able to greatly expand the variation of possible styles in NPR images generated using 3D models. We also want to emphasize that our method focuses on the problem of customizing view-dependent lines while previous works have only provided limited control over their stylization or simply focused on the customization of view-independent lines.

2   Algorithm

In this paper, we make the assumption that the inflections of contour lines have high probability to be chosen by artists as terminal points. We will start by describing the relationship between inflections points and surface curvature.

The apparent curvature κ_{app} is the curvature of the contours in image-space[19]. κ_{app} is positive at convex parts of contours, negative in the concave parts and zero at inflections. Koenderink[6] described the relationship between the apparent curvature κ_{app} and the Gaussian curvature K as follows:

$$\kappa_{app} = \frac{dK}{\kappa_r} \tag{1}$$

with d being the distance to the camera and κ_r the radial curvature.

Since visible occluding contours only appear where κ_r is positive, both κ_{app} and K have the same sign. Consequently, we use K instead of κ_{app} to divide the contours at inflections(where $K = 0$).

In the case of *suggestive contours*, the lines only appear at hyperbolic regions(where $K < 0$). As result, we cannot segment these lines in the same way as *occluding contours*.

2.1   Gaussian Curvature Areas

We segment the surface using the sign of the Gaussian curvature by separating the elliptic ($K > 0$) and the hyperbolic ($K < 0$) parts of the model (Fig. 2). We call these regions *Gaussian curvature areas*. The benefit of the Gaussian curvature segmentation is that not only it enables us to divide the line tracking problem into similar subproblems but also it is directly related to the inflection points of contour lines. In the case of *suggestive contours*, the zero-crossings of K cannot be related to inflection points. However, the *Gaussian curvature areas* are still useful to apply different styles and thresholds on different areas.

We make use of the connectivity data of the triangles as well as the zero-crossings of K to determine to which area each vertex belongs to. Afterwards, we pass the K zero-crossing data to a fragment shader in order to assign an unique color for each area. This shader also builds the boundaries between the areas by assigning different colors to each side of the triangles containing a zero-crossing of K. It should also be noted that, in the case of non-animated models, the Gaussian curvature is view-independent, i.e. constant, which means that the segmentation can be pre-computed. Additionally, we added the functionality of manually merging areas because the user may want to decide if a line should be segmented at the boundary between two areas or not.

Smoothing. Meshes with high level of detail usually results in a highly fragmented segmentation. Depending on the drawing style we want to replicate, we may want to ignore some of the surface detail in favor of a more simplified line segmentation.

Smoothing is commonly used for noise removal of rough meshes, e.g. 3D scan reconstructions of physical objects. A frequently used method for smoothing meshes is Laplacian smoothing. Laplacian smoothing can be thought of as the equivalent of lowpass filtering in signal processing. Desbrun et.al. [20] describes the discrete approximation of the Laplacian as a weighted sum of the one-ring neighbors of a vertex:

$$\mathcal{L}(x_i) = \sum_{j \in N} w_{ij}(x_j - x_i) \tag{2}$$

where x_j are the neighbors of the vertex x_i and N is the set of neighbor vertices.

For a given vertex, the most simple of the proposed approximations defines the Laplacian as the vector to the barycenter of its one-ring neighbors. This is also known as the *umbrella operator* and uses equal weights:

$$w_{i,j} = \frac{1}{m} \tag{3}$$

where m is the number of neighbor vertices.

The smoothed vertex positions can then be calculated as follows:

$$P_i(n + 1) = P_i(n) + \frac{1}{m} \sum_{j \in N} (P_j(n) - P_i(n)) \tag{4}$$

Fig. 2. Gaussian curvature areas separated by the boundary where $K = 0$ (red). The resulting areas can be classified into elliptic areas where $K > 0$ (green) and hyperbolic areas where $K < 0$ (blue).

Alternatively, Laplacian smoothing can also be directly applied to the values of the Gaussian curvature as follows:

$$K_i(n+1) = K_i(n) + \frac{1}{m} \sum_{j \in N} (K_j(n) - K_i(n)) \tag{5}$$

The results of both smoothing methods in Fig. 3, Fig. 4 and Fig. 5 show that as the number of iterations increases, the number of segmented areas decreases (Fig. 6). Applying Laplacian smoothing directly to the Gaussian curvature is slightly faster because no recalculation of normals and curvatures is needed (Table 1). Furthermore, the direct method tends to eliminate the over-segmentation caused by numerical instability. In comparison, the method that includes the recalculation yields better results because it does not modify as much the shape of the boundaries of the areas but the numerical instability of the approximation of K still produces unwanted areas. However, this problem can be solved by merging the unwanted areas as described in the following section.

Numerical Instability. For polygonal surfaces, K is just an approximation which can result in the generation of undesirable areas. We define the undesired areas as the areas where the minimum curvature κ_2 is around 0 and the sign fluctuates inconsistently.

In our case, we want to get rid of the areas which results in over-segmentation of the contour lines, i.e. the areas which are almost flat or are only bent in one direction.

We make use of a modified Sigmoid function to constrain the infinite values of the Gaussian curvature. The Sigmoid function is defined as:

$$s_\alpha(x) = \frac{1}{1 + e^{-\alpha x}} \tag{6}$$

where α defines the shape of the Sigmoid function.

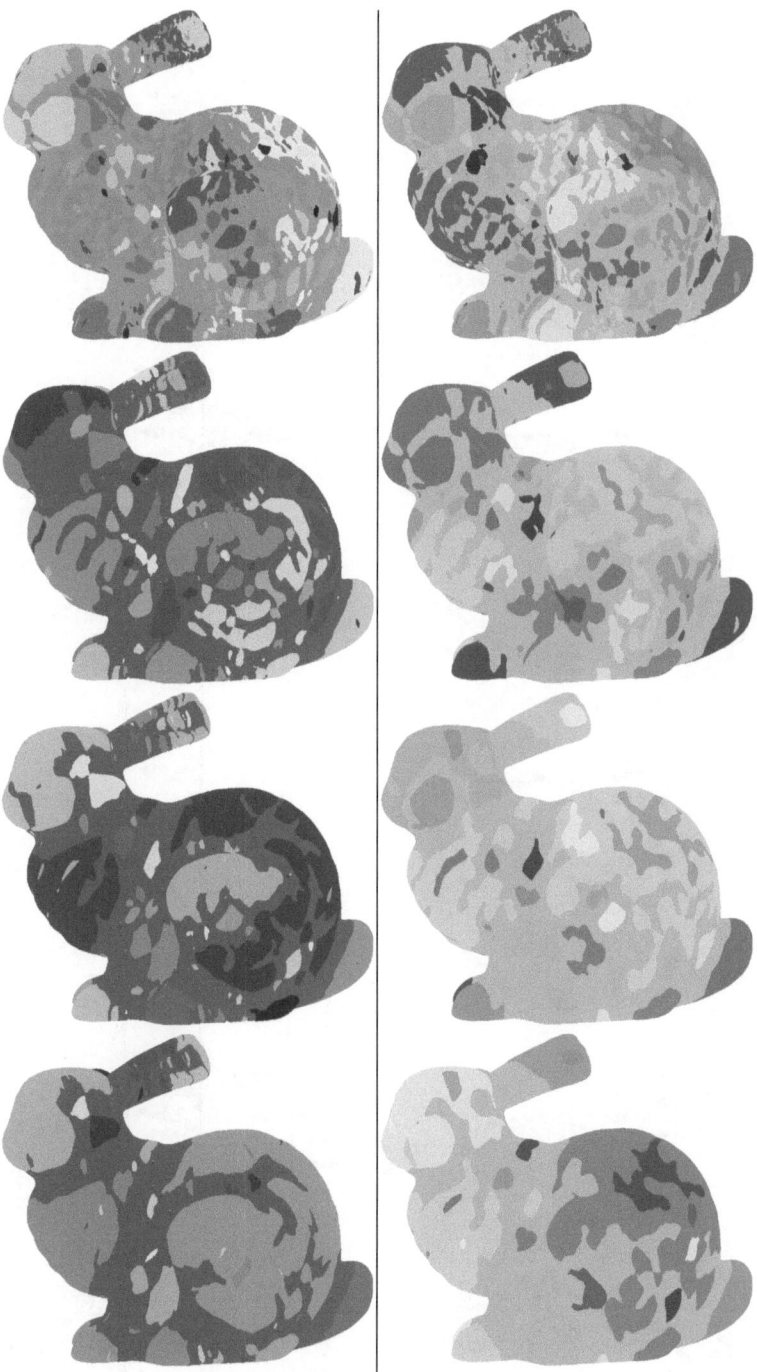

Fig. 3. Stanford bunny: initial segmentation and Laplacian smoothing applied to the vertices positions (left) and the Gaussian curvature (right) for 5, 25 and 100 iterations

Fig. 4. Stanford dragon: initial segmentation and Laplacian smoothing applied to the vertices positions (left) and the Gaussian curvature (right) for 5, 25 and 100 iterations

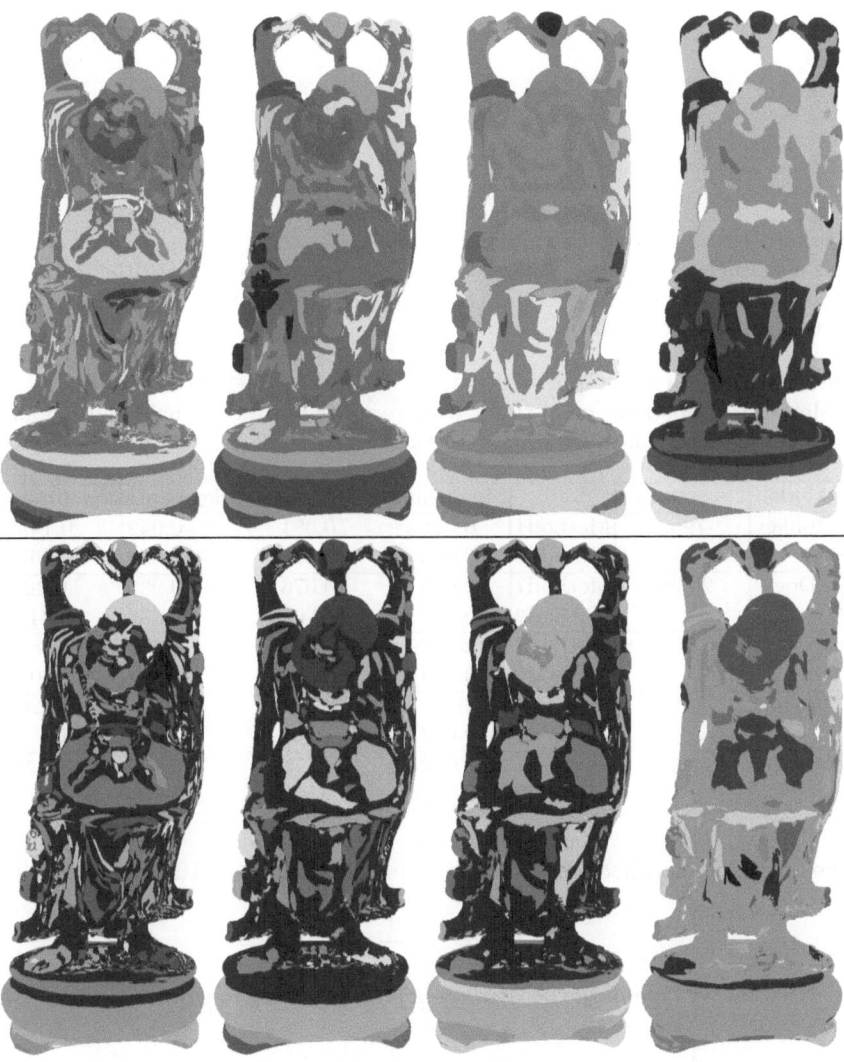

Fig. 5. Stanford buddha: initial segmentation and Laplacian smoothing applied to the vertices positions (top) and the Gaussian curvature (bottom) for 5, 25 and 100 iterations

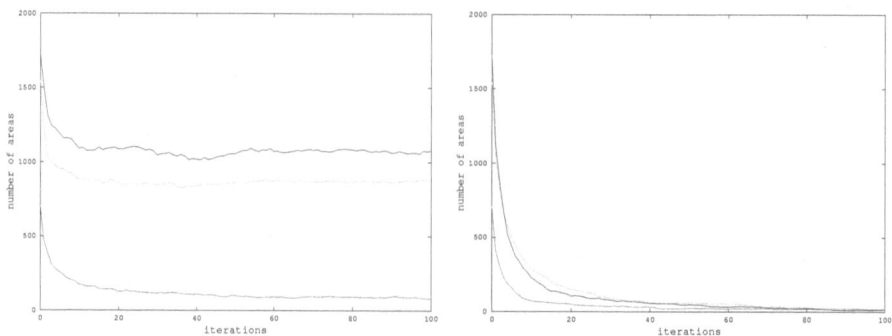

Fig. 6. For the method which applies Laplacian smoothing on the vertices and recalculates normals and vertices, the number of areas stabilizes (left). For the method that applies Laplacian smoothing to the Gaussian curvature values, the number of areas tends to one sigle area (right).

Table 1. Execution times (in seconds) for our smoothing and segmentation methods. Method1: Smoothing on vertices with recalculation of normals and curvatures. Method2: Smoothing on the Gaussian curvature values.

Model	No. vertices		Smoothing	Recalculation	Segmentation	total
Monkey	7952	Method1	0.026	0.081	0.042	0.149
		Method2	0.005	0.0	0.062	0.067
Dog	20909	Method1	0.009	0.076	0.235	0.32
		Method2	0.006	0.0	0.236	0.242
Bunny	34845	Method1	0.0050	0.102	1.476	1.583
		Method2	0.004	0.0	1.304	1.308
Dragon	50000	Method1	0.01	0.211	3.805	4.026
		Method2	0.007	0.0	3.748	3.755
Buddha	49990	Method1	0.012	0.179	3.138	3.329
		Method2	0.007	0.0	2.894	2.901

The following modified version takes values between 0 and 1 for positive values of x:

$$S_\alpha(x) = \frac{2}{1 + e^{-\alpha x}} - 1 \tag{7}$$

For each area, we calculate the average κ_2 of all the vertices contained inside it:

$$\bar{\kappa}_2 = \frac{1}{N} \sum_{i \in V} S_\alpha(|\kappa_{2_i}|) \tag{8}$$

where V is the set of vertices of the area.

Finally, we merge the areas which have only one adjacent area and fulfill the following condition (Fig. 7):

$$\bar{\kappa}_2 < \delta \tag{9}$$

where δ is an user-defined threshold.

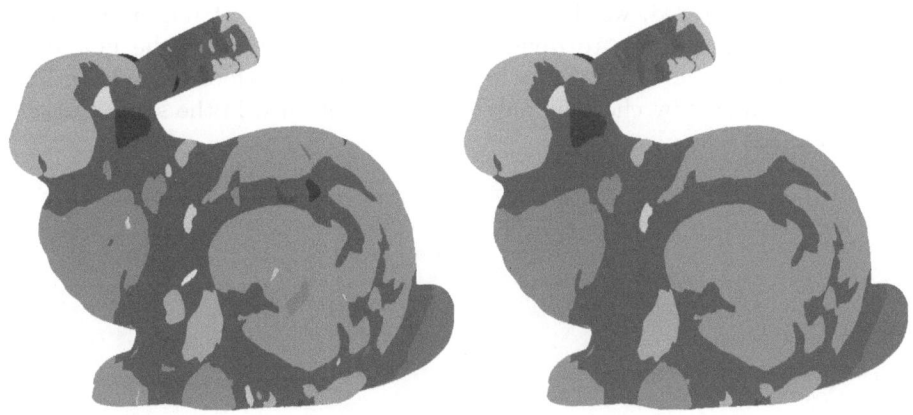

Fig. 7. The unwanted areas produced by numerical instability are eliminated

2.2   Generation of Tracked Areas

One of the main problems we face is that for view-dependent lines, the shape and position of each line changes depending on the viewpoint. Consequently, recognizing each contour line from frame to frame is essential to be able to stylize individual lines.

Line Tracking. In our method, we check the squared distance of both start and end of a given line with all terminal points of the lines of the next frame. For the line currently being checked, we define the points s^k and e^k as the start and end points respectively. A line in the frame k is considered the same as a line in frame $k - 1$ if the following conditions are fulfilled:

- s^k and e^k are matched to the same line in frame $k - 1$
- s and e are matched to different terminal points, i.e $s^{k-1} \neq e^{k-1}$

Additionally, we sample a number of equidistant points along each line and check the similarity of the matched lines using the Hausdorff distance $H(X, Y)$:

$$h(A, B) = \max_{a \in A}(\min_{b \in B}(d(a, b))) \tag{10}$$

where $d(a, b)$ is the Euclidean distance between points a and b.

$$H(X, Y) = max(h(X), h(Y)) \tag{11}$$

With X and Y being the sets of sampled points of the two lines being checked. Therefore, in order to prevent mismatches we add the following condition:

$$H(X, Y) < \delta \tag{12}$$

With δ being a distance threshold.

As previously stated, we decided to segment the lines at inflections points. This actually corresponds to dividing the lines as they cross the boundaries between *Gaussian curvature areas* in object-space. Therefore, we can optimize the tracking process by checking only the lines contained in the same *Gaussian curvature area*.

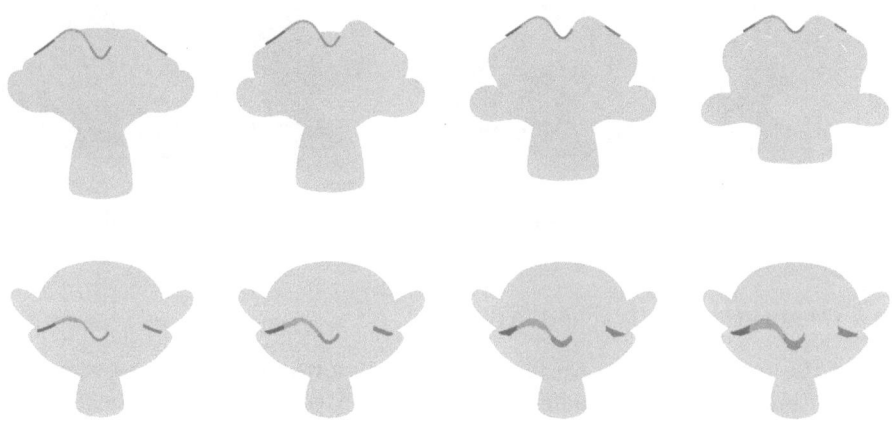

Fig. 8. Five lines of a 3D model as the viewpoint changes (up) and the evolution of their tracked areas (down)

Tracked Areas. As the camera position changes, view-dependent lines move across the surface until they eventually merge with other lines or completely disappear. Consequently, not all contour lines can be tracked at every viewpoint. It is then essential to be able to store and retrieve their references after arbitrary camera movements. Since contour lines can only appear inside a limited area, we store their references in a color-coded texture map containing the regions of the surface where each line has previously appeared (Fig. 8). We call these regions the *tracked areas*. It should be noted that the *tracked areas* can be considered as subsets of the *Gaussian curvature areas* (Fig. 9).

For any given line, we retrieve the reference from the texture map only if both of its terminal points and sampled internal points are in the same *tracked area*. The reference can then be used to recover the line stylization from the properties table. In our algorithm, the purpose of line tracking is limited to building the *tracked areas* corresponding to each contour line. Since these areas can be used to identify each line, pre-computing all the *tracked areas* would allow us to just retrieve the reference directly from the color-coded texture map, making further tracking unnecessary.

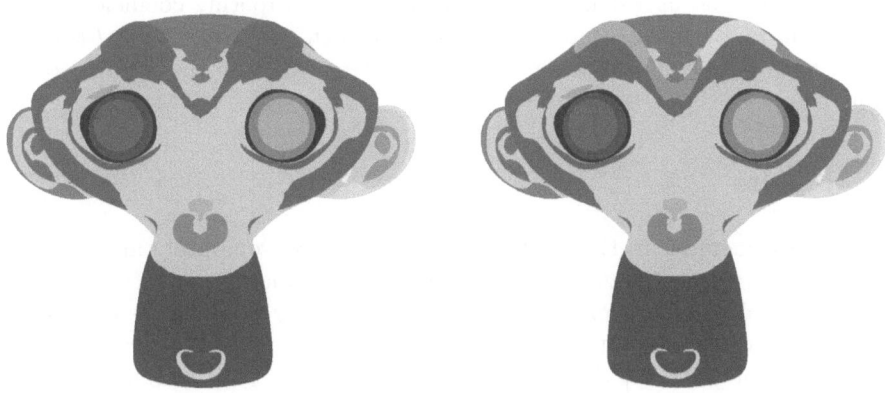

Fig. 9. The original segmentation (left) and the tracked areas of the same 5 lines tracked in Fig. 8, added as a subset of their corresponding Gaussian curvature area (right)

For high-definition meshes, if the camera movement step is not too small, a gap appears between the tracked line and its matched line of the next frame (Fig. 10). This gap area is located where the following condition is satisfied:

$$(n_k \cdot v_k)(n_{k+1} \cdot v_{k+1}) < 0 \tag{13}$$

where n is the surface normal and v the view direction.

In order to fill this gap, we make use of the triangles connectivity information to perform a search in the neighhbor triangles of the line being tracked. We limit the search to the triangles inside the gap, i.e. the enclosed region delimited by the boundaries of the Gaussian curvature area, the line being tracked and the matched line.

2.3   Line Rendering

We chose a commonly used method for line rendering that extrudes triangles strips along the zero-crossings in the normal direction. As opposed to other line primitive based methods, this rendering method enable us to change the width along lines as much as we want. We also added length dependent width and tapering[21] using the same modified Sigmoid function defined in (7) of section 2.1. We can obtain a variety of line shapes by changing the α coefficients of the Sigmoid functions. We can then calculate the width at a certain position of a line as follows:

$$W = \omega S_{\alpha_L}(L) S_{\alpha_T}(l) \tag{14}$$

With ω being the user-defined base width, α_T the tapering coefficient and α_L the length coeffficent. L represents the total length of the line while l is a scalar taking normalized values increasing as we move away from the nearest terminal point.

3   Results

In our implementation, the user can select each line separately and change its properties or select a Gaussian curvature area and modify at once all the lines contained inside it. The process to stylize a line only needs to be done for one viewpoint because its properties are preserved as the camera moves. As a result, our system not only frees the user from the tedious process of customizing all lines for every viewpoint but also, as opposed to previous stylization approaches[16, 17], we are able to stylize each line individually. For an experienced user, the process of stylizing the contour lines of the models shown in Fig. 11, 12 and 13 can be done in a few minutes. Additionally, we showed how unwanted areas caused by numerical instability can be eliminated, and also compared two smoothing methods for highly detailed models.

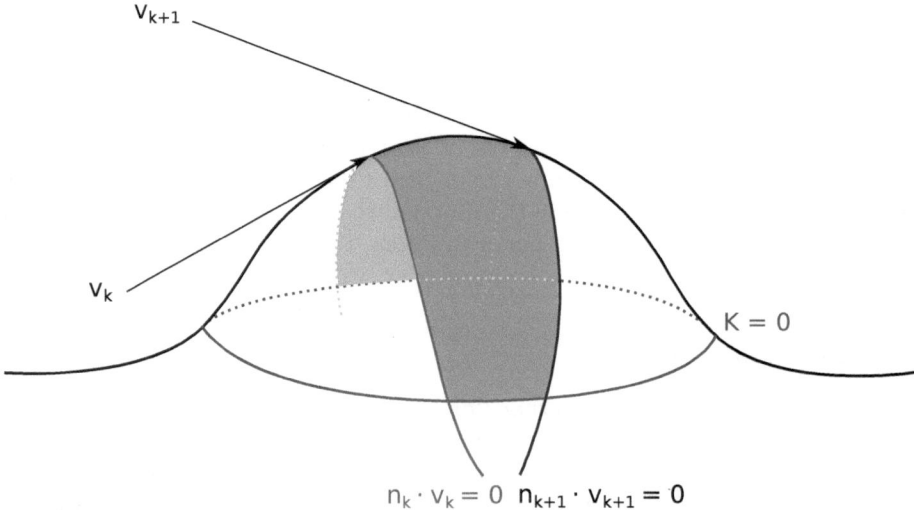

Fig. 10. A gap appears between the tracked lines in two consecutive frames (grey). The area to fill corresponds to the region inside the corresponding Gaussian curvature area where the product of $n \cdot v$ of two consecutive frames is negative.

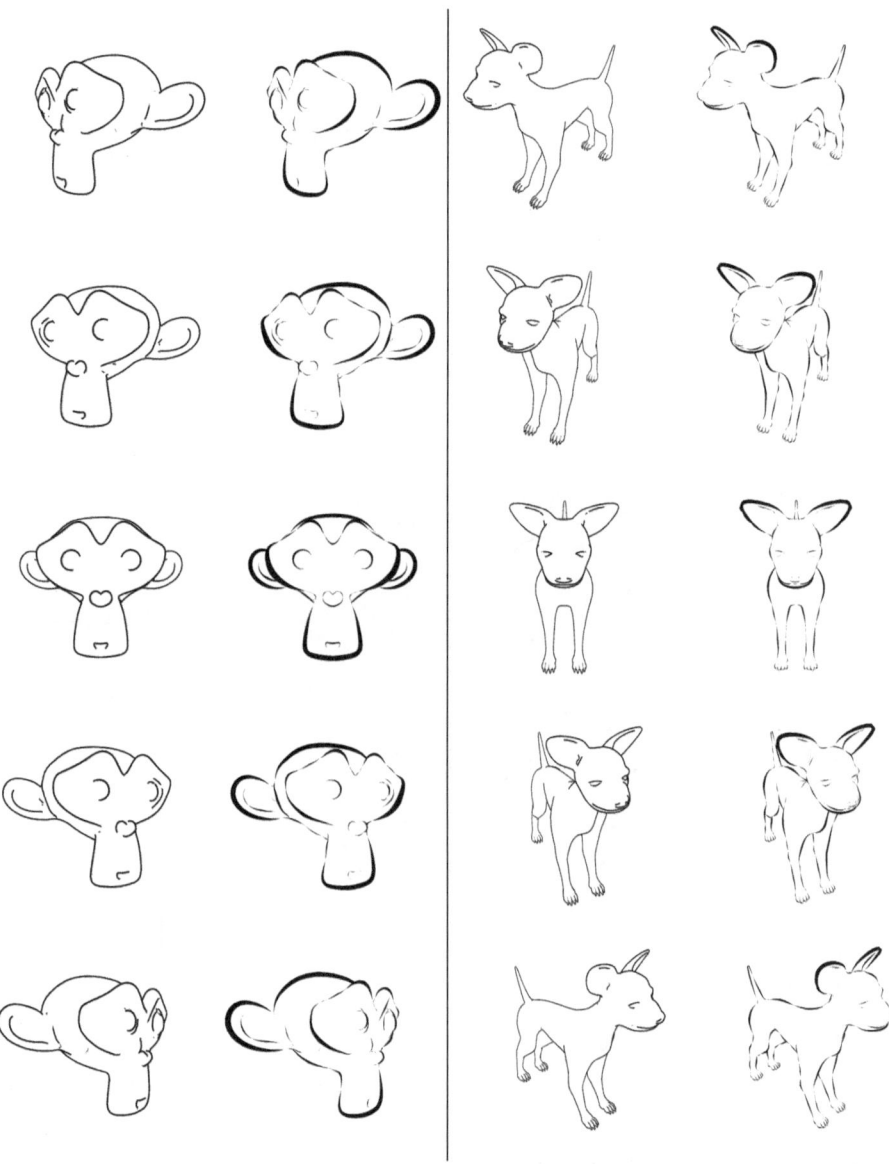

Fig. 11. Blender monkey (left) and dog (right) models without stylization and with *localized stylization* as the viewpoint changes (with suggestive contours)

Fig. 12. Stanford bunny (left) and Stanford dragon (right) models without stylization and with *localized stylization* as the viewpoint changes

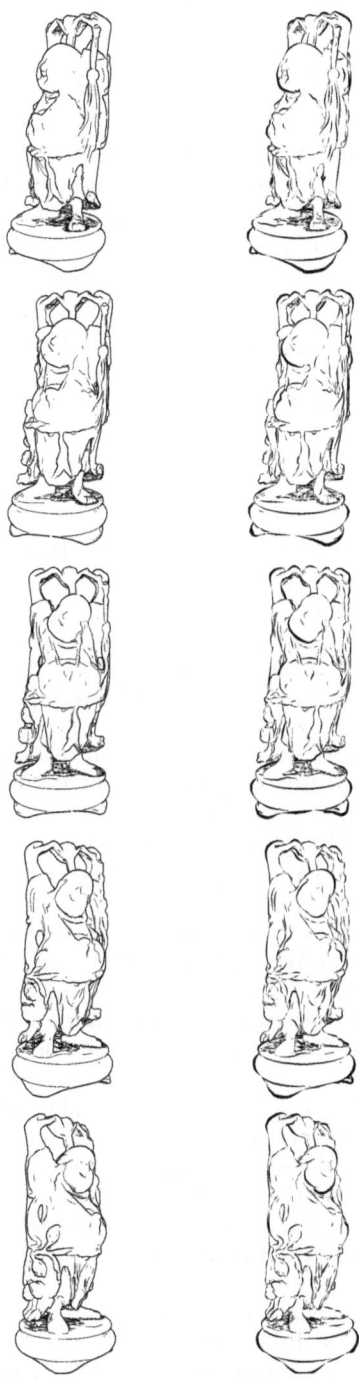

Fig. 13. Stanford buddha model without stylization and with *localized stylization* as the viewpoint changes (with suggestive contours)

4   Conclusion

We have proposed a method for *localized stylization* of *occluding contours* that preserves the properties of lines as the viewpoint change. However, future approaches should implement more robust tracking methods to prevent incorrect matches. Our system only provides control over the line shape and therefore we should extend the range of customizable properties. In addition, given that different lines may appear in common regions, we should add support for overlapping *tracked areas*. We should also note that our algorithm partially supports *localized stylization* of *suggestive contours* but it is still lacking compared to *occluding contours*. Finally, the segmentation of contour lines may be extended to consider other important points like the extremas of contour points as possible candidates for terminal points.

References

1. Cole, F., Golovinskiy, A., Limpaecher, A., Barros, H.S., Finkelstein, A., Funkhouser, T., Rusinkiewicz, S.: Where do people draw lines? Commun. ACM 55(1), 107–115 (2012)
2. Saito, T., Takahashi, T.: Comprehensible rendering of 3-d shapes. SIGGRAPH Comput. Graph. 24(4), 197–206 (1990)
3. Decaudin, P.: Cartoon looking rendering of 3D scenes. Research Report 2919, INRIA (June 1996)
4. Hertzmann, A.: Introduction to 3d non-photorealistic rendering: Silhouettes and outlines. In: Non-Photorealistic Rendering. SIGGRAPH 1999 (1999)
5. Lee, Y., Markosian, L., Lee, S., Hughes, J.F.: Line drawings via abstracted shading. In: ACM SIGGRAPH 2007 Papers, SIGGRAPH 2007. ACM, New York (2007)
6. Koenderink, J.J., et al.: What does the occluding contour tell us about solid shape. Perception 13(3), 321–330 (1984)
7. DeCarlo, D., Finkelstein, A., Rusinkiewicz, S., Santella, A.: Suggestive contours for conveying shape. ACM Trans. Graph. 22(3), 848–855 (2003)
8. DeCarlo, D., Finkelstein, A., Rusinkiewicz, S.: Interactive rendering of suggestive contours with temporal coherence. In: Proceedings of the 3rd International Symposium on Non-Photorealistic Animation and Rendering, NPAR 2004, pp. 15–24. ACM, New York (2004)
9. Ohtake, Y., Belyaev, A., Seidel, H.-P.: Ridge-valley lines on meshes via implicit surface fitting. ACM Trans. Graph. 23(3), 609–612 (2004)
10. Judd, T., Durand, F., Adelson, E.: Apparent ridges for line drawing. In: ACM SIGGRAPH 2007 Papers, SIGGRAPH 2007. ACM, New York (2007)
11. Kalnins, R.D., Davidson, P.L., Markosian, L., Finkelstein, A.: Coherent stylized silhouettes. In: ACM SIGGRAPH 2003 Papers, SIGGRAPH 2003, pp. 856–861. ACM, New York (2003)
12. Bénard, P., Cole, F., Golovinskiy, A., Finkelstein, A.: Self-similar texture for coherent line stylization. In: Proceedings of the 8th International Symposium on Non-Photorealistic Animation and Rendering, NPAR 2010, pp. 91–97. ACM, New York (2010)

13. Buchholz, B., Faraj, N., Paris, S., Eisemann, E., Boubekeur, T.: Spatio-temporal analysis for parameterizing animated lines. In: Proceedings of the ACM SIG-GRAPH/Eurographics Symposium on Non-Photorealistic Animation and Rendering, NPAR 2011, pp. 85–92. ACM, New York (2011)
14. Karsch, K., Hart, J.C.: Snaxels on a plane. In: Proceedings of the ACM SIG-GRAPH/Eurographics Symposium on Non-Photorealistic Animation and Rendering, NPAR 2011, pp. 35–42. ACM, New York (2011)
15. Bénard, P., Lu, J., Cole, F., Finkelstein, A., Thollot, J.: Active strokes: coherent line stylization for animated 3d models. In: Proceedings of the Symposium on Non-Photorealistic Animation and Rendering, NPAR 2012, pp. 37–46. Eurographics Association, Aire-la-Ville (2012)
16. Kalnins, R.D., Markosian, L., Meier, B.J., Kowalski, M.A., Lee, J.C., Davidson, P.L., Webb, M., Hughes, J.F., Finkelstein, A.: Wysiwyg npr: drawing strokes directly on 3d models. ACM Trans. Graph. 21(3), 755–762 (2002)
17. Grabli, S., Turquin, E., Durand, F., Sillion, F.X.: Programmable rendering of line drawing from 3d scenes. ACM Trans. Graph. 29(2), 18:1–18:20 (2010)
18. Chen, X., Golovinskiy, A., Funkhouser, T.: A benchmark for 3d mesh segmentation. ACM Trans. Graph. 28(3), 73:1–73:12 (2009)
19. Rusinkiewicz, S., Cole, F., DeCarlo, D., Finkelstein, A.: Line drawings from 3d models. In: ACM SIGGRAPH 2008 Classes, SIGGRAPH 2008, pp. 39:1–39:356. ACM, New York (2008)
20. Desbrun, M., Meyer, M., Schröder, P., Barr, A.H.: Implicit fairing of irregular meshes using diffusion and curvature flow. In: Proceedings of the 26th Annual Conference on Computer Graphics and Interactive Techniques, SIGGRAPH 1999, pp. 317–324. ACM Press/Addison-Wesley Publishing Co., New York (1999)
21. Saito, S., Kani, A., Chang, Y., Nakajima, M.: Curvature-based stroke rendering. Vis. Comput. 24(1), 1–11 (2007)

Image-Driven Haptic Rendering

Shahzad Rasool and Alexei Sourin

School of Computer Engineering, Nanyang Technological University, Singapore
{shahzadrasool,assourin}@ntu.edu.sg

Abstract. Haptic interaction requires the content creators to make haptic models of the virtual objects while it is not always possible or feasible, especially when it comes to using real images or videos as elements of interaction. We, therefore, propose tangible images and image-driven haptic rendering where a displayed image is used as a source of the force-feedback calculations at any pixel touched by the haptic device. We introduce the main idea and describe how it is implemented as a core algorithm for image-driven haptic rendering, as well as for a few particular cases of haptic rendering emphasizing colors, contours and textures of the objects displayed in the images. Implementations of the proposed method to desktop tangible image application and haptic video communication on the web are presented as a proof of concept.

Keywords: tangible images, tangible video, haptic interaction, image-driven rendering.

1 Introduction

While vision remains the most important cognition channel, the sense of touch significantly enhances our perception of the world around us. In human-computer interaction, touching is implemented using various haptic devices. The most common are desktop haptic devices, which are usually designed as robotic arms capable of digitizing their position in virtual space and delivering force-feedback to the user (Fig. 1).

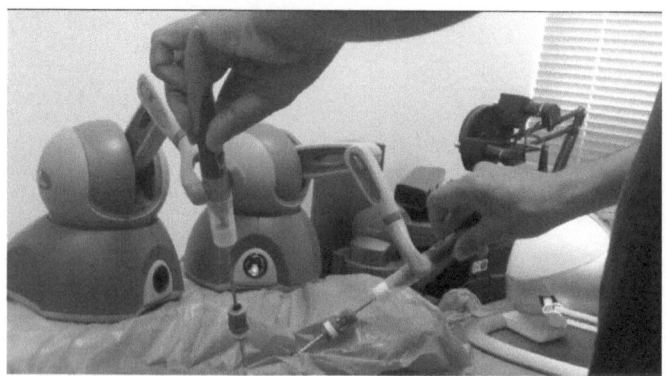

Fig. 1. Desktop haptic devices used for simulation of minimally invasive surgery

M.L. Gavrilova et al. (Eds.): Trans. on Comput. Sci. XXIII, LNCS 8490, pp. 58–77, 2014.
© Springer-Verlag Berlin Heidelberg 2014

Haptic interaction requires the content creators to make physical (haptic) models of virtual objects to be able to solve collision detection and force-feedback calculation tasks. These haptic models are usually based on polygon meshes, scalar fields or procedural models collocated in the modeling space with the geometric model of the virtual objects. However working with these models is not always possible or feasible when it comes to using real images or videos as elements of interaction.

As an alternative approach, we look at image-driven haptic rendering where a displayed image, real or simulated, is used as a source of force-feedback calculations at any pixel touched by the haptic device. The rationale for this approach lies in image-driven visualization, which, in certain cases, can be used as an alternative to the conventional method of 3D modeling followed by visual rendering to 2D image. The examples are various interactive panoramic images simulating walk-through in 3D environments, image-based travelling in interactive street views, and zooming views at compressed images. Hence, instead of creating haptic models and displaying 3D models of the objects as 2D images on the screen, we make maximum use of the final 2D computer generated images or actual photographs to understand the three-dimensionality of the objects depicted there and to calculate the feedback forces as if the haptic device interacted with the 3D scene displayed in the image. We do it without performing 3D reconstruction of the scene but by calculating in real time the feedback force for each pixel of the image "touched" by the haptic device.

We do not have an ambition to replace the traditional haptic modeling and 3D visualization but we foresee applications which can be implemented much faster and with a believable immersion when the image-driven approach is used. These are just a few possible scenarios of such haptic interactions:

1. There can be developed tools for haptic perception of the traditional visual interfaces as well as any visual information displayed on the computer monitor.
2. There can be cases of minimally invasive surgery training where the actual surgical images made tangible will teach the trainees how to move and apply the surgical tools while observing the surgical area on video monitor.
3. We can envisage networked video communication where one will not only see somebody in a video window but also will be able to touch this person based on the haptic rendering of the incoming streaming video data.

In this paper, we propose extensions to our previous work [1] where the image was assumed to have sharp discontinuities and ideal object contours. Here, we alleviate this assumption by catering for real edges that are usually represented by a gradual change in intensity values among neighboring pixels.

In Section 2, we review the existing approaches to image driven haptic interaction and motivate our research. In Section 3, we introduce the main idea of our approach and describe how it is implemented as a core algorithm for image-driven haptic rendering as well as the algorithms for a few particular cases of haptic rendering of different dominant colors, textures and contours of the objects displayed in the images. Applications of the proposed method to desktop tangible image application and haptic video communication on the web are presented in Section 4 as a proof of concept. In Section 5 we outline further challenges and then conclude the paper.

2   Related Work

Upon surveying the existing relevant works we concluded that the previous approaches to haptic interaction with images and videos mostly followed two ways:

1. Haptic interaction with the 3D objects reconstructed from the image, and
2. Haptic interaction based on deriving haptic forces directly from the image.

Reconstruction of 3D geometry from 2D images is usually based on using shading, focus, and texture data as well as multiple views of the scene. The techniques using shading information make a fundamental assumption that convex surfaces are illuminated brighter than concave surface. Often these techniques additionally assume a single directional light source placed at infinite distance and illuminating the scene, which exhibits Lambertian reflectance properties. Shadows and inter-reflections are usually neglected [2, 3]. Under these assumptions, the variation in intensity becomes a function of the local surface orientation. Using additional constraints, such as smoothness, the irradiance equation can be solved to generate a depth map. Recent methods aimed at eliminating unrealistic assumptions like orthographic projection [4] use PDE based approaches and/or formulate the shape from shading problem as polynomial [5]. There were also other methods proposed to generate an illusion of a relief surface from a single 2D image using shading and light source direction information [6]. In order to be able to reconstruct 3D shape from multiple views, a correspondence between the points in the two scenes needs to be established. Triangulation can then be used to recover a depth map of the scene using camera parameters and the generated disparity map [7]. Automatic establishment of dense and accurate correspondences between images is a challenging task and various techniques have been proposed to achieve a better performance. Thus, paper [8] presents a brief description of recent developments in determination of inter-image correspondences. Photometric stereo images taken from a single viewpoint under different lighting conditions can also be used for 3D reconstruction from images [9]. Some other methods of 3D reconstruction also exist including Shape from Focus/Defocus, Shape from Texture, etc. [10]. While reconstruction of 3D shapes from images is rather popular area of research, there were only a few attempts to use it for simulating haptic interaction with images. Shape from Shading by Tsai and Shah has been used to produce tangible images where the reconstructed 3D surface mesh is used as a depth map superimposed on a flat surface while forces are calculated at the contact point as a sum of normal and tangential forces [11]. A 3D model reconstructed from a stereo pair by triangulation is presented for visualization and haptic interaction in [12]. In [13], a 3D model reconstructed from multiple images is used for haptic rendering while auto-stereoscopic display is used for the model visualization. In [14], haptic interaction with a model reconstructed from stereo images captured by cameras mounted on shoulders of a blind user was proposed to enhance visually impaired users' navigation capabilities. In another work, Kim et al. [15] proposed a method to embed haptic information into 2D images using least significant bit manipulation for hiding haptic information in the image. The visual distortion produced by such manipulation is considered to be insignificant. At the time of interaction, a 3D polygon mesh is reconstructed from the decoded information and force is rendered based on interaction with this mesh.

Previous *works combining haptic interaction with image-driven visualization* have been done mainly in the context of assistive technology to enhance the interaction experience of visually impaired users or broadcast media. Based on these applications, the existing work has focused on making haptically perceivable contours and textures of the objects displayed in the image. Hence, a tool for image editing with a haptic device is presented in [16] where the user can trace the boundaries of the objects in the image. In [17], image segmentation hierarchy is used to provide various levels of detail for haptic perception of the edges in photographs for visually impaired users. In [18], edge detection and wavelets are used for providing different levels of detail for boundary curves in an image. Vector graphics is converted to haptic edges using gradient approximations in [19]. In [20], a boundary map is extracted from the image and edges are perceived as wedges peaking at the object boundaries. The techniques used in these works are evaluated in [21]. A two degree-of-freedom force feedback method is proposed in [22], where the pose of planar objects in the image is estimated and used to perturb the surface normal of each plane so that assistive or resistive forces can be applied to the haptic device.

There are also a few works on *image-based haptic texture generation*. For example, a direct method of haptic texture rendering is presented in [23], which uses color temperature and luminance to generate forces without generating a depth map. A similar direct haptic texture generation method presented in [24] uses image gradients based on Prewitt filters for force calculation. In [25], a method that uses wavelet and Fourier transforms to get a depth map of the scene for texture rendering is presented. Another method using Gaussian filters for smoothing the image was used in [26] to generate haptic textures from images. In [27], the Gaussian filter is replaced by an improved switching median filter to preserve fine details on the image.

Some broadcast applications techniques have also been proposed for *haptic interaction with videos* [28, 29]. These techniques require additional information for generating haptic forces. The examples of such data are scene depth [30] and trajectory to follow the client haptic device [31]. Extensions have been proposed to existing compression standards to include data required for feedback force generation apart from the color video [32, 33]. While these methods use 2D visualization, the collision detection and haptic rendering are performed on reconstructed 3D models of the scene, which requires powerful computers to achieve real-time performance.

Critically analyzing the existing approaches we have concluded that the current techniques of converting information extracted from images directly into haptic forces have limited performance. Some of them present only 2 degrees of freedom force feedback or have force stability flaws, others put stringent constraints on the input images. Similarly, the applicability of haptic perception of edges is quite limited. More importantly, the existing methods based on using individual images fail to provide haptic perception of the overall visible 3D geometry of objects in the scene and rather produce touch sensation for small perturbation of surface textures. 3D reconstruction followed by haptic rendering requires significant computational resources and often fails to provide high precision as well as overall consistency of the reconstructed scenes. Techniques proposed for broadcast media require extensive interactive preprocessing during the authoring stage.

We have therefore concluded that there is a room for research in direct haptic interaction with images without full 3D reconstruction. We understand though that it may be not possible to come up with a single method applicable to all images universally for producing feedback forces for perception of visible geometry, texture, edges and material properties. Instead, a set of methods with user adjustable parameters is needed where the user can tune the parameters best suited to the desired application.

3   Overall Approach to Haptic Interaction with Images

Ideally haptic interaction with 2D images should provide for perception of various features. These include geometry of objects, texture details for each object, physical properties, edges or boundaries of objects, etc. Difference in physical properties of various objects should be clearly perceptible. For example, the user should be able to feel the softness, elasticity of objects, as well as such effects in the scene as wind, liquid flow, etc., while being able to see the visual changes in the scene such as visual deformations of the objects when they are touched.

Our approach is based on the idea of obtaining during the run time the depth coordinate for each pixel "touched" by the haptic interface point (HIP) of the haptic device. We do it by interpreting the pixel color, as well as the colors of a few pixels in its vicinity, in terms of visible depth. Haptic feedback forces are then calculated at each pixel, which involves calculation of the force direction and force magnitude. The forces are calculated in such a way that there is no abrupt change of their directions and magnitudes resulting in jitter or sudden kick back motions of the haptic device handle. Additional samplings of the image in vicinity of the HIP are used to smooth interpolation and approximation of the force feedback. This approach still restricts images to be frontally illuminated to set a link between the shades of the colors and the visible points. To eliminate this constraint, we use, where it is feasible, stereo-images, subsequent frames of videos, as well as depth data obtained from RGBD depth-sensing cameras like Microsoft Kinect. Combination of all these methods turned images in what we call "tangible images" thus implementing the approach "what you see is what you touch".

There are three important cases that we highlight as important application modes.

The first case requires interpretation of color patterns on the visible surface of the objects as changes of colors rather than changes of their geometry. For example, while performing haptic rendering of an image of a face with fair complexion, the HIP will not be "diving" into dark eyes and hairs interpreting them as holes. It demands to filter out sudden changes of colors while performing the depth calculation task. The idea of the method can be explained as setting up a threshold value for the changes of dominant colors while analyzing pixels visited by the HIP. If the color change exceeds the threshold, it is assumed that the HIP continues to move along the surface of the displayed object with the same depth as that for the previous pixel.

Then, rather relative changes of the next dominant color are used for further depth calculations. Since real photographic images usually have blurred transitions at object boundaries, emphasizing the contrast of the input image helps to detect the color patterns.

The second special case pays accents to contours of the visible objects. This mode is essential for haptic interaction with graphical user interfaces or moving images. In contrast to the existing approaches, we do not detect and store edges of the objects but rather further extend the previously described approach with the color threshold while using it as a trigger for detecting the event of touching the contour of the object. Force profiles defined by mathematical functions are used to reliably keep the HIP outside the detected contour. This mode also permits to work with videos to detect the boundaries of the moving objects.

The third special case emphasizes tangible textures. This mode is useful when the object in the image has rather small overall changes of its geometry while the object's fine texture has to be explored. It is achieved by stretching the usable range of the image histogram. Any pixels that lie outside this range are clamped to the respective extreme of the chosen histogram range.

In the next section, we discuss the implementation details of the core algorithm and the three special cases.

4   Algorithm Implementation Details

The algorithm derives the depth coordinate for each pixel from the color information obtained from the image. Haptic forces are then calculated at each pixel from a small neighborhood around the pixel. In other words, colors are approximated to depth data, which is used for force calculation. Since this approximation assumes proportionality between colors and depth values, the algorithm works best with images taken with frontal illumination without specular highlights so that the image intensity matches the depth of the scene. This is feasible for a broad class of practical cyberworld applications including video communication and GUI augmentation, presented in Section 5. However, for certain applications, such as minimally invasive surgery simulation, special care must be taken as the rendered organs may have wet surfaces causing specular reflections. In such cases we can improve the algorithm performance by making adjustments for better approximation of the depth from the color, e.g. by using context aware filtering in the preprocessing stage.

The core algorithm works by converting the RGB input color to grayscale and inverting the image. The intensity of the pixels is then mapped to the depth values. Once the depth map has been estimated, the input image is used as a textured plane in an orthographically projected 3D space, and the haptic device workspace is mapped to the size of the image in xy–dimensions and to 0 to 2^8-1 levels in the z–dimension, mapping to the 256 levels of the depth map. The resulting mapping will be such that the brightest pixels, i.e. with the brightness value of 2^8-1, will correspond to the points closest to the viewer and those with intensity value of 0 will be the points located farthest from the viewer.

64   S. Rasool and A. Sourin

The idea of the algorithm is illustrated in Fig. 2 where the image of a frontally illuminated sphere is shown.

While the HIP is moving, the depth value at the pixel corresponding to the xy–coordinates of the HIP is tested against the z–coordinate of the HIP. A collision is detected if the HIP z–coordinate is greater than the depth value $z_{HIP}(x,y) > d(x,y)$, while the difference of the two is the depth of penetration of the HIP into the scene $p = \|z_{HIP}(x,y) - d(x,y)\|$. A small sampling matrix (Fig. 2d) with the HIP at its center follows the movement of the HIP and acquires the depth values of the pixels it overlaps with. These depth values are used to calculate the visible surface normal at the pixel visited by the HIP. Since the force is applied in the direction of the surface normal, it is normalized and scaled by the penetration depth to get the feedback force [34, 35]. Several adjustments are made to the calculated forces to remove inconsistencies in the estimated depth map due to noise and to provide stability. Hence, in order to allow for smooth perception of object boundaries, forces applied at previous frames are averaged and matched to the force calculated for the current frame. If a large mismatch in either magnitude or direction is observed, an average force is applied for the current frame ensuring that no sudden change in force occurs hence providing stable interaction. From our experiments, using a sampling matrix 5×5 and keeping track of the force feedback for up to 10 past locations of the HIP provides for an acceptable smoothness of the force feedback.

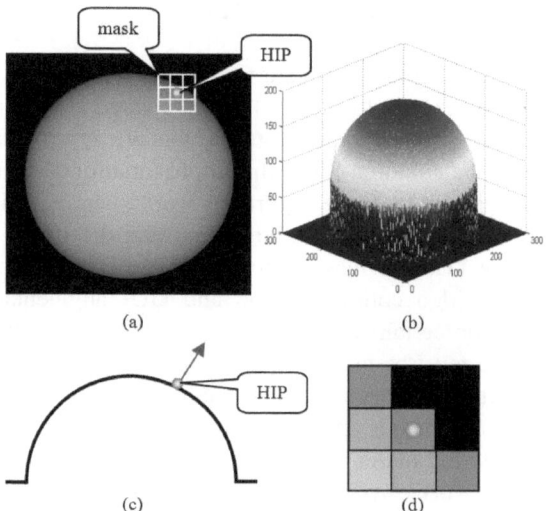

Fig. 2. (a) A 2D image with brightness reflecting heightmap of the scene, (b) corresponding heightmap, (c) surface felt by the haptic device (arrow shows the direction of force applied at the HIP), (d) content of the mask at the position indicated in (a)

While this approach produces believable perception of geometry, there may be images for which image intensity is not proportional to the height-map of the scene. To develop a system of image-based haptic interaction suitable for as many images as possible, the three special cases outlined in Section 3 are discussed here in greater detail.

4.1   Offset Mode

Let us consider for example, an image of a frontally illuminated face. A mole on the cheek or dark facial hair such as eyebrows or mustache will be perceived by the algorithm as a discontinuity in depth. Such a discontinuity will be interpreted as a deep hole or a cavity onto the face. To solve this problem, the haptic rendering algorithm switches to the '*offset*' mode, where the maximum difference between neighboring pixels at object boundaries is limited by a threshold value. If the color change exceeds the threshold, it will be considered as a *false discontinuity* and the HIP will continue to move along the surface of the displayed object with the same depth as that for the previous HIP position while the relative changes of the next dominant color will be used for further depth calculations. This is illustrated in Fig. 3 where a checkerboard image is used.

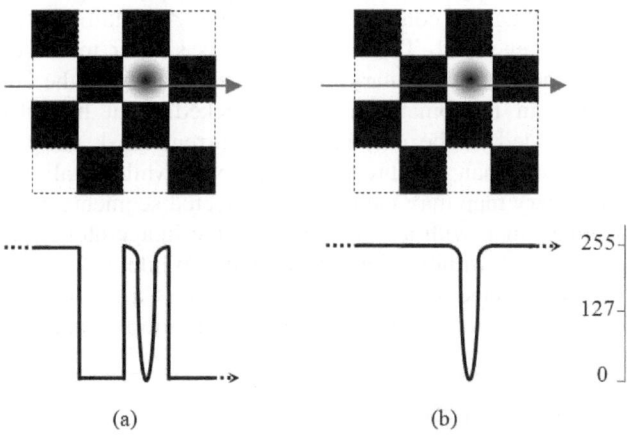

(a)   (b)

Fig. 3. Effect of using the offset mode on the perceived height-map: (a) test image in normal/default mode, (b) test image in the offset mode

It shows two input images overlaid with the position and direction of movement of the HIP while the respective height-maps perceived by the haptic device are displayed below along with the gray level scale on the right. Fig. 3(a) illustrates the perceived force feedback from the checkerboard pattern augmented with radial gradient if the default mode is used. In Fig. 3(b), the same pattern is used in the offset mode. As the HIP moves in the offset mode, the first discontinuity from white to black, being greater than the threshold, is ignored. As it enters the block with a radial gradient, a second discontinuity is encountered. This discontinuity, being larger in magnitude than the threshold value, is also ignored, and the height-map shown is perceived. This is done by using three masks of the same size centered at the HIP and following its movement in the xy-direction. These are *current mask* for storing the depth values in the neighborhood of the HIP at the current frame, *cached mask* for maintaining one frame depth mask memory, and the *force calculation mask* that is used to calculate the feedback forces. At every haptic frame, each entry of the cached mask is tested against the corresponding entry of the current mask. For the entries having an absolute difference greater than the threshold δ, the corresponding entry of the force calculation mask is copied from the cached mask. The rest of the entries are copied from the current mask, which is summarized as:

$$\delta_t^i = d_t^i - d_{t-1}^i$$
$$\forall \quad i \in \left\{1,2,3,...,MaskSize^2\right\} \tag{1}$$
$$D_t^i = \begin{cases} d_t^i & \delta_t^i < \delta \\ d_{t-1}^i & \delta_t^i > \delta \end{cases}$$

where d_t^i, d_{t-1}^i and D_t^i are the ith entries in the current mask, cached mask and the force calculation mask, respectively. At the end of the haptic frame, the force calculation mask is copied to the cached mask to be used in the next frame. This approach assumes a sharp transition from one dominant color to another, hence a sharp discontinuity in depth is assumed. However, real images may not necessarily have such properties. To handle such cases, we propose to preprocess the image interactively or automatically so that a binary image map having sharp discontinuities is produced by stretching the contrast of the image. An additional sampling *binary mask* matrix is thus generated. The binary mask is similar to the current mask. It carries the values read from the binary map. For each entry of the current mask, the corresponding entry in the binary mask is checked. If it has black values, the threshold value is added to the corresponding current mask entry. Therefore, any change in depth greater than the threshold is ignored while smaller changes remain perceivable. This binary map may include only selected segments or the entire image. Fig. 4 shows a binary map with a few regions of the image along with the feedback force rendered with and without the offset mode. While in the default mode the feedback forces are directed so as if the IKEA letters are carved deep inside the surface, in the offset mode the feedback forces remain orthogonal to the surface.

(a)   (b)

(c)   (d)

Fig. 4. Offset mode using a binary map. (a) 2D input image with blurry transitions, (b) the corresponding binary map with sharp discontinuities, (c) feedback forces in the default mode are directed as if the IKEA letters are carved deep inside the surface, (d) feedback forces in the offset mode are orthogonal to the surface.

4.2   Contour Emphasis

Contours or object boundaries are important visual cues for analyzing scenes haptically. In contrast to the existing approaches, we do not detect and store contours of the objects as their edges and boundaries but rather further extend the previously described color threshold case while using it as a trigger for detecting the event that the sudden change of colors is a result of touching the visible contour of the object. The event of crossing the contour can be then defined as an intensity discontinuity larger than a predefined or calculated threshold value. We propose to use mathematical functions to define the contour profiles that will have a variable width as a function of the speed of the HIP motion. This approach will not require generation of a contour map or image gradient but rather calculation of the forces from the pixels surrounding the HIP. Once the contour is detected, a two-dimensional force (i.e. 2 DOF forces) exerted parallel to the image plane will be calculated using the contour profile function and applied to the haptic device. For example, suppose the width of the contour is defined by a parameter Δ within which the feedback force is calculated by some mathematical distance function, e.g., $f = 1 - r^6 + 3r^4 - 3r^2$, where r is a distance (Fig. 5). Once the HIP encounters the intensity discontinuity, a distance δ will be calculated from the previous HIP position HIP_{t-1} to the current HIP position HIP_t. Various force profiles can be proposed to reliably keep the HIP outside the contour such as exponentials or inverse squares.

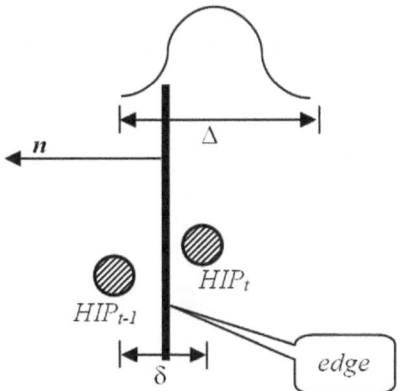

Fig. 5. An edge with width Δ, an associated normal n and a function defined edge profile

The magnitude of the force will be then calculated as:

$$\vec{v} = HIP_t - HIP_{t-1}$$

$$\delta = \|\vec{v}\| \tag{2}$$

$$r = \frac{\delta}{\Delta} - 1$$

$$\|F\| = \frac{\Delta}{2}\left(1 - r^6 + 3r^4 - 3r^2\right)$$

Besides the force profile for deriving the force magnitude, the force direction vector also has to be calculated. To link the direction of the force to the direction of motion when crossing the object contour, the angle between the HIP motion vector v and the contour normal n is checked by calculating a dot product $\cos\theta = \bar{v} \cdot \bar{n}$. If it is negative, i.e. the angle θ is greater than 90°, then the force direction has to be opposite to the contour normal, otherwise it is in the direction of the contour normal. Since two-dimensional forces are applied to the haptic device for contour perception, the third coordinate of the force is set to 0. In order to ensure a stable force, the distance δ is calculated in haptic device coordinates rather than in image pixel coordinates. This allows for sampling the function at a higher precision to avoid sudden increase or decrease of the force magnitude and ensure stability. Moreover, it is also important to consider the speed of motion of the haptic device handle. For example, if the HIP moves fast across the contour, the distance δ will exceed the contour width Δ very quickly and the force would be applied for a very short duration. Therefore, the contour width Δ is made directly proportional to the speed of motion of the HIP: $\Delta_{\min} + \| \text{velocity} \|$.

While this algorithm works for static contours, it requires some modification for moving objects. When the contour or an edge is detected and the force is applied as mentioned above, an *edge flag* is set. At the next frame in the haptic loop, if the edge flag is found to be set, the maximum force is applied to the haptic device as long as both the current HIP pixel and the *anchor pixel* (the pixel at HIP_{t-1} when the edge was found) have the same intensity values. This can happen either when the edge has moved over the current HIP pixel or it has moved over the anchor pixel, as shown in Fig. 6.

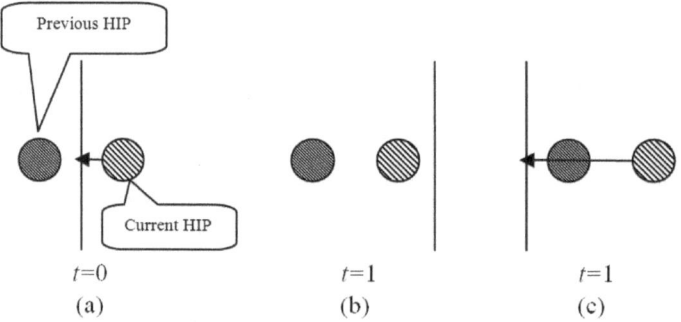

Fig. 6. Movement of an edge: (a) the edge is detected at $t = 0$, (b) the edge moves from left to right, (c) the edge moves from right to left

Here, the edge is detected at $t = 0$. At $t = 1$, the edge can move either to the position shown in (b) or to the position shown in (c). In case (b), since the current HIP pixel had a change in intensity after the last frame, we conclude that it has seen another edge. This means that the previous HIP position is not the anchor pixel any more. The new anchor position is the current HIP position with the previous color. The current

HIP position with the new color therefore becomes the current pixel. In other words, the pixel color of the HIP position has changed, the positions of the current and anchor pixel are the same, while their colors are different. Thus, the applied force becomes zero as the current intensity value differs from the new anchor position. In (c) case, the maximum force will continue to push the HIP toward the edge until it crosses the edge where the edge flag will be unset.

4.3   Texture Emphasis

The third special case allows for emphasizing surface micro-details for images which have a relatively small change in geometry. Under the core algorithm, these details would be perceived as small bumps on the surface but the texture emphasis mode stretches them to the entire depth range. Histograms of such images are concentrated within a small range instead of the entire 0 to 2^8-1 range. In the emphasized texture mode, based on the histogram of the image the user interactively selects the region (i.e. minimum and maximum grey levels) of the histogram to be stretched. The histogram is stretched so that the pixels having an intensity value lying outside the selected range are clipped to the respective extreme of the selected range. Then, each entry i of the force calculation mask is obtained according to the equation:

$$D_t^i = \frac{(2^8-1)(d_t^i - (2^8-1-g_{\max}))}{g_{\max} - g_{\min}} \tag{3}$$

where D_t^i is the ith entry of the force calculation mask, d_t^i is the ith entry of the current mask, and $g_{\max}$ and $g_{\min}$ are the values selected by the user as histogram range values. Recalling the mapping convention about location of the brightest parts and darkest parts of the scene, each mask entry is inverted, i.e. subtracted from 2^8-1 (hence the term $2^8 - 1 - g_{\max}$ is used in equation 3). Collision detection and haptic rendering will then be performed as discussed previously. The effect of texture emphasis in this way is illustrated in Fig. 7 where a 2D image with relatively small changes in geometry is shown along with the perceived surface before and after texture was emphasized. It can be seen from the histogram of the test image that it does not cover the entire range of gray level values and a significant portion of histogram is 'wasted' in a sense that those depth values do not occur in the scene. Therefore, the texture can be emphasized by stretching the histogram to the unused depth values.

5   Applications

The algorithm has been applied to haptic video communication on the web as a proof of concept. The developed application is used to select the chat window of a video conversation over Skype™. Pixel values are read from the screen into the current mask in the graphics thread at 30 frames per second. The mask is then used to calculate forces using the core algorithm (Fig. 8).

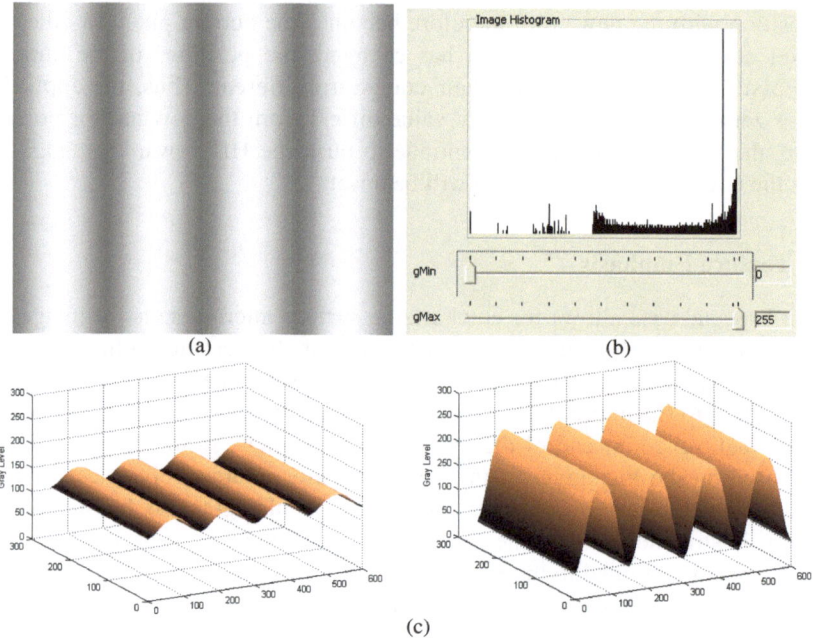

Fig. 7. Texture emphasis mode: (a) test image (b) the histogram generated by the developed application (c) the perceived surface before and after texture emphasis

Fig. 8. Haptic video communication: Proposed algorithm applied to video communication on the web. The direction of the haptic force at the current location of the HIP (at the nose) is shown as a red arrow.

The arrow displayed in the image shows the direction of the force applied to the haptic device at the current location of the HIP. Since color information does not always reflect the depth of the scene accurately, the perceived haptic sensation may not always be realistic. If the ground truth of the depth map can be transmitted with the color video stream, a better interaction experience can be ensured. Therefore, we have also used the Microsoft Kinect depth camera to capture the ground truth. When implemented for the networked video communication, it will allow for accurate perception of facial geometry at the client computer.

Alternatively, in order to avoid the cursor diving into the depth discontinuity arising in facial images due to hair such as eyebrows, mustaches, etc., the offset mode of the proposed system can be used, as it is illustrated in Fig. 9 (a).

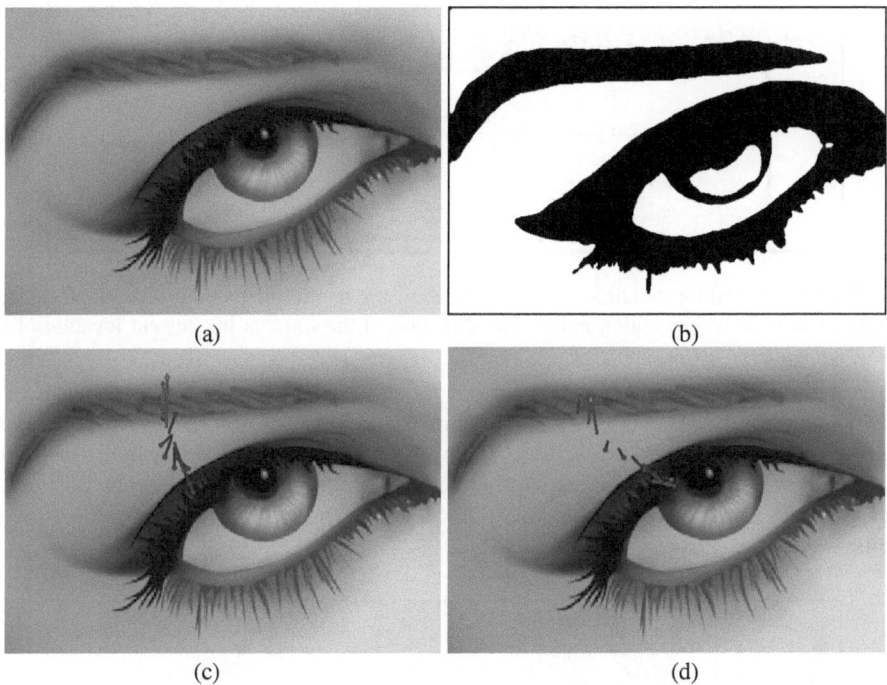

(a)   (b)

(c)   (d)

Fig. 9. Offset mode applied to facial images. (a) 2D input image with blurry transitions, (b) the corresponding binary map with sharp discontinuities, (c) force feedback in the default mode, (d) force feedback in the offset mode.

The binary map generated using contrast enhancement and image brightness manipulation is used to trigger the offset mode. There can be methods developed to generate such a binary map automatically based on image and histogram analysis. This will allow the offset mode with binary map to work with videos in real-time.

We have also implemented a pilot application for Microsoft Windows operating system which makes 'tangible' any window or region on the desktop screen. The control of the windows cursor is transferred to the haptic device and pixels are read from the screen in a small neighborhood around the cursor at every haptic frame. These pixel values are used to generate force feedback as described in Section 3. Various adjustable parameters such as the mask size, threshold value, stiffness value, etc. can be tuned to suitable values. An example of the desktop tangible image application is shown in Fig. 10 where the contour perception mode is enabled to perceive boundaries of the buttons in a dialog box. When combined with auditory output, this can be a useful tool for visually impaired users to interact with computers using graphical user interfaces.

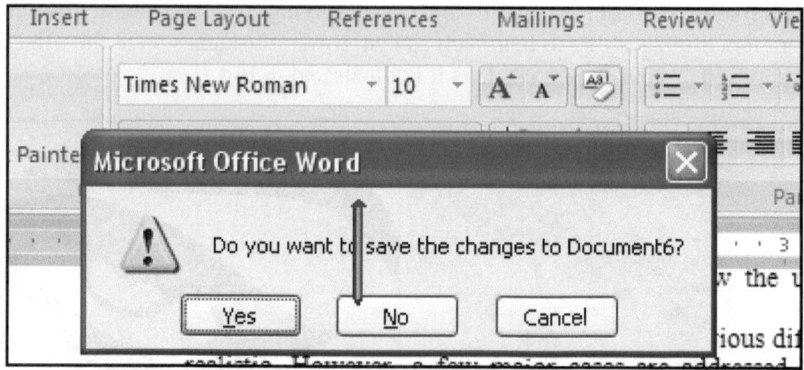

Fig. 10. Use of desktop tangible image application for haptic interaction with graphical user interfaces in contour perception mode. The direction of the force at the current location of the HIP is shown as an arrow.

As mentioned previously, the algorithm is suitable for interaction with moving objects as it works well in real-time. This is illustrated in Fig. 11, where the haptic device moves up and down following the hand movement of the other party in a Skype video conversation. The arrow shows the direction of force applied to the haptic device.

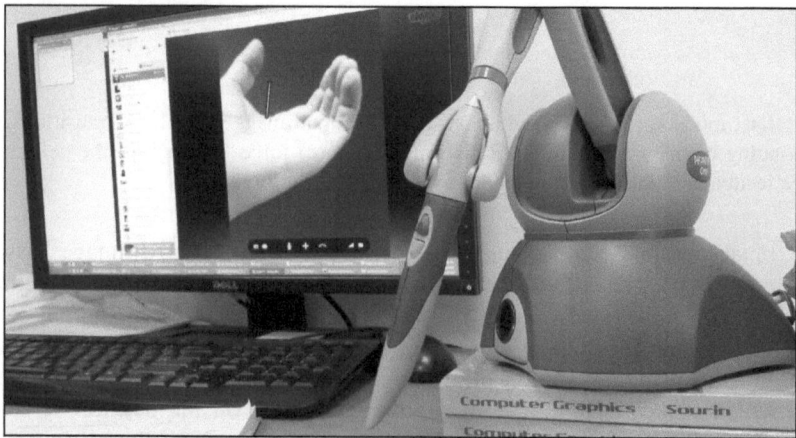

Fig. 11. Interaction with the moving object in haptic video communication. The handle of the haptic device moves up and down following the motion of the hand in the Skype window.

One more application of the proposed image-driven haptic interaction was done in arthroscopic surgery training [36] where actual surgical videos were converted to tangible images for training hand-eye coordination of the surgeons (Fig. 12). At the preprocessing stage, a panoramic image of the entire knee cavity is created by stitching some frames of a real arthroscopy video. This image is then visualized through a moving circular window which follows the motion of the virtual arthroscopic camera. The panoramic backdrop image is also augmented with a few 3D models of deformable tissues as well as models of the surgical instruments which will be seen by the camera. The images displayed on the virtual monitor are then nearly identical to those in the actual surgery.

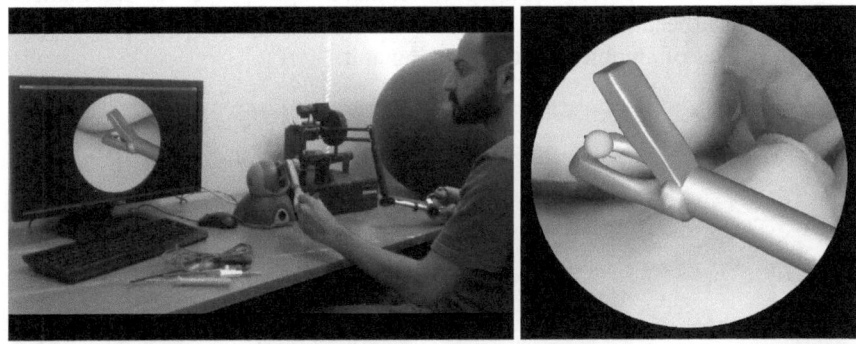

Fig. 12. Virtual haptic arthroscopy hand-eye coordination training based on tangible images which feels like the actual 3D surgical scenes

6   Challenges

While working with the developed pilot applications, we have identified cases which require further research and development. There are images for which the proposed algorithm will produce unrealistic results. This is due to how human vision and touch works in real life. For example, one interesting case is the bas-relief ambiguity. Let us consider a concave hemisphere lit by frontal illumination by a source at infinity. The inside of a concave hemisphere may appear to be the outside of a convex hemisphere. Such visual illusions occur in real life too and sometimes there is no way to tell the geometric structure or physical properties without manipulating the object. In such a case, other sources of depth information can be used to get a reference point of depth on the object surface, e.g., by using multiple views of the scene or depth sensors such as Microsoft Kinect.

Another issue that needs further attention is the association of material properties to different parts of the scene as perception of physical (material) properties of the objects is very important in the overall human touch experience. When using scenes composed of 3D models, each model can be defined as having specific physical properties. However, such a separation between objects is absent in a 2D image. Therefore, the image has to be segmented into regions of uniform physical properties. Moreover, material properties must be assigned to each region. For example,

Fig. 13(a) shows an image captured during a minimally invasive arthroscopic surgery. The image is segmented automatically, using a brightness threshold, to produce a segmentation map shown in Fig. 13(b). While this is sufficient for illustration purposes, sophisticated interactive image segmentation techniques can be used to extract a better approximation of human tissue. Different haptic properties are assigned to different parts of the image interactively. In this case, the physical properties are set so that the haptic cursor is allowed to penetrate into the tissue once it is in the white region on the segmentation map. A highly viscous effect is activated to give an illusion of cutting through the tissue. The original image is still used as a visual guide for the haptic interaction. While automatic image segmentation is a well-researched topic, development of an algorithm that assigns properties automatically is a challenging task because even in the real world it is often not possible to judge the physical properties of an object just by looking at it.

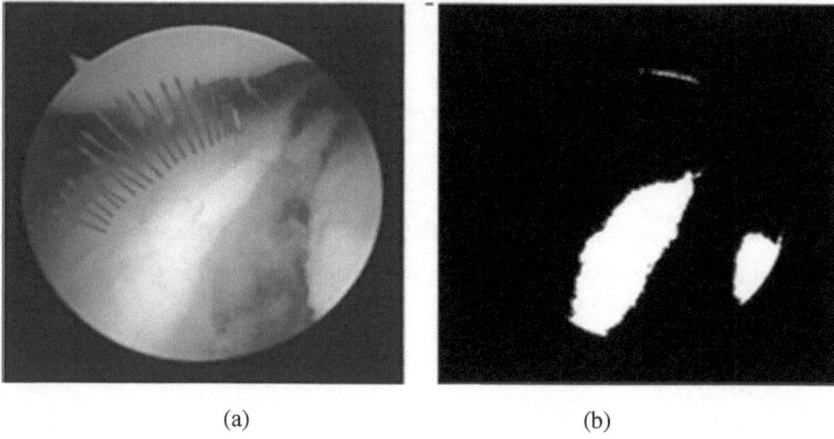

(a)   (b)

Fig. 13. Haptic rendering of physical properties, (a) actual image with arrows showing direction of force rendered, (b) segmentation map

7   Conclusion

We have proposed an approach for haptic interaction with 2D images where a displayed image, real or simulated, is used as a source of the force-feedback calculations at any pixel touched by the haptic device. This is done by interpreting the pixel color, as well as the colors of the pixels in its vicinity, in terms of visible depth. Haptic feedback forces are then calculated in such a way that there is no abrupt change of their values resulting in jitter or sudden kick back motions of the haptic device handle. Three novel enhancements for various types of images have also been proposed. First, a method of predicting geometric consistency at color discontinuities has been presented. Second, a new technique for haptic perception of static and moving edges has been proposed. Lastly, we have introduced a texture emphasis technique based on observing image histogram. This is achieved without full 3D reconstruction or an edge map generation. The three algorithms along with the core algorithm have been implemented into a single application which allows for touch interaction with the Windows desktop screen. A number of user adaptable parameters allow for tuning the algorithm best suited for the image being haptically explored.

As a part of the future work we intend to explore two possible directions for physical property assignment. Firstly, a database of different physical properties can be created and after image segmentation, regions can be interactively classified into having a set of predefined physical properties from this database. Secondly, object detection can be used to associate physical properties. The derived forces will be combined with the forces generated by the core algorithm either in the form of accelerating or decelerating forces for friction, or as a varying stiffness constant for surface hardness. We also intend to devise various mapping functions to get a better estimate of depth from the color information in the image.

Acknowledgments. This project is supported by the Ministry of Education of Singapore Grant MOE2011-T2-1-006 "Collaborative Haptic Modeling for Orthopaedic Surgery Training in Cyberspace", and by the Russian Foundation for Basic Research Grant 12-07-00157-a "Virtual Modeling of Minimally Invasive Surgery Operations". The project is also supported by Fraunhofer IDM@NTU, which is funded by the National Research Foundation and managed through the multi-agency Interactive & Digital Media Programme Office hosted by the Media Development Authority of Singapore.

References

1. Rasool, S., Sourin, A.: Image-Driven Haptic Rendering in Virtual Environments. In: 2013 International Conference on Cyberworlds, CW (2013)
2. Durou, J.-D., Falcone, M., Sagona, M.: Numerical methods for shape-from-shading: A new survey with benchmarks. Computer Vision and Image Understanding 109(1), 22–43 (2008)
3. Zhang, R., et al.: Shape from Shading: A Survey. IEEE Trans. Pattern Anal. Mach. Intell. 21(8), 690–706 (1999)
4. Breuss, M., et al.: Numerical algorithms for perspective shape from shading. Kybernetika 46(2), 207–225 (2010)
5. Ecker, A., Jepson, A.D.: Polynomial shape from shading. In: 2010 IEEE Conference on Computer Vision and Pattern Recognition (CVPR), San Francisco, USA (2010)
6. Alexa, M., Matusik, W.: Reliefs as images. In: ACM SIGGRAPH 2010 Papers, pp. 1–7. ACM, Los Angeles (2010)
7. Longuet-Higgins, H.C.: A computer algorithm for reconstructing a scene from two projections. Nature 293(5828), 133–135 (1981)
8. Szeliski, R.: Stereo correspondence. In: Computer Vision, pp. 467–503. Springer, London (2011)
9. Vogiatzis, G., Hernández, C.: Practical 3D Reconstruction Based on Photometric Stereo. In: Cipolla, R., Battiato, S., Farinella, G. (eds.) Computer Vision. SCI, vol. 285, pp. 313–345. Springer, Heidelberg (2010)
10. Szeliski, R.: 3D reconstruction. In: Computer Vision, pp. 505–541. Springer, London (2011)

11. Li, J., Song, A., Zhang, X.: Haptic Texture Rendering Using Single Texture Image. In: 2010 International Symposium on Computational Intelligence and Design, ISCID (2010)
12. Shi, Y., Pai, D.K.: Haptic display of visual images. In: IEEE Virtual Reality Annual International Symposium, Albuquerque, USA (1997)
13. Basdogan, C.: From 2D images to 3D tangible models: autostereoscopic and haptic visualization of Martian rocks in virtual environments. Presence: Teleoper. Virtual Environ. 16(1), 1–15 (2007)
14. Di Stefano, L., Mattoccia, S.: Real-Time Stereo within the VIDET Project. Real-Time Imaging 8(5), 439–453 (2002)
15. Kim, S.-C., Kyung, K.-U., Kwon, D.S.: Haptic annotation for an interactive image. In: 5th ACM International Conference on Ubiquitous Information Management and Communication, ICUIMC 2011. ACM, Seoul (2011)
16. Kagawa, T., et al.: A Study of Haptic Interaction for Image Edition Tools. In: International Conference on Complex, Intelligent and Software Intensive Systems, Krakow, Poland (2010)
17. Lareau, D., Jochen, L.: Haptic rendering of photographs. In: 2012 IEEE International Workshop on Haptic Audio Visual Environments and Games, HAVE (2012)
18. Pai, D.K., Reissell, L.M.: Haptic interaction with multiresolution image curves. Computers & Graphics 21(4), 405–411 (1997)
19. Krufka, S.E., Barner, K.E., Aysal, T.C.: Visual to Tactile Conversion of Vector Graphics. IEEE Transactions on Neural Systems and Rehabilitation Engineering 15(2), 310–321 (2007)
20. Wang, Q.: Translation of graphics to haptic boundary representation, Department of Electrical and Computer Engineering, McGill University, p. 65 (1999)
21. Way, T.P., Barner, K.E.: Automatic visual to tactile translation. II. Evaluation of the TACTile image creation system. IEEE Transactions on Rehabilitation Engineering 5(1), 95–105 (1997)
22. Kim, S.-C., Kwon, D.-S.: Haptic interaction with objects in a picture based on pose estimation. In: Multimedia Tools and Applications, pp. 1–22 (2013)
23. Li, J., Song, A., Zhang, X.: Image-based haptic texture rendering. In: Proceedings of the 9th ACM SIGGRAPH Conference on Virtual-Reality Continuum and its Applications in Industry, pp. 237–242. ACM, Seoul (2010)
24. Vasudevan, H., Manivannan, M.: Tangible Images: Runtime Generation of Haptic Textures From Images. In: Proceedings of the 2008 Symposium on Haptic Interfaces for Virtual Environment and Teleoperator Systems, pp. 357–360. EEE Computer Society, Reno (2008)
25. Adi, W., Sulaiman, S.: Haptic Texture Rendering Based on Visual Texture Information: A Study to Achieve Realistic Haptic Texture Rendering. In: Badioze Zaman, H., Robinson, P., Petrou, M., Olivier, P., Schröder, H., Shih, T.K. (eds.) IVIC 2009. LNCS, vol. 5857, pp. 279–287. Springer, Heidelberg (2009)
26. Juan, W., Aiguo, S., Chuiguo, Z.: A novel haptic texture display based on image processing. In: IEEE International Conference on Robotics and Biomimetics, ROBIO 2007, Sanya, China (2007)
27. Xu, S., et al.: An improved switching vector median filter for image-based haptic texture generation. In: 2012 5th International Congress on Image and Signal Processing, CISP (2012)
28. O'Modhrain, S., Oakley, I.: Adding interactivity: active touch in broadcast media. In: Proceedings of the 12th International Symposium on Haptic Interfaces for Virtual Environment and Teleoperator Systems, HAPTICS 2004, Chicago, USA (2004)

29. Mee Young, S., et al.: Touchable Video and Tactile Audio. In: 11th IEEE International Symposium on Multimedia, ISM 2009, San Diego, USA (2009)
30. Cha, J., et al.: 3D video player system with haptic interaction based on depth image-based representation. IEEE Transactions on Consumer Electronics 52(2), 477–484 (2006)
31. Gaw, D., Morris, D., Salisbury, K.: Haptically Annotated Movies: Reaching Out and Touching the Silver Screen. In: 14th Symposium on Haptic Interfaces for Virtual Environment and Teleoperator Systems, Alexandria, USA (2006)
32. Bayakovski, Y., et al.: Depth image-based representations for static and animated 3D objects. In: Proceedings of the International Conference on Image Processing 2002, Rochester, USA (2002)
33. Cha, J., Eid, M., Saddik, A.E.: Touchable 3D video system. ACM Trans. Multimedia Comput. Commun. Appl., TOMMCAP 5(4), 1–25 (2009)
34. Rasool, S., Sourin, A.: Tangible images. In: SIGGRAPH Asia 2011 Sketches. ACM, Hong Kong (2011)
35. Rasool, S., Sourin, A.: Haptic interaction with 2D images. In: Proceedings of the 10th International Conference on Virtual Reality Continuum and Its Applications in Industry, pp. 13–22. ACM, Hong Kong (2011)
36. Rasool, S., Sourin, A.: Image-driven virtual simulation of arthroscopy. The Visual Computer 29(5), 333–344 (2013)

Multi-touch Interface and Motion Control Model for Interactive Character Animation

Masaki Oshita

Kyushu Institute of Technology
Iizuka, Fukuoka, Japan

Abstract. In this paper, we propose a new method for interactive motion control with a multi-touch interface. A user of our system can touch and drag character's body parts to control its motion. The character's full body motion is driven by our interactive motion control model based on the movement of a few body parts which are directly manipulated by the user via the multi-touch interface. We propose a method for determining 3-dimensional positions of controlled body parts from 2-dimensional touch inputs based on the character's local coordinates and drag speed. We introduce a point-based pose representation which consists of the positions or orientations of a small number of primary body parts. Based on the representation, we develop a motion control model that includes modules for tracking, balance, inter-body interaction, relaxing and self-collision avoidance. The character's pose is reconstructed from the point-based pose representation. We present our experimental results to show that our framework can realize various natural-looking motions.

Keywords: motion control, multi-touch interface, computer animation, character animation.

1 Introduction

Tablet computers that support multi-touch inputs have recently become commonplace. Although many applications control character motion in the virtual environment, most use virtual buttons or stroke gestures for selecting actions. Multi-touch input is a simple substitute for gamepads or keyboards. The strengths of multi-touch are underutilized. Using multi-touch, users should be able to control character motion freely and intuitively rather than simply executing predefined actions.

In theory, using inverse kinematics (IK), a user can change a character's pose by dragging its body part. However, this kind of interface is not suitable for controlling a character's motion in interactive applications, for two primary reasons. First, because multi-touch inputs on the screen are 2-dimensional, 3-dimensional position and orientation of body parts cannot be easily controlled. Second, since multiple body parts must be moved in a coordinated way to realize natural-looking motion, a user must control multiple body parts, which is very difficult. For example, to execute a punch motion, in addition to the hand, the pelvis and trunk should also be moved.

M.L. Gavrilova et al. (Eds.): Trans. on Comput. Sci. XXIII, LNCS 8490, pp. 78–97, 2014.
© Springer-Verlag Berlin Heidelberg 2014

Fig. 1. Examples of interactive motion control with multi-touch interface. The red circles represent touch inputs.

A statistics-based model for IK (style-based IK [1]) can be a solution for these problems. Using a large number of example poses, natural-looking pose and motion can be synthesized based on touch inputs. Oshita [2] applied this approach for a multi-touch interface for motion control. However, because different example data sets are required for each kind of actions, this approach requires a large number of examples and a mechanism to switch data sets automatically. Moreover, it is difficult to execute new types of actions whose example poses are not provided in advance.

In this paper, we propose a new method for interactive motion control with a multi-touch interface. A user of our system can touch and drag a character's body parts to control its motion. Unlike the data-based approach (the statistics-based IK) discussed above, we take a model-based approach. The character's full body motion is driven by our interactive motion control model based on the movement of a few body parts which are directly manipulated by the user via the multi-touch interface. Our motion control model can perform various motions without preparing any example poses (Figure 1).

Our method for determining 3-dimensional positions of controlled body parts from 2-dimensional touch inputs is based on the character's local coordinates and drag speed. We introduced a point-based pose representation which consists of the positions or orientations of a small number of primary body parts (pelvis, hand, foot, trunk and head). Based on this representation, we developed a motion control model that includes modules for tracking, balance, inter-body interaction, relaxing and self-collision avoidance. The character's pose is reconstructed from the point-based pose representation. We present our experimental results to show that our framework can realize various natural-looking motions.

Even though our method can accept a number of multi-touch inputs, in our experience it is difficult for a user to control multiple touches simultaneously. With our method, a user needs to control the movement of only one or a few primary body parts to perform an action. The motion control model then generates the full body motion accordingly.

This paper is an extended version of our previous work [3]. We describe more specific details of our motion control model (Section 6). We also provide a result from a user test which is a comparison with conventional mouse-based interface for posing a character (Section 7).

The remainder of this paper is organized as follows. Section 2 reviews related work. Section 3 shows the system overview. Sections 4, 5 and 6 explain our methods for pose representation, interpretation of multi-touch inputs, and the motion control model, respectively. Section 7 presents the experimental results and discussion. Finally, Section 8 concludes this paper.

2   Related Work

2.1   Point-Based Pose Representation

We used a point-based pose representation in this research. Representing a pose by using points is an efficient way to handle character motion. Jakobsen [4] represented a character as a set of connected particles for an efficient physics simulation. However, he did not consider reconstructing a full body pose. Popović and Witkin [5] reconstructed full body motion using an optimization process. These approaches are not applicable to our research.

Similar pose representations to our method which use the positions and orientations of primary body parts have been used in previous research [6][7]. The difference between these studies and our method is that they used their representation for encoding existing motions for motion editing or retargetting. Kulpa et al. [6] used a numerical IK for limbs. Neff et al. [7] included the center of mass position in the pose representation and computed the ankle joints accordingly during pose reconstruction. We didn't take such approaches to avoid redundancy and achieve robust and efficient method.

2.2   Motion Control Interface

There are several existing multi-touch interfaces for interactive motion control. Krause et al. [8] applied conventional IK to a character model based on multi-touch inputs for animation. Kip and Nguyen [9] proposed a system to control one arm and hand of a character using a multi-touch interface by changing several parameters to blend arm and hand postures. Oshita [2] applied a statistics-based IK (style-based IK [1]). Although this approach successfully generates natural-looking full-body pose and motion based on multi-touch inputs, as explained in Section 1, it requires a large number of examples and a mechanism to switch data sets automatically. Moreover, it is difficult to execute new types of actions whose example poses are not provided. On the other hand, our research used a model-based approach and our motion control model makes it possible to perform various motions without preparing any example poses.

There are many methods for controlling a character's motion by using a single point or trajectory. Generating locomotion along with a given trajectory is common [10]. However, the type of motion is limited to walking or running. Throne et al. [11] introduced gesture-based motion selection. Based on gestures drawn along a trajectory, their system inserts predefined motions such as a jump or flip. Oshita [12] proposed a stroke-based motion selection technique that chooses an appropriate action according to the initial and terminal points of a single stroke drawn on the screen. With these systems [11][12], users can simply select actions but the postures and speed of the actions are fixed and cannot be controlled. Igarashi et al. [13] proposed a spatial keyframing animation technique. This approach enables changing a character's pose continuously based on the cursor position. To use this technique, key postures must be placed at appropriate positions depending on a specific action.

Some systems allow a user to specify a number of trajectories and constraints for motion creation [14] and deformation [15]. However, with these systems, the user is expected to prioritize the inputs. Our methods uses multiple inputs and control modules and prioritizes them automatically.

2.3   Motion Control Model

There are various approaches for motion control and synthesis based on user input. A combination of physics simulation and physics-based controllers [16][17] is one approach. A controller determines joint torques based on a target pose, balancing, etc. and the physics simulation generates physically valid motions. However, designing a stable controller is difficult and different controllers must be designed for each kind of action.

Space-time optimization is another approach [5][18]. It synthesizes a continuous motion based on given constraints such as footsteps and timings so that the generated motion minimizes an objective function that evaluates its physical validity. However, this approach generate a motion sequence and requires computational time. Therefore, it is difficult to apply it for interactive motion control.

Previous researches has applied optimization (Quadratic Programming) for computing the pose of the next frame instead of a motion sequence [19][20] to realize interactive motion generation. These controllers are designed for autonomous control instead of user control and also require computational time.

In contrary to these approaches, we developed a kinematics based controller. Our controller considers physics in part but directly changes the positions and orientations of body parts rather than using physics simulation or optimization. Our controller is designed to move the character's full body naturally based on the user's inputs.

3   System Overview

The structure of our framework is shown in Figure 2. We use an intermediate point-based pose representation for motion control (controlled pose). Multi-touch inputs from the user are interpreted and represented as constraints in the same pose representation.

In addition to constraints for controlling the character's pose, when the character is moved over a certain distance, a moving motion (step) is executed. In this case, the target position of the moving motion is sent to the motion control module.

The skeletal structure of the character is given to the system in advance. It includes the information on the shape and weight of the body parts. Shape

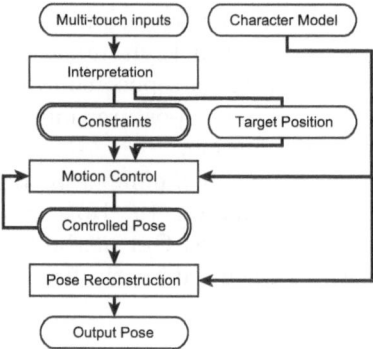

Fig. 2. Data flow in the proposed framework

information is necessary for self-collision avoidance, and weight information is necessary for balance control.

The user can also control the camera using multi-touch interface. A swipe can control the camera direction and pinch-in and -out can control zoom (the distance from the camera to the character).

4   Point-Based Pose Representation

Our intermediate point-based pose representation $\mathbf{P}$ includes pelvis position $\mathbf{p}_{pelvis}$, hand positions $\mathbf{p}_{r\_hand}$, $\mathbf{p}_{l\_hand}$, foot positions $\mathbf{p}_{r\_foot}$, $\mathbf{p}_{l\_foot}$, trunk orientation $\mathbf{q}_{trunk}$ and head orientation $\mathbf{q}_{head}$; 5 positions and 2 orientations as shown in Figure 3. All positions and orientations are represented in the absolute (world) coordinates.

In general, there are several ways to represent a rotation such as quaternion, axis-angle, 3×3 matrix and Euler angles. Although any of these can be used with our method, in the following explanation, we treat them as 3×3 matrices such that the product of two rotations $\mathbf{q}_b\mathbf{q}_a$ equates to the combination of two rotations. $\mathbf{q}^{-1}$ represents the inverse of the rotation. $\mathbf{q}\mathbf{v}$ denotes the rotation of a vector $\mathbf{v}$. In this paper, $|\mathbf{q}|$ represents the rotational angle and $w\mathbf{q}$ represents the scaling of the rotational angle.

4.1   Pose Reconstruction

The character's output pose $\mathbf{X}$ is represented by the position and orientation of the pelvis and rotations for all joints as $\mathbf{X} = \{\mathbf{p}_{pelvis}, \mathbf{q}_{pelvis}, \mathbf{q}_i(i = 1...n)\}$ where n is the number of joints. Our method reconstructs this output pose from our intermediate pose representation $\mathbf{P} = \{\mathbf{p}_{pelvis}, \mathbf{p}_{r\_hand}, \mathbf{p}_{l\_hand}, \mathbf{p}_{r\_foot}, \mathbf{p}_{l\_foot}, \mathbf{q}_{trunk}, \mathbf{q}_{head}\}$. Figure 3 shows the difference between the conventional pose representation and our point-based pose representation. In our experiments, we used a character model which has 15 joints in the conventional pose representation as shown in Figure 3. The pose reconstruction follows 4 steps as explained below:

conventional
pose representation

our point-based
pose representation

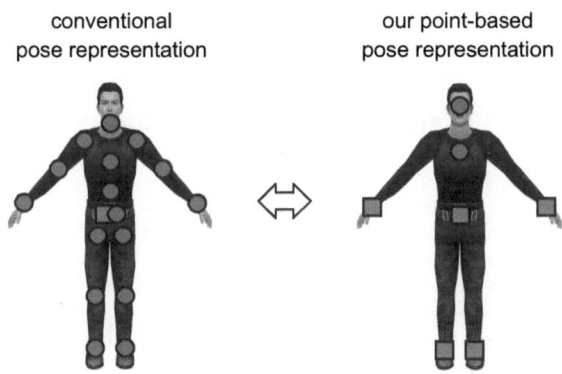

Fig. 3. Pose representation. A blue rectangle represents a position and a read circle represents a rotation (orientation).

Pose Reconstruction for Pelvis Position, Pelvis Orientation and Back Joints. The pelvis position of the intermediate representation is simply used for the pelvis position $\mathbf{p}_{pelvis}$.

Pelvis orientation and back joint rotations are computed from trunk orientation $\mathbf{q}_{trunk}$. The number of back joints depends on the skeleton model. In general, the back joint rotations can be computed from the total rotation of the back joints by distributing the total rotation to each back joint in specific ratios [21]. Our method determines pelvis orientation in addition to the back joint rotations. We divide the trunk orientation into horizontal rotation $\mathbf{q}_{trunk\_h}$(1DOF) and front-back and right-left rotations $\mathbf{q}_{trunk\_v}$(2DOF). The horizontal rotation is assigned to pelvis orientation. The other rotations are distributed into pelvis orientation $\mathbf{q}_{pelvis}$ and back joints $\mathbf{q}_{i(back)}$ with a specific weight $w_{pelvis\_back\_ratio}$. In our implementation, we use $w_{pelvis\_back\_ratio} = 0.5$.

$$\mathbf{q}_{trunk} = \mathbf{q}_{trunk\_v}\mathbf{q}_{trunk\_h} \tag{1}$$

$$\mathbf{q}_{pelvis} = ((w_{pelvis\_back\_ratio})\mathbf{q}_{trunk\_v})\mathbf{q}_{trunk\_h} \tag{2}$$

$$\mathbf{q}_{i(back)} = (1 - w_{pelvis\_back\_ratio})\mathbf{q}_{trunk\_v} \tag{3}$$

If the skeleton model contains more than one back joints, the total back rotation $\mathbf{q}_{i(back)}$ can be further distributed to each back joint with specific weights. The number of back joints of a human character model can be 19 at most [21]. Typically a character model with from one to three back joints is used. In our implementation, we used a character model with two back joints as depicted in Figure 3.

Pose Reconstruction for Neck Joints. The neck joint rotations are computed from trunk and head orientations.

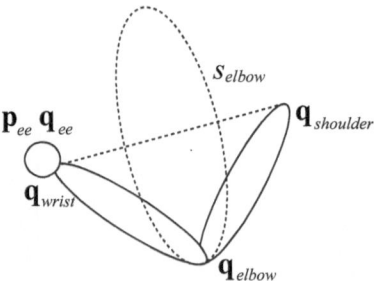

Fig. 4. Analytical inverse kinematics for a limb

$$\mathbf{q}_{i(neck)} = \mathbf{q}_{head}(\mathbf{q}_{trunk})^{-1} \tag{4}$$

Pose Reconstruction for Limb Joints. After the pelvis and trunk states are determined, limb joints rotations are computed from the end-effector (hand or foot) position. In the followings explanation, we take the case of an arm to make the explanation easier, although the same method is applied to legs too.

In general, as shown in Figure 4, an analytical IK [22] determines the rotation of limb joints (3 DOF shoulder joint $\mathbf{q}_{shoulder}$, 1 DOF elbow joint $\mathbf{q}_{elbow}$ and 3 DOF wrist joint $\mathbf{q}_{wrist}$) based on the relative position and orientation of the end-effector from the shoulder $\mathbf{p}_{ee}$, $\mathbf{q}_{ee}$ and swivel angle of the elbow s_{elbow}. Since we determined the wrist angle joint rotations differently as explained in the next subsection, if we focus on shoulder (3 DOF) and elbow (1 DOF) joints, their rotations can be determined based on hand position $\mathbf{p}_{ee}$ (3DOF) and swivel angle s_{elbow}(1 DOF).

How swivel angle is determined is important. If analytical IK is used for changing an existing pose, the swivel angle of the original pose can be retained. Because of the need to generate arbitrary poses in our case, such an approach is not applicable. It is known that the swivel angle depends on the end-effector position [23]. Therefore, we determined the swivel angle from the hand position based on examples that are prepared in advance.

We prepared sets of normalized relative hand positions and swivel angles as examples. Given a hand position, we blend nearby samples to determine swivel angle. We use Radial Basis Function (RBF) to compute the weight of each example depending on hand position.

$$s_{elbow} = \sum f_i(\mathbf{p}_{ee})s_i \tag{5}$$

$$f_i(\mathbf{p}_{ee}) = exp(-(|\mathbf{p}_i - \mathbf{p}_{ee}|/r_i)^2) \ (if \ |\mathbf{p}_i - \mathbf{p}_{ee}| < r_i) \tag{6}$$

where $f_i(\mathbf{p}_{ee})$ is the RBF for each example $\{\mathbf{p}_i, s_i, r_i\}$. In our implementation, we use about 10 examples for each limb which are tuned manually. Alternatively, it is possible to use motion capture data to create more accurate samples.

Although we used example data here, because these examples are common for all types of poses and actions, it is not necessary to prepare separate sets

Fig. 5. Examples of swivel angles

of examples for each type of action, unlike a statistics-based posture synthesis [1][2].

Figure 5 shows poses that are generated from the examples. The colors represent the weights computed from the hand position. Note that each example has a swivel angle and not a pose.

Pose Reconstruction for Hand and Foot Joints. Since we do not use hand and foot orientations, wrist and ankle rotations $\mathbf{p}_{wrist}$, $\mathbf{p}_{ankle}$ are determined automatically. Unless the character is performing a gesture or holding an object in the environment, neither is considered in our system, it is natural to keep the wrist and foot rotations in the rest pose. Therefore, we simply set the joint rotation to zero after limb joint rotation is determined.

When an end-effector (typically foot) is contacting the ground, the foot must be kept horizontal. Also, when the foot is near the ground, the ankle joint must be flexed or extended to prevent the foot from penetrating into the ground. Similar to trunk orientation control, ankle rotation is set, when the foot is near or on the ground.

5   Interpretation of Multi-touch Inputs

In this section, we explain how to interpret multi-touch inputs to determine constraints in the point-based pose representation form. A user can touch and drag the pelvis, hand, foot, trunk and head of the character. Since we use multi-touch inputs, multiple body parts can be touched and dragged at the same time. In this paper, we did not take inputs on the middle of limbs (e.g. upper arm, forearm, elbow, etc.); limbs can be controlled only by moving the end-effectors (hand and foot). Although a person has 10 fingers, from our experience, we can control at most two or three touches at the same time. Therefore, the limited number of controllable body parts in our method is considered reasonable.

Our method treats each touch input as the spatial translation of the touched body part. The biggest challenge is how to determine 3-dimensional positions of controlled body parts. When a user touches and drags a body part on the 2-dimensional screen, the touched position on the screen represents a line in the 3-dimensional scene. There is no simple way to determine a unique point on the line.

We solved this problem by introducing several assumptions. First, when a person performs motions, the pelvis, hand and foot are generally moved in either front-back or right-left direction relative to the person. For example, for punch and kick motions, the body parts are moved in the front-back direction. For a waving hand and arm extending motion, the body parts are moved in the right-left direction. Although some complex motions include movements in combinations of both front-back and left-right directions, in many cases the body parts are moved on one plane. We determined in which plane the touched body part should be moved depending on the character's orientation and the camera direction.

A second assumption is to move the selected body part (hand or foot) in a perpendicular direction to the screen. When a hand or foot is moved away from the trunk on the screen, there is not much freedom of movement in the perpendicular direction, because arm and leg lengths are limited. However, when the hand or foot is moved toward or near the trunk, it may be moved in the perpendicular direction. When the hand or foot is moved toward the camera, it is likely that they are dynamic motions such as a punch or kick which would require quick movement. Therefore, the resultant translation in the perpendicular direction is based on the speed of the body part being controlled by the user. Although this may not be the case all of the time, we consider that this is a reasonable assumption.

In addition to these assumptions, self-collision avoidance is considered. For example, when a hand is moved toward the trunk on a plane that crosses the trunk, the arm can penetrate into the trunk. In this case, the hand position is adjusted to a position where such penetration does not happen.

5.1   Translation of Pelvis, Hand and Foot

Based on the above approach, we determined the target position of pelvis, hand or foot as follows:

Translation on a Hyper Plane. Based on the first assumption above, when a body part (pelvis, hand or foot) is touched and dragged on the screen, it is moved on either the XY, ZX or YZ hyper plane which is defined by the local coordinates of the character as shown in Figure 6.

X, Y and Z axes are determined based on pelvis orientation. Y axis is always $(0, 1, 0)$, while X and Z axes are determined from the horizontal pelvis orientation. Then, among these axes, the one whose inner product with the camera vector (camera direction) $\mathbf{d}_{camera}$ is the largest is chosen as the normal vector that defines the hyper plane. The hyper plane is defined by the normal vector $\mathbf{n}$ and the current position of the controlled body part $\mathbf{p}_{current}$ as follows

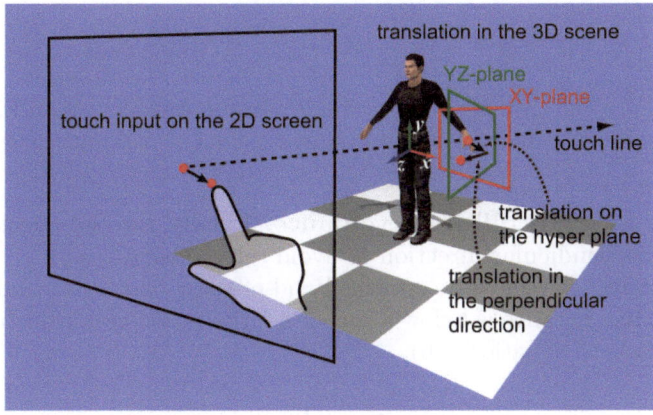

Fig. 6. Touch interpretation

$$\mathbf{n}(\mathbf{p} - \mathbf{p}_{current}) = 0 \tag{7}$$

The touch line where the controlled body part exist is defined as follows

$$\mathbf{p} = t\mathbf{d}_{touch} + \mathbf{p}_{camera} \tag{8}$$

where $\mathbf{d}_{touch}$ is the normalized vector from the camera to the touch point and $\mathbf{p}_{camera}$ is the camera position. From equations (7) and (8), the target position of the controlled body part on the hyper plane is computed.

Translation in the Perpendicular Direction. Based on the second assumption above, position is adjusted in the direction perpendicular to the screen. This adjustment is applied to end-effectors (hand and foot) but not to the pelvis. When the speed of a dragged end-effector is faster than the threshold, its position is adjusted in proportion to speed.

There are two directions for the perpendicular vector. The body part should be moved forward from the character. The moving direction vector $\mathbf{d}_{forward}$ is determined as follows.

$$\mathbf{d}_{forward} = \begin{matrix} \mathbf{d}_{touch} & (if\ \mathbf{d}_{z\_axis} \cdot \mathbf{d}_{touch} > cos45°) \\ -\mathbf{d}_{touch} & (if\ \mathbf{d}_{z\_axis} \cdot \mathbf{d}_{touch} < cos45°) \\ \mathbf{0} & (otherwise) \end{matrix} \tag{9}$$

where $\mathbf{d}_{z\_axis}$ is the Z axis of the character's pelvis. Although it is possible to apply this translation on any camera direction in theory, throughout our tests, we found that it does not work well when the body parts are moved on the YZ plane (when the camera is on the side of the character). Therefore, we limit this control when the angle between $\mathbf{d}_{z\_axis}$ and $\mathbf{d}_{touch}$ is less than 45°.

The position of the end-effector is adjusted in the direction of $\mathbf{d}_{forward}$ based on the velocity of the end-effector $\mathbf{v}$.

$$\mathbf{p'} = \mathbf{p} + \frac{|\mathbf{v}| - v_{th}}{v_s}\mathbf{d}_{forward} \quad (if \ |\mathbf{v}| > v_{th}) \tag{10}$$

where v_{th}, v_s are the threshold and scaling parameters. We tuned those parameters empirically. In our implementation, we use $v_{th} = 1.0$ and $v_s = 0.2$.

Translation for Self-collision Avoidance. Finally, the end-effector is moved in the same perpendicular direction to avoid self-collision.

The distances between the controlled end-effector and other body parts are computed. If the distance is below a threshold, the position is adjusted using the similar equation to equation (10).

$$\mathbf{p'} = \mathbf{p} + k\mathbf{d}_{forward} \tag{11}$$

In this case, the scaling parameter k is computed based on the distance and the threshold.

For collision detection and distance computation between body segments, any existing method can be used. The method for representing the shapes of body segments is also flexible. A simplified representation such as a bounding box or ellipsoid makes distance computation easier. In our implementation, we represented each body part as an oriented bounding box [24].

5.2   Rotation of Trunk and Head

Because we use the rotations of the trunk and head in our point-based pose representation, we interpreted the touch and drag of a point on a body part as their rotation.

The translation of the touched point of the trunk or head is computed the same way as the computation for pelvis translation $\mathbf{p'}_{touched}$. The touched point on the body depends on the point where the user touches first. Based on the translation of the touched point, the trunk rotation that satisfies it is computed $\Delta\mathbf{q}_{trunk}$ as follows.

$$(\mathbf{p'}_{touched} - \mathbf{p}_{back}) = \Delta\mathbf{q}_{trunk}(\mathbf{p}_{touched} - \mathbf{p}_{back}) \tag{12}$$

where $\mathbf{p}_{touched}$ is the initial position of the touched point without trunk rotation and $\mathbf{p}_{back}$ is the back joint position. Because the touched point is on the surface of the character's body, when the touched body is moved downward on the screen, the character bends forward, and when the touched body is moved upward on the screen, it bends backward.

5.3   Execution of Moving Motion

As explained in Section 3, when the pelvis is moved over a large distance, this is interpreted as moving in a step and the target position is computed.

Fig. 7. Touch interpretation for the pelvis

Figure 7 shows the touch interpretation for the pelvis. The horizontal movement of the pelvis is limited within the support polygon computed from foot positions (see Section 6.2). Vertical movement of the pelvis is limited by leg length and minimum duck height. When the pelvis is moved within this range, the input is interpreted as pelvis translation. When the pelvis is moved outside this range, the input is interpreted as moving motion (step) and the target position is computed.

The target position $\mathbf{p}_{move}$ is computed by computing the crossing point of the viewing vector with the plane that is parallel to the ground and crosses the pelvis of the character. To keep the step distance within a reasonable range, the distance between $\mathbf{p}_{move}$ and the current pelvis position is limited within a specific range (0.5m $\sim$ 0.8m in our implementation). Note that up-down touch movement on the screen controls front-back step direction.

6   Motion Control Model

In this section, we describe our motion control model that determines the output pose $\mathbf{P}_{output}$ based on the constraints from multi-touch inputs $\mathbf{P}_{input}$ and the previous pose $\mathbf{P}_{prev}$. These are represented by the intermediate point-based pose representation described in Section 4.

Our motion control model includes several modules and each of them determines an output pose. The output pose is computed by blending the results of all modules.

$$\mathbf{P}_{output} = (\sum \frac{w_i}{\sum w_i} \mathbf{P}_i) \tag{13}$$

where $\mathbf{P}_i$, w_i are the output pose and weight of each control module and $i =$ *tracking, balance, inter_body_ interaction, relaxing and self_collision_avoidance.* Note that all modules may not determine all parameters. For example, when there is no user input, the tracking control does not produce its output pose and weight. High priority is given to tracking, balance and self collision avoidance while low priority is given to inter body interaction and relaxing.

The concepts behind our each control module are not new. We designed these models based on our intermediate point-based pose representation. Our models directly change positions and orientation rather than using physics simulation. We introduced simple approximations and parameters for these modules. We argue that our framework is very simple and easy to implement, but also powerful and flexible.

In the remainder of this section, we briefly describe our approach for implementing each controller.

6.1 Tracking Control

Tracking control is for satisfying input constraints from the multi-touch interface. The output of the tracking control module $\mathbf{P}_{tracking}$ uses input constraints as $\mathbf{P}_{tracking} = \mathbf{P}_{input}$.

When an end-effector (hand or foot) is controlled by the user and the target position is within the reachable range of the limb, only the end-effector position is changed. However, when the target position is outside of the reachable range, the pelvis and the trunk should be moved to reach the target position. In such case, the pelvis position $\mathbf{p}_{pelvis}$ and the trunk orientation $\mathbf{q}_{trunk}$ are changed accordingly as follows.

$$\Delta\mathbf{p}_{root} = \mathbf{p}_{root}^{input} - \mathbf{p}_{root} \tag{14}$$

$$(\Delta\mathbf{q}_{trunk}(\mathbf{p}_{trunk} - \mathbf{p}_{back}) - (\mathbf{p}_{trunk} - \mathbf{p}_{back})) + \Delta\mathbf{p}_{pelvis} = \Delta\mathbf{p}_{root} \tag{15}$$

where $\Delta\mathbf{p}_{root}$ is the required translation of the root of the limb (shoulder). $\mathbf{p}_{trunk}$ and $\mathbf{p}_{back}$ are the positions of the trunk and back joints, respectively. First, the trunk orientation $\Delta\mathbf{q}_{trunk}$ is computed to satisfy $\Delta\mathbf{p}_{root}$ as much as possible. Then, the pelvis translation $\Delta\mathbf{p}_{pelvis}$ is computed to satisfy the remaining required translation $\Delta\mathbf{p}_{root}$.

Also, while an end-effector (foot) is contacting the ground, tracking control keeps the current foot position. When no constraint is specified to a body part, the tracking control does not handle the body part, as result, the body part is controlled by other modules.

Since the priority of tracking control should be high, $w_{tracking}$ is set to 1.0 (the highest weight).

6.2 Balance Control

Balance control maintains the balance of the character. Our balance control module controls pelvis position and trunk orientation to keep the projection of the center of mass of the character within its support polygon.

First, based on the character's current state, the position of the center of mass and its projection to the ground $\mathbf{p}_{com}$ is computed. The support polygon S is also computed based on the positions and contact conditions of the feet. Then it is determined if $\mathbf{p}_{com}$ is within S. If not, the closest point to $\mathbf{p}_{com}$ within S is computed as $\mathbf{p}'_{com}$. To maintain the character's balance, the center of mass is moved from $\mathbf{p}_{com}$ to $\mathbf{p}'_{com}$.

$$\Delta \mathbf{p}_{com} = \mathbf{p}'_{com} - \mathbf{p}_{com} \tag{16}$$

The translation of the upper body (position of the pelvis) $\Delta \mathbf{p}_{pelvis}$ and the rotation of the upper body (orientation of the trunk) $\Delta \mathbf{q}_{trunk}$ are computed to move the center of mass within the support polygon $\Delta \mathbf{p}_{com}$, when it is found to be outside the support polygon.

$$M \Delta \mathbf{p}_{pelvis} = w_{pelvis} \Delta \mathbf{p}_{com} \tag{17}$$

$$M(\Delta \mathbf{q}_{trunk}(\mathbf{p}_{trunk} - \mathbf{p}_{back}) - (\mathbf{p}_{trunk} - \mathbf{p}_{back})) = w_{trunk} \Delta \mathbf{p}_{com} \tag{18}$$

where M is the total mass of upper body. The required translation of the center of mass $\Delta \mathbf{p}_{com}$ is distributed to the translation of the pelvis position $\mathbf{p}_{pelvis}$ and the orientation of the trunk $\mathbf{q}_{trunk}$ with a specific ratio w_{pelvis} : $w_{trunk} = w_{pelvis\_trunk\_ratio} : 1 - w_{pelvis\_trunk\_ratio}$. In our implementation, we use $w_{pelvis\_trunk\_ratio} = 0.5$.

Since the priority of balance control is as high as tracking control, $w_{balance}$ is set to 1.0 too.

6.3 Inter-Body Interaction Control

This control is for simulating the physical interface between connected body parts. When a person moves his or her body part (e.g. an arm), any connected body part (e.g. trunk) also moves a little even if he or she tries to keep it still because there is physical influence between the connected body parts.

This module controls trunk orientation based on the velocities of end-effectors and the positions of end-effectors based on the velocity of the trunk. Because it is difficult to simulate this kind of effect accurately even with physics simulation, because it also requires realistic muscle stiffness models, we chose to scale the velocities of connected body parts.

The change of trunk orientation $\Delta \mathbf{q}_{trunk}$ is computed as follows.

$$\mathbf{v}_i = (\mathbf{p}_i - \mathbf{p}_i^{prev})/\Delta t \tag{19}$$

$$\Delta \mathbf{q}_{trunk}(\mathbf{p}_{trunk} - \mathbf{p}_{back}) - (\mathbf{p}_{trunk} - \mathbf{p}_{back}) = w_{ee\_to\_trunk} \Delta t \mathbf{v}_i \tag{20}$$

where $\mathbf{p}_i, \mathbf{p}_i^{prev}$ are the current and previous end-effector positions, $w_{ee\_to\_trunk}$ is the influence from the end-effector velocity to the trunk orientation. In our implementation, we use $w_{ee\_to\_trunk} = 2.0$.

The end-effector position is computed as follows.

$$\mathbf{v}_i = ((\Delta \mathbf{q}_{trunk}(\mathbf{p}_i - \mathbf{p}_{trunk}) - (\mathbf{p}_i - \mathbf{p}_{trunk})) + (\mathbf{p}_{pelvis} - \mathbf{p}_{pelvis}^{prev}))/\Delta t \tag{21}$$

$$\mathbf{p}'_i = \mathbf{p}_i + w_{trunk\_to\_ee} \Delta t \mathbf{v}_i \tag{22}$$

We use $w_{trunk\_to\_ee} = 0.2$. This is not applied to the end-effector (feet) that is contacting on the ground.

Since the priority of this control is low, a low value is set to $w_{interaction}$ (0.1 in our implementation).

6.4   Relaxing Control

Relaxing control is for moving the body parts to the rest pose when there is no user input. We introduced this module because it looks unnatural if the character stops in an unnatural pose. This module keeps the trunk vertical, lowers arms and legs, and maintains the head elevation within certain limits.

The trunk orientation is computed by

$$\mathbf{q}_{trunk} = \mathbf{q}_{trunk_v} \mathbf{q}_{trunk_h} \tag{23}$$

$$\mathbf{r} = \mathbf{q}_{trunk_v}^{-1} \tag{24}$$

$$\mathbf{q}'_{trunk} = \begin{matrix} \mathbf{q}_{trunk_h} & (if \; |\mathbf{r}| \leq v_{trunk} \Delta t) \\ \frac{v_{trunk} \Delta t}{|\mathbf{r}|} \mathbf{r} \mathbf{q}_{trunk} & (if \; otherwise) \end{matrix} \tag{25}$$

where $\mathbf{q}_{trunk_h}$ and $\mathbf{q}_{trunk_v}$ are decomposition of the trunk rotation into the horizontal orientation and the other component. The rotation $\mathbf{r}$ makes the trunk orientation closer to $\mathbf{q}_{trunk_h}$ in a predefined angular speed v_{trunk}.

Each end-effector positions is computed by

$$\mathbf{p}'_i = \mathbf{p}_i + \Delta t \mathbf{g} \; (if \; \mathbf{p}_{i,y} > h_{ee}) \tag{26}$$

where $\mathbf{g} = (0, v_{ee}, 0)$ is a predefined spatial speed. This equation is applied when the position of the end-effector is higher than the predefined height h_{ee}.

When there is no input to the head. The head is moved based on the trunk. However, this does not look natural. When a person moves, the head elevation is kept horizontal. To realize such head movements, the head orientation $\mathbf{q}_{head}$ is computed by the same equation with equation (25).

Since the priority of this control is low, a low value is set to $w_{relaxing}$ (0.1 in our implementation).

There are more sophisticated methods for gazing (head and eye orientation) control. However, such control is not considered in our motion control model, because as such methods work only on a virtual environment with other characters and objects which can be gazing targets and those are not considered in our current system.

6.5   Self-collision Avoidance Control

Self-collision avoidance requires care because we cannot know if self-collision will occur until the output pose is computed. Therefore, an interim output pose is computed without self-collision avoidance. If there is any self-collision, this control is then applied repeatedly until on self-collision problem exists.

This module solves self-collision between limbs and trunk by moving limbs. Assuming the limbs didn't penetrate into the trunk on the previous frame, the self-collision can be fixed by moving the limb (end-effector position) toward the state of the previous frame.

$$\mathbf{p}'_i = t\mathbf{p}_i + (1-t)\mathbf{p}_i^{prev} \qquad (27)$$

where $t(0 < t < 1)$. t is reduced from 1 to 0, until the collision is resolved.

However, in case that the trunk is also moving, moving the limbs to the previous state may not solve the collision. In such case, the limb (end-effector position) is moved outward as follows.

$$\mathbf{p}'_i = \mathbf{p}_i + \epsilon(\mathbf{p}_i - \mathbf{p}_i^{root}) \times \mathbf{d}_z \qquad (28)$$

where $\mathbf{p}_i^{root}$ is the position of the root of the limb (shoulder) and $\mathbf{d}_z$ is the z-axis of its local coordinates. ϵ is a small displacement for each step. This step is repeated until the self-collision is avoided.

Note there is the difference between this module and the method described in Section 5.1. The former deals with self-collision during motion control, while the latter is for interpreting multi-touch inputs. Both are important for not only avoiding self-collision but also for generating natural motion from the touch and drag inputs.

Since the priority of this control is high, $w_{self\_collision\_avoidance}$ is set to 1.0.

6.6   Step Motion Control

When a step is executed and its target position is sent from the interface module, the motion control generates a step motion. In our implementation, we used a similar model to that to that used by [25]. During action control, the pelvis and feet are controlled based on a procedural action model. The full body motion is automatically generated by our motion control framework.

The step control determines trajectories of the pelvis and feet. First, the goal position of both feet $\mathbf{p}_{r\_foot}^{goal}$, $\mathbf{p}_{l\_foot}^{goal}$ are computed from the given goal position of the pelvis $\mathbf{p}_{pelvis}^{goal}$ so that the relative positions is kept before and after step as follows.

$$\mathbf{p}_{r\_foot}^{goal} = \mathbf{p}_{pelvis}^{goal} + (\mathbf{p}_{r\_foot}^{initial} - \mathbf{p}_{pelvis}^{initial}) \qquad (29)$$

Our step control generate one cycle of step, that is, a leg is moved first and the other leg follows. The leg that is near to the target position is moved first. For example, when the character steps to the right, the right leg is moved first. The first moving leg is determined based on the target position.

The step action is executed in two phases; preparation and execution phases. During preparation phase, the pelvis is moved over the first supporting leg so that the character can move the moving leg. During execution phase, one cycle of step is executed. The trajectories of the pelvis and feet during those phases can be approximated by linear trajectories [25]. The durations of those phases are determined based on the length of the trajectories.

Fig. 8. Mouse-based interface for comparison. The position and orientation of a joint or end-effector can be controlled by dragging a handle.

7   Results and Discussion

We have implemented our interface and tested it. Some of the resulting motions are shown in Figure 1 and the accompanying video. Various simple actions such as posing, reaching, stepping, gestures (nodding, pointing, waving), fighting actions (punch, kick) and combinations can be created by using our interface. As explained in Section 1, even though our method can take multi-touch inputs, it is difficult for a user to control many parts simultaneously. Based on our experiments, we found that using one to three touches at the same time is enough when performing typical actions. Each action typically has one primary limb (e.g. an arm for punch). One touch can be used to control its end-effector. Also, one touch can be used to control the body (pelvis and/or trunk). The rest of the body is driven by our motion control model.

We conducted a user test to show the efficiency of our multi-touch interface. Because there is no alternative common interface that can control full-body motion of a charter interactively, it is difficult to compare our interface for motion control tasks. Therefore, in this user study we evaluated our interface for posing control tasks. We compared our interface with a conventional mouse-based pose editing interface where a joint rotation or position can be manipulated using handles displayed on the screen as shown in Figure 8. The blue and red spheres on the character represent controllable end-effectors and joints, respectively. This kind of interface is commonly used in commercial animation systems such as maya, max and softimage. Although only one body can be controlled at a time, its position and rotation can be controlled precisely.

Seven subjects who have basic knowledge of computer animation participated in the user test. During the experiment, a target pose was showed to the subject and he or she was asked to make the same pose by using one of the interfaces. The system determines that the task is completed when the maximum distance between the positions of all joints in the target and controlled poses becomes below the threshold (10 cm in our experiment). The five target poses used in our experiment are shown in Figure 9. The required times for making each target pose from the initial pose were measured. Each subject used both interfaces.

Fig. 9. Target poses used in the user test

Table 1. Results from the user test. Average times for making each target pose.

Pose no.	Mouse interface	Multi-touch interface
1	27.4 s	8.6 s
2	33.2 s	9.9 s
3	34.7 s	11.9 s
4	76.2 s	25.6 s
5	132.5 s	40.1 s

The average times for the posing tasks are shown in Table 1. For all target poses, our multi-touch interface was more efficient than the mouse-based interface. From our observation, the subjects first tried to make the lower body pose by using one or two touches and by changing the view direction if necessary. They then made the upper body pose by using multi-touch. This is because the relaxing control module lowers the arms if the user stops touching them. Since body orientation cannot be controlled by our multi-touch interface, it seemed that the subjects found it difficult to make some poses such as pose no. 4. The subjects also found it difficult to control end-effector positions when two hands are close to each other such as pose no. 4, because multiple touches cannot point the same position. The pose no. 5 took time the most, because the all feet and hands must be controlled both in front-back and right-left directions.

Using our interface, the user can make his or her avatar perform their own actions. This will be useful in many applications such as communication in virtual environments using avatars or fighting games. Conversely, performing all motions using our interface may not be realistic. Making a combination of our interface and conventional interfaces available and allowing users to choose may be a more practical option.

There are limitations in our interface. Control is focused on the pose of a standing character and performing moving motions other than stepping was not considered in this paper. There are existing methods for such movement control [10][11] and our system can be integrated with these.

Because of the constraints of using inputs on a 2-dimensional screen, it is not possible to control which direction the character is facing, because the touch inputs are interpreted as translation or tilt of the controlled body parts and rotation is not considered. It may be possible to extend our system to include different methods of interpretation or to make it possible to switch between different interfaces. However, such extension makes the interface more complicated. Seeking a balance between freedom of control and usability is an important area for future research. Although our motion control model takes physics into account, it is not driven by physics simulation and may not always be physically correct. For example, pose and motion is limited so that the character never falls. We believe hat this is a reasonable constraint, but a user may want the character to perform a falling motion.

8   Conclusion

In this paper, we proposed a framework for controlling a character using a multi-touch interface. Although our framework is very simple, various kinds of motions can be realized using our interface without using any examples. Our interface is easy to implement and can be used by many tablet computers.

Acknowledgment. This work was supported in part by a Grant-in-Aid for Scientific Research (No. 24500238) from the Japan Society for the Promotion of Science (JSPS).

References

1. Grochow, K., Martin, S.L., Hertzmann, A., Popović, Z.: Style-based inverse kinematics. ACM Transactions on Graphics 23(3), 522–531 (2004)
2. Oshita, M.: Multi-touch interface for character motion control using example-based posture synthesis. In: International Conference on Computer Graphics, Visualization and Computer Vision (WSCG 2012), pp. 213–222 (2012)
3. Oshita, M.: Multi-touch interface for character motion control using model-based approach. In: International Conference on Cyberworlds 2013, pp. 330–337 (2013)
4. Jakobsen, T.: Advanced character physics. In: Proceedings of Game Developer's Conference 2001 (2001)
5. Popović, Z., Witkin, A.: Physically based motion transformation. In: SIGGRAPH 1999, pp. 11–20 (1999)
6. Kulpa, R., Multon, F., Arnaldi, B.: Morphology-independent representation of motions for interactive human-like animation. Computer Graphics Forum (Eurographics 2005) 24(3), 343–352 (2005)
7. Neff, M., Kim, Y.: Interactive editing of motion style using drives and correlations. In: Eurographics/ACM SIGGRAPH Symposium on Computer Animation 2009, pp. 103–112 (2009)
8. Krause, M., Herrlich, M., Schwarten, L., Teichert, J., Walther-Franks, B.: Multi-touch motion capturing. In: ACM International Conference on Interactive Tabletops and Surfaces 2008, p. 2 (2008)

9. Kipp, M., Nguyen, Q.: Multitouch puppetry: Creating coordinated 3d motion for an articulated arm. In: ACM International Conference on Interactive Tabletops and Surfaces 2010, pp. 147–156 (2010)

10. Park, S.I., Shin, H.J., Shin, S.Y.: On-line locomotion generation based on motion blending. In: ACM SIGGRAPH Symposium on Computer Animation 2002, pp. 105–111 (2002)

11. Thorne, M., Burke, D., van de Panne, M.: Motion doodles: An interface for sketching character motion. ACM Transactions of Graphics (SIGGRAPH 2004) 23(3), 424–431 (2004)

12. Oshita, M.: Motion control with strokes. Computer Animation and Virtual Worlds 16(3-4), 237–244 (2005)

13. Igarashi, T., Moscovich, T., Hughes, J.F.: Spatial keyframing for performance-driven animation. In: ACM SIGGRAPH/Eurographics Symposium on Computer Animation 2005, pp. 253–258 (2005)

14. Dontcheva, M., Yngve, G., Popović, Z.: Layerd acting for character animation. In: SIGGRAPH 2003, pp. 409–416 (2003)

15. Callennec, B.L., Boulic, R.: Interactive motion deformation with prioritized constraints. Graphical Models 68, 175–193 (2006)

16. Hodgins, J.K., Wooten, W.L., Brogan, D.C., O'Brien, J.F.: Animating human athletes. In: SIGGRAPH 1995, pp. 71–78 (1995)

17. Faloutsos, P., van de Panne, M., Terzopoulos, D.: Composable controllers for physics-based character animation. In: SIGGRAPH 2001, pp. 251–260 (2001)

18. Liu, C.K., Popović, Z.: Synthesis of complex dynamic character motion from simple animations. ACM Transactions on Graphics (SIGGRAPH 2002) 21(3), 408–416 (2002)

19. Jain, S., Ye, Y., Liu, C.K.: Optimization-based interactive motion synthesis. ACM Transactions on Graphics 28(1), Article No. 10 (2009)

20. Macchietto, A., Zordan, V., Shelton, C.R.: Momentum control for balance. ACM Transactions of Graphics (SIGGRAPH 2009) 28(3), Article No. 80 (2009)

21. Monheit, G., Badler, N.I.: A kinematic model of the human spine and torso. IEEE Computer Graphics and Applications 11(2), 29–38 (1991)

22. Tolani, D., Goswami, A., Badler, N.I.: Real-time inverse kinematics techniques for anthropomorphic limbs. Graphical Models and Image Processing 62(5), 353–388 (2000)

23. Yonemoto, S., Arita, D., Ichiro Taniguchi, R.: Real-time human motion analysis and ik-based human figure control. In: Workshop on Human Motion 2000, pp. 149–154 (2000)

24. Gottschalk, S., Lin, M., Manocha, D.: Obbtree: A hierarchical structure for rapid interference detection. In: SIGGRAPH 1996, pp. 171–180 (1996)

25. Wu, C.-C., Medina, J., Zordan, V.B.: Simple steps for simply stepping. In: Bebis, G., et al. (eds.) ISVC 2008, Part I. LNCS, vol. 5358, pp. 97–106. Springer, Heidelberg (2008)

Efficacy of a Virtual Environment for Training Ball Passing Skills in Rugby

Helen C. Miles[1], Serban R. Pop[1], Simon J. Watt[1], Gavin P. Lawrence[1],
Nigel W. John[1], Vincent Perrot[2], Pierre Mallet[2],
Daniel R. Mestre[2], and Kenton Morgan[3]

[1] Bangor University, Bangor, United Kingdom, LL57 1UT
n.w.john@bangor.ac.uk
[2] Aix-Marseille Université, CNRS, ISM UMR 7287 13288, Marseille cedex 09, France
daniel.mestre@univ-amu.fr
[3] Rygbi Innovations Cyf., United Kingdom

Abstract. We have designed a configurable virtual environment to train rugby ball passing skills. Seeking to validate the system's ability to correctly aid training, two experiments were performed. Ten participants took part in ball passing activities, which were used to compare the combinations of different user positions relative to the physical screen, the use of stereoscopic presentation and the use of a floor screen to extend the field of view of the virtual scene. Conversely to what was expected, the results indicate that the participants did not respond well to simulated target distances, and only the users physical distance from the screen had an effect on the distance thrown.

Keywords: distance perception, stereoscopy, rugby.

1 Introduction

There is a great deal of interest in training sporting skills using virtual environments (VEs), for example handball [1], [2], tennis [3], [4], [5], golf [6], [7], [8], baseball [9], [10], [11], cycling [12] and swimming [13]; and discussion concerning the validity of VEs as a training tool for a wide array of different activities [14], [15], [16]. The discussions focus on the possibility of detrimentally affecting the user by teaching a new skill incorrectly or spoiling a skill the user already possesses by providing a training platform that lacks vital cues or provides superficial cues that are not present in the real world. There is no universally accepted method of validating VEs; technologically benchmarking VEs is difficult when each can be quite unique in their software and hardware configuration. Despite this, however, there are a growing number of examples of VEs (and simulators [17]) being regularly used as part of real training regimes in professional sports [18]. Such VEs must therefore be carefully designed with consideration to affordances and feedback, ensuring that any limitations or assistance provided by the VE do not leave gaps in the users learning or dependencies on certain information [19].

M.L. Gavrilova et al. (Eds.): Trans. on Comput. Sci. XXIII, LNCS 8490, pp. 98–117, 2014.
© Springer-Verlag Berlin Heidelberg 2014

We have designed a configurable VE to assist in the training of rugby skills using rugby ball passing as the test case. A focus on passing skills has been made because it is a fundamental core skill in rugby; previous work has been undertaken in lineout [20], [21], [22] and attack interception [23], [24], [25], [26] skills training. The experiments detailed in this paper investigate the technology that was initially chosen for the proposed system, with a focus on the ability to perceive virtual distances correctly within the VE.

2   Related Work

For sport-based VEs, it is important to constrain the user as little as possible and allow the freedom of movement that they would normally experience when playing the sport. Data projection to a large screen is the most common approach, e.g. [3], [5]. A head-mounted display (HMD) is likely to interfere with the physical activity of the user, as many require large cables trailing from the headset to transfer the visual data. They also prevent the user from seeing their own hands, requiring the use of an avatar; this in turn can lead to issues with latency.

Many systems also employ stereoscopic technology to augment the sense of depth in the virtual scene: shutter glasses were the most popular type of stereo technology over anaglyphic and polarisation glasses [1], [27]. However, the potential detriment of using stereo technology has not been discussed.

The above issues are discussed in more detail in [28]. This review covers both the state-of-the-art technology currently used to build a VE and a number of other issues involving the training of a user in a task involving ball sports. The investigation of these issues has provided the motivation and a knowledge base on which to build the VE for Rugby Skills Training (VERST). This paper describes the VERST system and presents the results of initial experiments using a rugby ball passing task. We describe the development of a physics engine for a rugby ball in flight, and an investigation of the effect of stereoscopic technology and the physical screen configuration on the user's ability to perceive virtual distances correctly.

3   Building a Virtual Environment for Rugby Skills Training

The VE, which can be seen in Fig. 1 and Fig. 3, placed the subject in the centre of the field of play in a model of the Millennium Stadium in Cardiff, Wales. Circular archery-style targets of fixed size (1m diameter) were presented to the user, with the centre of the target 1m above the ground. The user holds a real tracked rugby ball (which is tethered to the ceiling or attached to the wrist of the player to prevent any damage to the equipment), and must throw the ball to hit the targets. The data from the tracked ball is input into the physics engine to produce a predicted flight path, shown with a virtual ball.

Development of the VERST software began with implementing a physics engine to handle the virtual flight path of the ball. It employs a simple ballistic model based on work by Bray and Kerwin [29] on football free kicks, and by Vance et al [30] on the aerodynamics of a rugby ball in flight, which provided drag and lift coeffients. The solution to the flight path of the rugby ball can then be estimated in real-time using the Runge-Kutta 4th Order method. The required input data for this model is the last position vector at which the ball was recorded for continuity between the real and computed movement, and a Cartesian velocity vector based on an average of several velocity estimates taken as the ball was tracked.

To test the accuracy of the physics model, a series of real ball throws (passes) were captured in a motion capture laboratory at Bangor University. The laboratory was equipped with 12 Vicon cameras covering an area of approximately 5×5m in the centre of the room, so allowing for only relatively short throws. The cameras were able to capture a full throw with sufficient accuracy and precision, at a rate of 250 Hz. Once the data had been collected, the throws were compared with a Matlab implementation of the physics model. This highlighted the necessity of controlling the capture window to ensure the correct section of the real ball's flight is captured. This lead us to design the ball capturing system to be a small capture window placed approximately 50cm in front of the user; with the participant in a fixed position, which would allow only the capture of the ball after being released from the participant's hands.

To begin evaluating the VERST system, an experiment was designed to examine the effects of display technology on the task of hitting a target with a rugby ball.

3.1   Issues in Depth Perception

In a virtual training exercise involving targets at different distances, it is vital that depth perception in the scene be as accurate as possible. Using stereoscopic technology to augment the sense of depth in VERST is therefore an aspect that we want to investigate. Stereo displays have been shown to provide a greater sense of presence in the environment [31] and provide a more accurate sense of object size [32]. However, they can potentially also cause a range of other issues, including discomfort (see [33]). Cues to the target distance were also available from monocular depth cues, principally the angular size of the targets at the eye, and height in the visual field.

Depth compression within VEs using both HMDs [34], [35] and large screen displays [36], [37] has also been previously reported but is not well-understood. Standard methods of evaluating the perception of distance in VEs are verbal judgments [36], [38] and blind walking [39], [40]; blind throwing [41] has also been used. Sahm et al [41] found a distance underestimation of 30% between distances of 3-6m using a HMD, while Piryankova et al [37] found a distance underestimation of approximately 25% for an experiment using a large screen immersive display. See the review by Renner et al [42] for an overview.

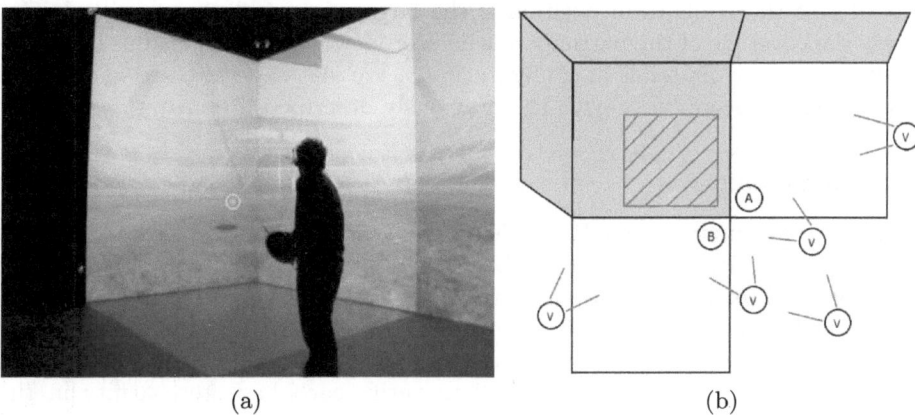

(a)   (b)

Fig. 1. (1a) The VERST system during experiment 1. (1b) A top-down view of the screen configuration, the darker sections highlight the screens, the 'A' and 'B' markers show the two positions the participant stands during the experiment. The 'V' markers give the position of the Vicon cameras and the hatched area indicates the approximate capture area.

4   An Initial Evaluation of the Efficacy of VERST

Because of the uncertainty of the effects of stereoscopic technology, and display technology, on the ability of the user to perform our ball passing task, experiment 1 on VERST was to evaluate the suitability of the technology. The performance of the physics engine was also scrutinized, as the results of the trials rely heavily on an accurate representation of the movement of the ball. The key factors to be investigated in this experiment were: (1) stereoscopic versus non-stereoscopic presentation, (2) the use of a floor screen to cover more of the user's field-of-view, and (3) the position of the physical display, where the surface structure is specified by focus cues and a visible outline.

Participants could not see the virtual trajectory of the ball in this experiment. There were two reasons for this. Firstly, we did not want them to adjust their technique to any flaws that may be present in the physics model at this time; we must be confident that it is correctly modeling the ball's movement before exposing users to any potential detriment of training to a non-natural system. Secondly, as the experiment is attempting to measure any distortions in the perception of the virtual target, using the ball throw as the dependent measure, subjects must not be allowed to adapt to any distortions; the perceptual system adapts to systematic distortions quickly, and so allowing feedback would result in excellent performance regardless of any depth distortion problems, thereby preventing measurement of any distortions.

We hypothesize that the participants should respond more accurately to distance in the trials where the floor panel increases the coverage of the participant's field-of-view and stereoscopic cues are available (configurations 1 and 5, see table 1). In the trials from position B the larger right wall screen will also increase the coverage of the participant's field-of-view; this would lead us to expect the best results from trials in configuration 5. We also expect to see some depth compression in accordance with the previously described literature.

4.1 Participants

Four male participants aged 21, 25, 26 and 38 years took part in this preliminary study. The participants had each being playing rugby for a minimum of 10 years for local teams, and played in a variety of team positions. All participants were right-handed and reported having normal, unimpaired vision, or wore their typical corrective lenses (glasses or contact lenses). Participants' stereo vision was tested using the Randot SO–002 to verify each had stereoacuity in the normal range.

Each was observed in a real-world throwing task for a distance of 9m to verify their ability to perform passes accurately in the correct distance range. The task was performed indoors to ensure there were no external wind forces affecting the pass, to mirror the conditions of the VE in the experiment.

4.2 Equipment

The VERST system was implemented in the 3DVIA Virtools software package and presented in a CAVE-like virtual reality system (Fig 1). The hardware consists of three 3×4m rear-projected wall screens and a 3×3m floor projected from above. Each screen had a resolution of 1400×1050 pixels and the screens were seamlessly joined to provide a visually continuous projection surface. The left wall was at 90 degrees from the front wall, while the right wall was "open" (aligned with the front wall), giving an L-shape configuration, to allow the user more space and for efficient placement of the motion tracking system. Stereoscopic projection is achieved using Infitec technology with two DLP projectors per screen.

A tracking system (ArtTrack), using infrared recognition of passive markers placed on the subjects glasses, was used to record the subject's head position and orientation and to update the stereoscopic images relative to the subject's point of view in real time (with a frame rate of 60 Hz). The two eyes' images were presented simultaneously and the images were correctly geometrically projected for each eye; prior to the experiment, the interpupillary distance (IPD) of each participant was measured using an Essilor Digital Corneal Reflection Pupilometer (CRP) in order to tailor the separation of the stereoscopic images to each individual. The whole projection system was controlled by a cluster of synchronized PCs.

A real rugby ball was suspended from the ceiling of the building, tracked by five Vicon cameras indicated in Fig. 1b with 'V' markers. The participants were positioned at either A or B (marked in Fig. 1b); the white squares in Fig. 1b represent two platforms raised approximately 10cm from the ground either side of the CAVE floor screen. The capture area (marked by the red hatched box in

Fig. 1b) was positioned far enough away from the user that they would have to reach unnaturally to have their hands within it.

4.3   Experimental Design

Three variables were used to determine a testing configuration: (1) position of the participant (position A/B in Fig. 1b); (2) whether stereoscopic presentation was active or not (S/NS); and (3) whether the floor screen was active or not (F/NF). The three variables produced eight different configurations as shown in table 1.

Virtual targets were considered in a range of 5–15m away from the participant into the virtual scene. For each configuration, the participant was presented with 7 target distances with 5 repetitions of each target distance rotated around the azimuth of the user. This resulted in each participant throwing 280 trials. The eight configurations were randomized across participants to remove any order bias.

Table 1. Configurations as defined by each set of variables

Configuration Number	Position A/B	Stereo (S)/ No Stereo (NS)	Floor (F)/ No Floor (NF)
1	A	S	F
2	A	S	NF
3	A	NS	F
4	A	NS	NF
5	B	S	F
6	B	S	NF
7	B	NS	F
8	B	NS	NF

4.4   Procedure

Once the experiment began, the program automatically assigned the seven target distances randomly between 5 and 15m at random angles rotated around the position of the participant (obtained from the tracked glasses). A beep signified the start of the trial, and the participant had 5 seconds to attempt the throw. This ensured that the participant could not have time to study the target and contemplate the distance, and to encourage the participant to react to his first instincts.

If the user failed to throw the ball in time or the Vicon cameras did not successfully capture the motion of the ball, they were awarded one further attempt at the same trial. Despite there being an existing physics model, the virtual ball was not shown to the user so that they could not make any corrections to their method or adjust their attempts to compensate for any failings in the system.

The participant was prevented from knowing whether they had successfully hit any of the targets during or after the experiment. After the participant had completed the experiment, they were asked to provide some verbal feedback on the system.

For each trial, the following data were collected: (1) position of the participant from the tracked glasses; (2) position of the target in the VE; (3) the motion data of the real ball collected by the Vicon system; (4) the data that would have been input for the physics engine (position and velocity vectors).

4.5   Results

The straight distance thrown by all four participants, as a function of the virtual target distance, is plotted in Fig. 2a; the five repeat trials to the same target distance are plotted as a single averaged data point.

During the experiment it was observed that participant 4 was constantly throwing the real ball with much less force than the other participants. This participant had been observed successfully throwing 9m distances with little effort prior to the experiment, and appeared to be struggling to accept the safety of throwing the real ball so close to the screen. It was found that participant 4 accounted for the lower group of results in Fig. 2a, consistently throwing between 3–5m distances for all target distances (with a standard deviation of less than 0.5m for each group of trials). To prevent this lower group from distorting the results of the other three participants, only participants 1–3 will be considered when investigating the distance, as shown in Fig. 2b.

In Fig. 2c the data from Fig. 2b are plotted as a series of linear best-fit lines labeled by configuration. This graph demonstrates much poorer scaling between the virtual distance and the thrown distance than we had expected to see, although the slopes do progress upwards slightly between 6–9m. Because the participants were throwing at targets suspended 1m above the ground rather than a target placed on the ground plane, it is not necessary for the participant to throw the exact distance to hit the target, so throws travelling beyond the target distance for the closer targets may not present a problem. To look at the difference between the variables in greater detail, each of the three will be discussed in turn.

Comparison of the different configurations using ANOVA revealed that there was no significant difference in the distances thrown from the two different positions ($F(1,68) = 0.22, p = 0.64$), with stereoscopy active/inactive ($F(1,68) = 0.18, p = 0.67$) or the floor screen active/inactive ($F(1,72) = 0.14, p = 0.71$).

It was noted that there were a great number of trials where the ball missed the target to the left or right. Exploring this revealed that all participants threw too far to the left in 82% of the trials from position B, and threw too far to the right in 51% of the trials from position A (in this instance participants 2–4 threw 66% of the trials to the right but participant 1 threw only 10% of the throws to the right). Exploring the statistics of the misses with ANOVA verified that there was a significant effect on the left misses from position B ($F(1,40) = 108.3, p = 6.04E - 13$), and right misses from position A ($F(1,40) = 69, p =$

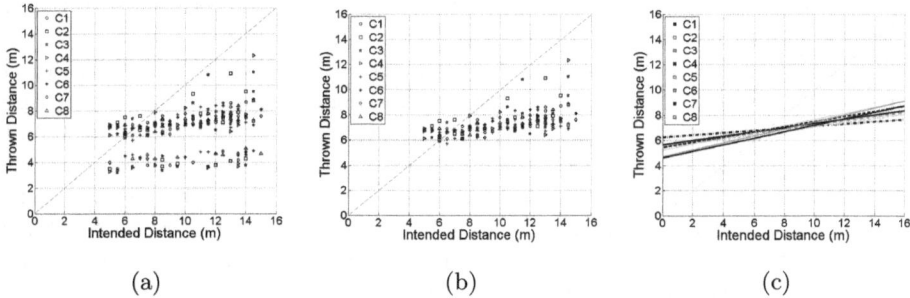

Fig. 2. Each configuration is plotted in a different shade (c1-8). The dashed line denotes the 1:1 ratio of the two axes. (2a) All participants, the average distance thrown as a function of target distance. (2b) Participants 1–3, the average distance thrown as a function of target distance. (2c) Participants 1–3, the average distance thrown as a function of target distance from (2b) presented as a series of best-fit lines.

$3.07E - 10$). Positioning in the CAVE was the only variable influencing this; the number of misses left and right were very evenly spread between the stereo on/off (left: $F(1, 40) = 0.34, p = 0.56$; right: $F(1, 40) = 0.17, p = 0.68$) and the floor projection on/off (left: $F(1, 40) = 0.87, p = 0.36$; right: $F(1, 40) = 1.01, p = 0.32$) variables.

Participant 1 had been in the CAVE previously for other studies; the difference in results, the lower number of misses to the left and right of the target compared to the other three participants is perhaps due to this previous experience. The other three participants had not undertaken any previous experiments at the CAVE used for the experiment, or any other to our knowledge.

Verbal feedback from the participants included two noting that the distances appeared correct to them, and one noting that he used the pitch markings in the virtual scene to aid him. Two of the participants stated that they noticed no difference when the variables were switched, while a third had noticed the floor being changed but not the stereo. Finally, two of the participants commented that it was "strange" and difficult to perform the task while unable to see the virtual ball. None of the participants noted any nausea or discomfort at any point during or after the experiment.

4.6   Conclusions

In this preliminary study, it was found that the participants did not respond well to the simulated distances with most throws travelling between 6–9m with little regard to the depicted target distance. The use of stereoscopy and the use of a floor screen did not significantly affect the distance thrown by the participant. It was noted that the physical position of the participant and the position of the target they were aiming at may have influenced them to over-rotate their throw to the left and right. It is also possible that the participants were unintentionally aiming the throw closer to the diagonal across the floor screen–the longest physical space to throw; for this reason the L-shape configuration of the CAVE may not be appropriate to the task of throwing a rugby ball at a virtual target.

One of the participants was unable to make any throws beyond 5m, which nullified the training potential of the system for them. It appeared that they were unable to accept the safety of the system, and were fearful of hitting the CAVE walls with the ball. It is conceivable that improving the sense of presence the system provides might assist the participant's performance. This demonstrates that the use of this VE for training will not be suitable for all users, as it is likely that some other users will experience similar problems in accepting the virtual content and ignoring the physical distance.

This experiment showed that, for this VE, users were unable to correctly perceive the distances; further work must be done to understand the reasons for this. The position of the user, the use of stereoscopic presentation and the use of a floor screen to extend the coverage of the user's field of view did not significantly affect the distance estimations made by the participants. Finally, it was found that the shape of the CAVE may not be suitable to this throwing task, as the participants were found to over–rotate their throws.

5   Further Evaluation of the Depth Perceived in VERST

The main focus of experiment 2 was to investigate the use of different screen shapes, considering whether this might have affected the results of the throwing task. Participants performed the same task as in the first experiment, using both curved and flat screens. We were given access to a different facility than that used for experiment 1, with both high fidelity curved and flat display environments. However, because the tracking systems available at the new facility only operate at 60 Hz, they would not provide sufficient tracking support for the throwing task. In order to use both the screens, a verbal estimation task was performed with both configurations, and the throwing task with the flat screen only, with the intention of using the verbal results to draw comparisons between the curved and flat screens, and theorise about the performance of the participants in the throwing task using the curved screen. The results from the two experiments are not expected to be perfectly matched for each participant [43], [44], [45], but it is possible that some comparison between the results may be found.

Based on Renner et al's [42] review of distance perception experiments, the distances in the verbal estimation task are expected to be underestimated by approximately 26%.

5.1   Participants

Six participants aged 20–54 years took part in experiment 2. For this experiment, the participants were not required to have extensive previous experience playing rugby; five of the participants had played only at school or college level, while one had played for a local team. Five of the participants were right-handed, while the sixth was left-handed; all reported normal or corrected-to-normal vision. Participants were all found to have stereoacuity in the normal range using random dot stereograms.

Each was observed in a real-world throwing task to verify their ability to perform passes accurately in the correct distance range. As with experiment 1, the task was performed indoors to ensure there were no external wind forces affecting the pass, to mirror the conditions of the VE in the experiment.

5.2   Equipment

The VERST system was implemented in the Unity 3D and MiddleVR software packages and presented on a flat (shown in Fig. 3a) and a curved power wall (shown in Fig. 3b).

(a)   (b)

Fig. 3. Participants during the experiment using the flat (3a) and curved (3b) screens

The curved screen was 2m tall with an arc length of 11m (cord length approximately 8m). The screen was rear-projected by 8 separate projectors that ran on either a single unit or a cluster of 8 PCs, depending on the demands of the application. The screen had a resolution of 8500×1920 pixels. An ART tracking system consisting of 12 cameras was fixed around the edges of the screen; the cameras were able to track multiple objects in front of the screen at 60 Hz.

The flat screen was 6m wide and 2.1m tall with a resolution of 3387×1200 pixels from 4 projectors. The laboratory housing the flat screen was equipped with a 12-camera Vicon system that covered the entire floor area in front of the screen by placing the cameras high on the walls all around the room. The cameras were able to capture movement at 250 Hz, making it more than capable of capturing high-speed ball movements.

Both screen configurations had stereoscopic projection, presented through tracked shutter glasses, which allowed the scene to be geometrically projected correctly for each user. Before the experiment, each participant's IPD was measured using a basic IPD ruler, and taken into account in the stereo projection.

The change of location for the second experiment meant that the real ball could not be suspended from the ceiling, so a bungee and wrist strap were used for the throwing experiment (see Fig. 3a). The capture area for the ball was determined during each trial as being 1m in front of the user (based on their position from the tracked glasses).

5.3 Experimental Design

Two variables were used to determine a testing configuration: (1) whether stereoscopic presentation was active (S) or not (NS); and (2) the physical distance of the participant from the screen (Near [1m], Medium [3m] and Far [4m]–the throwing task used only Medium and Far). The two variables produced six different configurations as shown in table 2.

Virtual targets were considered in a range of 5–10m away from the participant into the virtual scene. For each configuration, the participant was presented with six target distances with three repetitions of each target distance rotated around the azimuth of the user. This resulted in each participant throwing 288 trials. The six configurations were randomized across participants to remove any order bias.

Table 2. Configurations as defined by each set of variables

Configuration No. (Verbal Task)	Configuration No. (Throwing Task)	Participant's Distance from the Screen	Stereo (S)/ No Stereo (NS)
1	-	Near	S
2	1	Medium	S
3	2	Far	S
4	-	Near	NS
5	3	Medium	NS
6	4	Far	NS

5.4 Procedure

The two screen configurations were alternated for each participant; when the participant was ready they were lead to the first room and performed the verbal task. If they were in the curved screen laboratory, they then moved straight to the flat screen room, but if they were in the flat screen laboratory they remained to perform the throwing task before moving to the curved screen room.

For both tasks, the participant would stand at the instructed position for each configuration of both tasks. A bull's-eye style target would appear in the virtual playing field in front of them; they would have five seconds to react to the target by either stating the target distance or throwing the ball at the target. For the throwing task, the participant was prevented from knowing whether they had successfully hit any of the targets during or after the experiment.

For the verbal task, the participants were asked to provide an answer in whole metres. The participants were not given any information about the range of target distances, and any comments or questions regarding the distance of the targets or the participant's three positions were neither confirmed nor denied by the experimenter.

For all of the trials in both of the verbal and throwing experiments, the following data were collected: (1) position of the participant from the tracked glasses; (2) position of the target in the virtual space and the distance from the participant; (3) the amount (in degrees) the target was rotated around the participant; (4) the start and completion timestamps for each configuration and the whole experiment. For each of the trials in the verbal experiment, the distance estimate by the participant was noted as the experiment progressed; as the target distances were shuffled prior to each participant performing the experiment, the experimenter only knew the range of possible distances. For each of the trials in the throwing experiment, the following additional data were also collected: (1) the position and velocity vectors that would have been input for the physics engine; (2) the position the ball would land at according to the physics engine. After both the verbal estimation experiment and the throwing experiment, the participants each completed a copy of the Witmer & Singer Presence Questionnaire [46].

5.5   Results

Verbal Experiment. First, the individual target distances were analysed (across all participants and configurations, with both the flat and curved screens); the results are plotted in Fig. 4. Medians and inter-quartile ranges are used instead of mean and standard deviation because the distance estimates were made in whole metres.

The data in Fig. 4 shows that the target distances were mostly overestimated, target distances of 5, 6, 8 and 9m only having the lower 25% of the results underestimated (for 7 and 10m target distances, the lower quartile fell 1m under the distance they were intended to perceive). The median results for 6 and 7m targets are 3m above the intended distance, while the 5 and 8-10m targets were 2m above. The inter-quartile range indicates that 50% of the estimates were within a range of up to 6m across all target distances.

2×2 repeated measures ANOVA was conducted on the mean estimated distance values of the verbal task, revealing that the use of stereoscopy did not significantly affect the estimates made using either the curved ($F(1, 168) = 2.14, p = 0.15$) or flat ($F(1, 204) = 0.24, p = 0.63$) screens; the combined mean estimated distances were also not significantly affected by the use of stereoscopy ($F(1, 348) = 0.48, p = 0.49$).

The position of the participant relative to the screen (at Near, Medium and Far distances using both the curved and flat screen) was found to have a significant effect ($F(2, 342) = 28.18, p = 0$) on the estimated distances; target distances were perceived as nearer the closer the participant to the screen. The position of the participant was found to significantly affect the estimated distance when

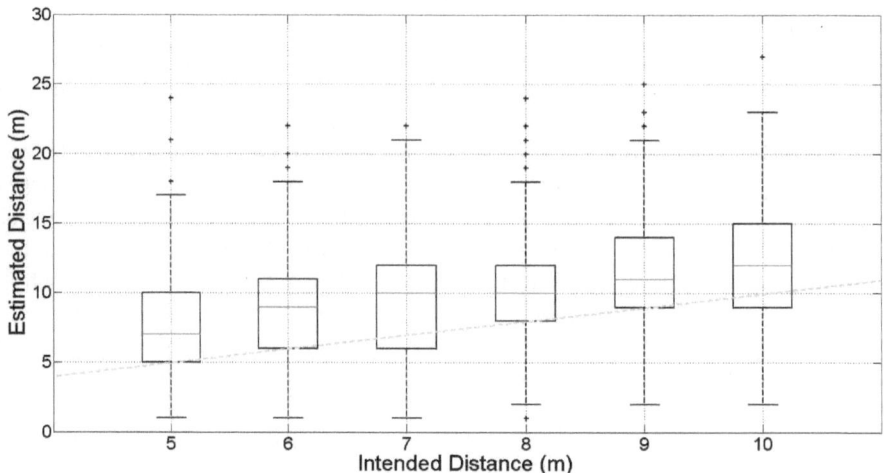

Fig. 4. Results of the verbal task. Intended perceived distance between 5–10m is plotted against the distance estimated by all participants. The dashed line represents the 1:1 ratio of the two axes.

using the curved screen ($F(2, 162) = 80.25, p = 0$), but not the flat screen ($F(2, 198) = 1.9, p = 0.15$) (see Fig. 5).

Whether the estimates were made using the curved or flat screen was found to have a significant effect ($F(1, 348) = 40.4, p = 0$), with mean estimates made using the flat screen consistently overestimated 2–3m farther than those made using the curved screen.

Throwing Experiment. The mean results of the throwing experiment are plotted in Fig. 6. The results do not appear to be scaled to the intended target distances, with results ranging from 2–30m regardless of the target distance.

2×2 repeated measures ANOVA was conducted on the mean thrown distance values of the throwing task, showing no significant effect from the use of stereoscopy/no stereoscopy ($F(1, 132) = 0.4, p = 0.53$) or the distance of the participant from the screen (Medium and Far distances away, $F(1, 132) = 2.18, p = 0.14$).

Presence Questionnaire. The Presence Questionnaire was used to assist in gaining an understanding of the participants' attitudes towards different aspects of the VERST system. Comprising of 24 questions, it rates the (1) realism; (2) the possibility to act in the virtual world; (3) the quality of the interface; (4) the possibility to examine the virtual world; (5) a participant's self-evaluation of their performance inside the VE; (6) sounds used in the VE (not used in VERST); and (7) haptics used in the VE.

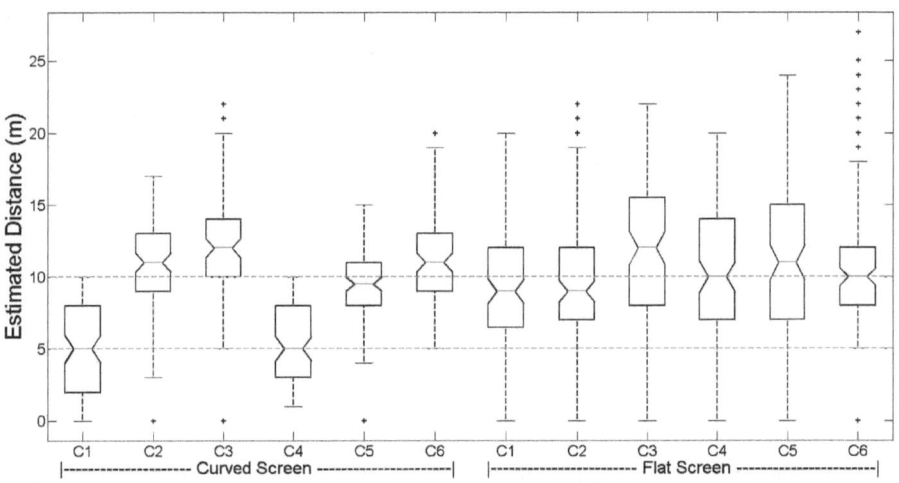

Fig. 5. Results of the verbal task separated into the estimations made under different configurations (see table 2) using the curved and flat screens. The horizontal dashed lines mark the range of target distances intended to be perceived (5–10m).

The results of the Presence Questionnaire are summarised in table 3. No group had significantly different results to the other four, $F_{(4, 25)} = 0.91, p = 0.47$, although the Possibility to Examine group has a lower score overall than the other four groups.

Table 3. Presence Questionnaire Group Results

Group	Maximum Possible Score	VERST Median Score	VERST Inter-Quartile Range
Realism	49	37	3
Possibility to Act	28	23	4
Quality of Interface	21	11	4
Possibility to Examine	21	17	2
Self-Evaluation of Performance	14	13	4
Haptics	14	10	1
Total	133	101	7

5.6   Conclusions

In terms of execution, the second experiment was performed in a similar manner to experiment 1. Differences included the use of the wrist strap rather than a ceiling tether, and a combination of spherical markers attached using hook

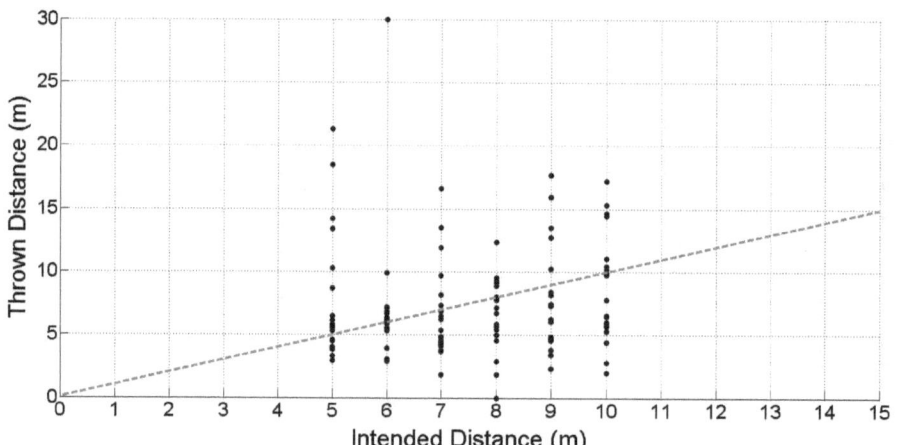

Fig. 6. Distance thrown according to the results of the physics engine plotted against the intended target distance. The dashed line represents the 1:1 ratio of the two axes.

and loop tape and flat, circular markers for tracking the ball. The wrist strap proved to be difficult to use, like the ceiling tether, resulting in the participants concentrating less on the task and more on the potential of the ball to hit them during the bungee's post-throw reflex. While the spherical markers were held solidly during most of the trials, as the ball hit the ground, the markers would occasionally be knocked off.

The participants responded to the verbal experiment with better scaling to the intended target distances than the throwing experiment. The verbal estimates were generally overestimated by participants, which conflicts with previous similar experiments [42]. The curved and flat screens were found to affect the verbal estimates, with the flat screen estimates tending to be higher than the curved screen.

The use of stereoscopy was not found to have a significant effect on the estimations being made in either the verbal or throwing experiments. A significant effect of participant's physical distance from the screen was found for the verbal estimation task, but not the throwing task. The results of the Presence Questionnaire showed that the participants had a positive attitude towards their immersion experience in VERST.

Comparing the results of the verbal and throwing tasks in the second experiment (see Fig. 7) showed an effect of the measurement type, where verbal estimates were tending to be larger than throws. Verbal estimates were scaled well to the intended target distance, although they were overestimated, while distances thrown displayed no scaling.

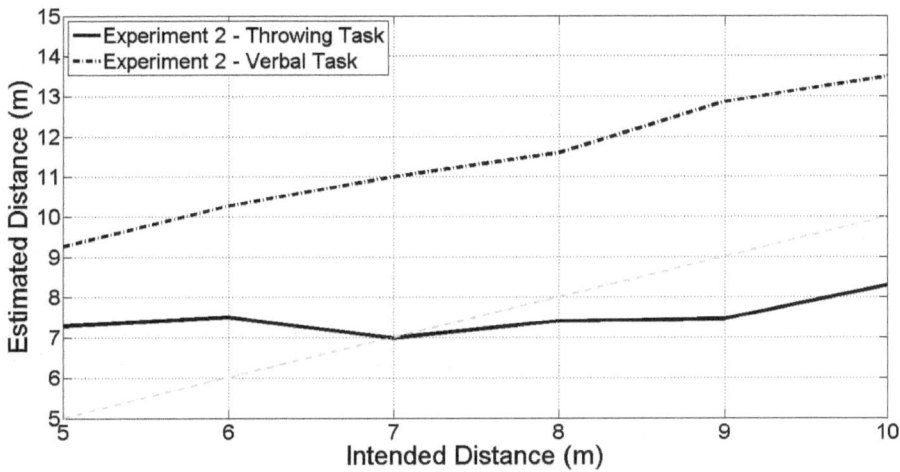

Fig. 7. Estimated distance during the verbal (dashed line) and the throwing (solid line) experiments plotted against the intended distance. The lighter-coloured dashed line represents the 1:1 ratio of the two axes.

6   Summary and Conclusions

Two experiments were performed to measure the users' perception of egocentric distance to virtual targets. The first experiment, performed in a CAVE, was based on four participants throwing the tethered ball at 280 targets at 5–15m under three experimental variables: the position of the participant relative to the screen, the use of the floor screen and the use of stereoscopy. The second experiment consisted of a throwing task performed using a flat screen, and a verbal estimation task performed using flat and curved screens; experimental variables were the distance of the participant from the screen and the use of stereoscopy. For the second experiment, a smaller range of distances was used: 5–10m.

The use of stereoscopy was not found to significantly affect the verbal estimations or thrown distances from either experiment; neither was the use of the floor screen in experiment 1. The position of the participants did affect the distances percieved: in the first experiment, the position of the participant affected the direction of the throw, while for the second experiment, the further the participant from the screen, the further they percieved targets.

The mean throw distance data from both experiments are plotted in Fig. 8. That the participants were able to perceive a scaling in distance during the verbal experiment, but not to do the same during the throwing tasks suggests that they may have been uncomfortable with throwing the ball towards the screen.

A Presence Questionnaire was administered to the participants after the second experiment was performed, which showed that most of the participants had a highly positive attitude towards their immersion experience.

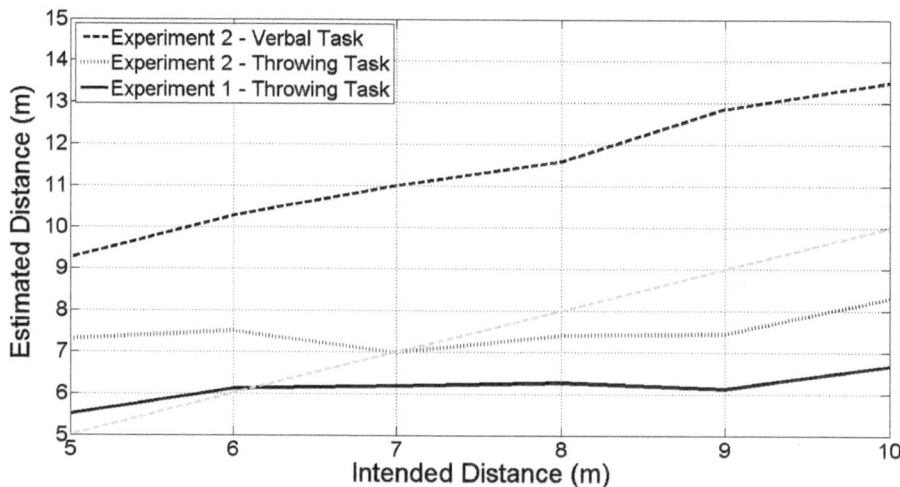

Fig. 8. Comparison of the average estimated distance between the verbal and throwing tasks in the two experiments as a function of the intended distance. The lighter-coloured dashed line represents the 1:1 ratio of the two axes.

VERST has proved to be a useful platform for investigating the optimal set up of a VE for training ball passing skills in rugby. The system will be improved as a result of the experiments carried out and a validation of skills transfer from the VE to the rugby pitch will be an important part of our future work. We will also explore training of skills from other ball sports.

Acknowledgments. The experiment was undertaken at the Centre for Virtual Reality of the Mediterranean (CRVM) at Aix–Marseille University, France, and the Hartree Centre at the Science and Technology Facilities Council, Daresbury, UK. The associates of Bangor University wish to thank both facilities for their hospitality and support during the experiment, particularly Terry Hewitt from the Hartree Centre, and Joss Petit and Chris Greive from OPTIS Northern Europe who supported the experiments at Daresbury.

This project is jointly–funded by a Knowledge Economy Skills Scholarship (KESS), the European Social Fund (ESF), Bangor University and Rygbi Innovations. The research leading to these results has been partially supported by the European Community's Research Infrastructure Actiongrant agreement VISIONAIR 262044–under the 7th Framework Programme (FP7/20072013).

References

1. Bideau, B., Multon, F., Kulpa, R., Fradet, L., Arnaldi, B., Delamarche, P.: Using virtual reality to analyze links between handball thrower kinematics and goalkeepers reactions. Neurosci. Lett. 372(1-2), 119–122 (2004)

2. Bideau, B., Kulpa, R., Menardais, S., Fradet, L., Multon, F., Delamarche, P., Arnaldi, B.: Real handball goalkeeper vs. virtual handball thrower. Presence–Teleop. Virt. 12(4), 411–422 (2003)
3. Xu, S., Song, P., Chin, C.L., Chua, G., Huang, Z., Rahardja, S.: Tennis Space: an interactive and immersive environment for tennis simulation. In: ICGIP, pp. 652–657 (2009)
4. Brunnett, G., Rusdorf, S., Lorenz, M.: V-Pong: an immersive table tennis simulation. IEEE Comp. Graph. 26(4), 10–13 (2006)
5. Li, Y., Shark, L.K., Hobbs, S.J., Ingham, J.: Real-time immersive table tennis game for two players with motion tracking. In: IEEE–IV, pp. 500–505 (2010)
6. Kelly, P., Healy, A., Moran, K., O'Connor, N.E.: A virtual coaching environment for improving golf swing technique. In: ACM–MM SMVC, p. 51 (2010)
7. Govil, A., You, S., Neumann, U.: A video-based augmented reality golf simulator. In: ACM–MM, pp. 489–490 (2000)
8. Ahn, S.H., Kang, K.B., Kim, E.J., Kim, S.J., Lee, J.W., Song, C.G.: Interactive 3D Golf Simulator. LNCS (2006)
9. Gray, R.: Behavior of college baseball players in a virtual batting task. J. Exp. Psychol. Human 28(5), 1131–1148 (2002)
10. Fink, P.W., Foo, P.S., Warren, W.H.: Catching fly balls in virtual reality: a critical test of the outfielder problem. J. Vis. 9(13(14)), 1–8 (2009)
11. Syamsuddin, M.R., Kwon, Y.M.: Simulation of baseball pitching and hitting on virtual world. In: CISIS, pp. 663–667 (2011)
12. Chung, J., Xu, K., Colaco, A., Schmandt, C., Li, V.O.K.: My Second Bike: a tv-enabled social and interactive riding experience. In: IEEE–CCNC, pp. 1–5 (2010)
13. Fels, S., Kinoshita, Y., Takama, Y., Yohanan, S., Gadd, A., Takahashi, S., Funahashi, K.: Swimming across the Pacific: a VR swimming interface. IEEE Comp. Graph. 25(1), 24–31 (2005)
14. John, N.W.: Design and implementation of medical training simulators. Virtual Reality 12(4), 269–279 (2008)
15. Hays, R.T., Jacobs, J.W., Prince, C., Salas, E.: Flight simulator training effectiveness: a meta-analysis. Mil. Psychol. 4(2), 63–74 (1992)
16. Crivella, R., Daly, B., Schaaf, R., Ventura, D., Camill, T., Hodgins, J., Pausch, R.: Training for physical tasks in virtual environments: tai chi. In: IEEE–VR, pp. 87–94 (2003)
17. Thales Group: Thales tackles scrum simulation Thales Group Press Release (June 04, 2013), http://tinyurl.com/lnbp358 (accessed: May 28, 2013)
18. Westcott, R.: Trying out Fernando Alonso's Ferrari F1 simulator. BBC News website (April 19, 2013), http://www.bbc.co.uk/news/technology-22218163 (accessed: May 28, 2013)
19. Ruffaldi, E., Bardy, B., Gopher, D., Bergamasco, M.: Feedback, affordances, and accelerators for training sports in virtual environments. Presence–Teleop. Virt. 20(1), 33–46 (2011)
20. Chong, A.K., Mileburn, P., Newsham West, R., ter Voert, M., Croft, H.: Recent practical applications of close-range photogrammetry for complex motion study. ISPRS J. Photogramm. XXXVII(Part B5), 921–926 (2008)
21. Chong, A.K., Croft, H.: A photogrammetric application in virtual sport training. Photogramm. Rec. 24(125), 51–65 (2009)
22. Brook, P., Croft, H., Mann, S.: Laser based line-out simulator. NACCQ, 265 (2007)
23. Bideau, B., Kulpa, R., Vignais, N., Brault, S., Multon, F., Craig, C.: Virtual reality, a serious game for understanding performance and training players in sport. IEEE Comp. Graph. 30, 14–21 (2010)

24. Brault, S., Bideau, B., Kulpa, R., Craig, C.: Detecting deceptive movement in 1 vs. 1 based on global body displacement of a rugby player. IJVR 8(4), 31–36 (2009)
25. Brault, S., Bideau, B., Kulpa, R.: How the global body displacement of a rugby player can be used to detect deceptive movement in 1 vs. 1. Laval–Virtual, 161–166 (2009)
26. Brault, S., Bideau, B., Craig, C., Kulpa, R.: Balancing deceit and disguise: how to successfully fool the defender in a 1 vs. 1 situation in rugby Hum. Movement Sci. 29(3), 412–425 (2010)
27. Vignais, N., Bideau, B., Craig, C., Brault, S., Multon, F., Delamarche, P.: Does the level of graphical detail of a virtual handball thrower influence a goalkeepers motor response? J. Sport Sci. Med. 8(4), 501–508 (2009)
28. Miles, H.C., Pop, S.R., Watt, S.J., Lawrence, G.P., John, N.W.: A review of virtual environments for training in ball sports. Comput. Graph. 36(6), 714–726 (2012)
29. Bray, K., Kerwin, D.G.: Modelling the flight of a soccer ball in a direct free kick. J. Sport Sci. 21(2), 75–85 (2003)
30. Vance, A.J., Buick, J.M., Livesey, J.: Aerodynamics of a rugby ball. J. Appl. Mech. 79(2), 021020-1–021020-5 (2012)
31. Ijsselsteijn, W., Ridder, H., Freeman, J.: Effects of stereoscopic presentation, image motion, and screen size on subjective and objective corroborative measures of presence. Presence–Teleop. Virt. 10(3), 298–311 (2001)
32. Luo, X., Kenyon, R., Kamper, D., Sandin, D., DeFanti, T.: The effects of scene complexity, stereovision, and motion parallax on size constancy in a virtual environment. In: IEEE–VR, pp. 59–66 (2007)
33. Watt, S.J., MacKenzie, K.J.: 3D media and the human visual system. Emerging Technologies for 3D Video: Creation, Coding, Transmission, and Rendering, 349 (2013)
34. Creem-Regehr, S.H., Willemsen, P., Gooch, A.A., Thompson, W.B.: The influence of restricted viewing conditions on egocentric distance perception: implications for real and virtual indoor environments. Perception 34(2), 191–204 (2005)
35. Willemsen, P., Colton, M., Creem-Regehr, S.H., Thompson, W.B.: The effects of head-mounted display mechanics on distance judgments in virtual environments. In: APGV, pp. 35–38 (2004)
36. Alexandrova, I., Teneva, P.: Egocentric distance judgments in a large screen display immersive virtual environment. In: APGV (2010)
37. Piryankova, I.V., de la Rosa, S., Kloos, U., Bülthoff, H.H., Mohler, B.J.: Egocentric distance perception in large screen immersive displays. Displays 34(2), 153–164 (2013)
38. Interrante, V., Ries, B., Anderson, L.: Distance perception in immersive virtual environments, revisited. In: IEEE–VR, pp. 3–10 (2006)
39. Thomson, J.A.: Is continuous visual monitoring necessary in visually guided locomotion? J. Exp. Psychol. Human 9(3), 427–443 (1983)
40. Steinicke, F., Bruder, G., Hinrichs, K.: Transitional environments enhance distance perception in immersive virtual reality systems. APGV 1(212), 19–26 (2009)
41. Sahm, C.S., Creem-Regehr, S.H., Thompson, W.B., Willemsen, P.: Throwing versus walking as indicators of distance perception in similar real and virtual environments. ACM Trans. Appl. Percept. 2(1), 35–45 (2005)
42. Renner, R., Velichkovsky, B., Helmert, J.: The perception of egocentric distances in Virtual Environments. ACM Comput. Surv. (to appear, 2014)

43. Bridgeman, B., Gemmer, A., Forsman, T., Huemer, V.: Processing spatial information in the sensorimotor branch of the visual system. Vision Res. 40(25), 3539–3552 (2000)
44. Parks, T.E.: Visual-illusion distance paradoxes: a resolution. Atten. Percept. Psychophys. 74(8), 1568–1569 (2012)
45. Goodale, M.A., Milner, A.D.: Separate visual pathways for perception and action. Trends Neurosci. 15(1), 20–25 (1992)
46. Witmer, B.G., Singer, M.J.: Measuring Presence in Virtual Environments: A Presence Questionnaire. Presence–Teleop. Virt. 7(3), 225–240 (1998)

Preparing for International Operations and Developing Scenarios for Inter-cultural Communication in a Cyberworld: A Norwegian Army Example

Ekaterina Prasolova-Førland[1], Mikhail Fominykh[1], Ramin Darisiro[2],
Anders I. Mørch[3], and David Hansen[4]

[1] Norwegian University of Science and Technology, Trondheim, Norway
[2] Norwegian Armed Forces, Oslo, Norway
[3] University of Oslo, Oslo, Norway
[4] Centre for International and Strategic Analysis, Oslo, Norway
{ekaterip,mikhail.fominykh}@ntnu.no, rdarisiro@fhs.mil.no,
anders.morch@iped.uio.no, david.hansen@strategiskanalyse.no

Abstract. Understanding culture is an integral part of international operations in developing countries and conflict zones. Cultural encounters in countries such as Afghanistan might introduce a number of challenges. This article presents the experiences with the CAMO project (Cultural Awareness in Military Operations) seeking to address these challenges. While game-based simulations are to an increasing degree used for military training, most of such systems are expensive to develop. The goal of this project has been to create a low-cost simulation in the 3D virtual world of Second Life for pre-deployment cultural awareness training among Norwegian military personnel preparing for service in Afghanistan. We provide a detailed description of the methodology and training scenarios, based on examples of cultural challenges the participants were expected to face. We also report the results of evaluation of the system with the cadets of the Norwegian Military Academy. Finally, we discuss how the proposed methodology could be extended for non-military use, since due to the gradual withdrawal of troops from Afghanistan training cultural awareness among civilian personnel becomes more important.

Keywords: cultural awareness, military training, game-based simulations.

1 Introduction

In this paper, we present the results of the CAMO project (Cultural Awareness in Military Operations). The goal of the project has been to create an inexpensive and flexible game-based simulation for training cultural awareness among military personnel preparing for international operations (Afghanistan), which has the potential to be reused for civilians working in the area.

Overcoming cultural distances requires externalizations [1,2] in the form of boundary objects [3] that have meaning across the boundaries of the individual knowledge systems [4]. In this way, boundary objects allow different knowledge systems and

M.L. Gavrilova et al. (Eds.): Trans. on Comput. Sci. XXIII, LNCS 8490, pp. 118–138, 2014.

communities to interact by providing a shared reference that is meaningful within both parts. Another way to overcome cultural distances is by 'perspective taking', which means to see a point of view from another person's position and then to act as though one were that person. Social scientists have studied how people take on the perspective of the other when they act on shared objects e.g., boundary objects. For example, during economic exchange, both buyer and seller must take each other's perspectives towards the shared object of exchange for proper understanding. Role-playing is a technique for learning perspective taking [5].

3D cyberworlds provide interesting possibilities for creating boundary objects. Game-based simulations and role playing in 3D cyberworlds have also been used for military training and as general learning and teaching methods for a long time [6,7]. They provide engaging learning experience and are used for demonstrating complex concepts in an intuitive way. Game-based simulations and educational role playing may have both positive and negative impacts (as discussed e.g., in [8]) that we considered in our design. We are also aware of the fact that the technology we apply may impose a number of limitations in terms of generalization, transfer, and application in real life settings [9].

An example of a complex concept that can be demonstrated and learnt in a 3D cyberworld is operational culture. Understanding culture is a basic component of operational planning, training, and execution. There are a number of commercially available game-based simulations and cyberworlds for training operational culture including systems such as Tactical Iraqi and First Person Cultural Trainer [10-12]. Such systems are typically very expensive to develop and primarily single-player, providing no or very limited support for collaborative learning and team training. In addition, there are no or very few possibilities for the user to generate own scenarios and modify existing ones, something that might be of high importance when the political situation in the region of interest suddenly changes. At the same time, there is a lack of research-based methods for using game-based simulations in military training [13], especially in the area of cultural awareness/operational culture. The use of such systems requires aids for scenario development, training practices, and performance measurement tools that currently do not exist [13].

The CAMO project seeks to address these challenges. The project is a joint effort between the Norwegian Defense University College, the Norwegian University of Science and Technology, the University of Oslo, and the Bjørknes College. The ADL (Advanced Distributed Learning) section at the Norwegian Defense University College has been coordinating the project. Other participants include Norwegian Military Academy, Norwegian Defense Language and Intelligence School, Telemark Battalion, and Norwegian Defense Media Center. Apart from developing the simulation, the project aims at creating research-based methodology, guidelines, and tools for developing 3D educational simulations for future use in the Norwegian Armed Forces [14].

As a starting point for developing such a methodology, we studied publicly available literature and guidelines for operational culture training, such as "Operational Culture for the Warfighter: Principles and Applications" [15] and recommendations for developing cross-cultural competencies at the US Department of Defense [16]. We have also studied scenario methodologies developed at the UK Human Factors Integration Defence Technology Centre [17] and the Royal Netherlands Army/TNO Defense, Security & Safety/Delft University of Technology [18], which are well developed and rather systematized, but are primarily focused on tactical/operational tasks and not on operational culture. Therefore, these methodologies have been developed further during the project to be adjusted to the goals of the CAMO project [14]. Since the existing literature on Afghani operational culture is rather fragmented and/or classified, it was decided to use subject matter experts within the Norwegian Armed Forces and Norwegian academia as the major source of information for the scenarios.

In the following, we present the results of the project, including a detailed description of the scenario examples. We shortly outline the implementation of the virtual environment, and present the evaluation results with four data excerpts. We also discuss how the resulting methodology and design principles could be further developed and extended for civilian use in Afghanistan and other developing countries.

2   Background

A Norwegian military force operating in foreign countries would, regardless of the composition and organizational affiliation, have a need for culture-related knowledge – in order to carry out their missions in a best possible way (either missions taking place in Afghanistan, Sudan, Syria, the Balkans or other areas of operation). In brief, there are major cultural differences between what a Norwegian soldier is used to from Norway, and even other international operations, and what one is met with on the ground in Afghanistan – whether it is in Kabul or in a district such as Maymanah, Northern Afghanistan.

In this paper, the concept of culture is specified to encompass cross-cultural issues covering general operational culture, including aspects related to gender, language, and cultural artifacts, limited to tactical scenarios in Afghanistan. This is considered to be of primary relevance for the forces of Provincial Reconstruction Teams (PRT), Military Observation Teams (MOT), tactical mentors that operate in cooperation with local Afghan forces (Afghan National Army-ANA and Afghan National Police ANP), and Special Operations Forces (SOF). It would also be relevant to the staff officers serving in the International Security and Assistance Force (ISAF) headquarters, as well as other contributions, such as field hospital personnel, mine-clearing personnel, Norwegian police elements in Afghanistan, and other smaller units and individual officers serving in other NATO / UN positions in Afghanistan. In a wider context, some other actors, such as embassy personnel, non-governmental organizations and media personnel, could also benefit from the learning insights and knowledge derived from the project presented in this paper.

Since Afghanistan is very complex and ethnically diverse, it was necessary to prioritize, focusing in particular on the cultural aspects typical of the Pashtun ethnic group. However, the learning goals of this project caught up the cultural aspects of a more general character – with validity beyond Pashtuns – to the extent that was appropriate and necessary to describe the cultural aspects. Furthermore, the project also focuses on the generic aspects of culture, such as religion, social norms, and gender aspects.

Operational culture in this context means practical, specific, and applicable knowledge about cultural issues related to, among other things, cultural artifacts: distinguishing a mosque from other buildings, rhetorical and linguistic factors: religion (Islam), myths, folklore and superstition, crime and local conflicts, interpersonal relationships, power, position, and social conditions.

Practically applicable knowledge means knowledge that a single soldier, a patrol, a team, or others should be able to use in their everyday work in interaction with and in the analysis of friendly as well as hostile local citizens and social structures in general – with the intent to implement their operations in the best possible way. Another perspective on cultural awareness/operational culture can be found in [19], which states that cultural awareness (in general) is about "Norwegian forces' understanding of the local [cultural] context in the operational area and their approach to local moral, ethical, cultural and legal borders, in cooperation with both the civilian population, allied military and the enemy."

Both definitions emphasize the importance of identifying the relevant aspects of culture that affect military operations and that helps us to understand the effects of our actions in the light of the socio-cultural composition of the operational environment. Focus on culture allows (theoretically) military units and partners to use knowledge of foreign culture for the following purposes:

- Understanding the specific socio-cultural motives for action (or non-action)
- Understanding enemy mindset
- Exerting influence on the population
- Improving interaction with other actors in the area of operation
- Justifying own actions

The above points also constitute the overall learning goals for this project. The practically applicable knowledge was conveyed through practical learning objectives that had been embedded into the simulated training including a virtual Afghan village and local 'Afghans' in a cyberworld based on Second Life (SL) platform.

3   Cultural Challenges and Scenario Development

The methodology for scenario development used for the CAMO project is based on a systematized set of learning goals and associated 'mini-scenarios', to obtain the maximum reusability of the content. Each 'mini-scenario' comes with a set of 'cues' [18], associated reactions from the gaming environment or feedbacks from the 'game master'. Cues can be defined as "the perceptual elements of the environment that influence the challenging decisions" [20,18].

These mini-scenarios provide a basis for requirements for the virtual environment for every 'scene'/gaming sequence and the associated scripts for the role players, especially the 'Afghans'. The scripts were not hardcoded, and the role-players were free to interpret them in personally meaningful ways. Based on the consultations with the subject experts, the following major categories of learning goals were identified:

- T. Tactics: general tactics (in a concrete cultural context) e.g. identifying threats based on the relevant cues from the environment
- G. Gender: interacting with women in tribal/clan communities e.g. how to act towards Afghan women
- R. Religion: dealing with religious customs, practice, and symbols, such as recognizing a village mosque
- S. Socializing: observing local customs, e.g. dealing with children, visiting a house
- L. Language: basic language skills for simple tasks like polite greeting, asking for directions, identifying security threats, interactions between the interpreter, the locals, and the squad.

Though being initially identified for the project setting (focusing on international operations in Afghanistan), these categories are generally applicable for operational culture training and, as discussed later, for cultural awareness training of civilian personnel. Each of the learning goals categories are split into sub-categories, providing a basis for the corresponding mini-scenarios, for example:

- Tactics sub-goal T1. Identifying possible threats
- Religion sub-goal R1. Correct behavior during a prayer
- Religion sub-goal R2. Food during Ramadan
- Gender sub-goal G1. Close contact with local women
- Social interaction sub-goal S3. Dealing with children
- Language sub-goal L1. Basic polite phrases in local language.

Each of the learning sub-goals is further detailed with corresponding cues, appropriate reactions, typical mistakes, and typical responses in case of mistake. Below is an example of such a detailing for a gender-related learning sub-goal (see also Tables 1-2):

Learning sub-goal G1: Close contact with local women

- Cues: a local woman asks for/needs (medical) assistance
- Appropriate reaction: a female soldier approaches the woman, talks to her and provides necessary assistance
- Typical/possible mistake: a male soldier approaches the woman, talks to her and in the worst case touches her while attempting to provide assistance
- Typical response in case of mistake: the woman (other locals) gets upset/hostile, further efforts are needed to resolve the situation

The scenario consists of eight 'scenes' with associated places in the virtual environment called 'zones' (Fig. 1). Each scene consists of a set of learning sub-goals with corresponding cues. Before the start of the role-play, a 'mission order' was provided in the form of a short video. It contained the following information: threat level is medium, it is Ramadan, it is Friday, it is about 12.45 pm when the squad enters the village, and the squad does not know where the village chieftain and his house is, but they have an appointment to meet him in the village. The purpose of the meeting is to obtain information about possible Taliban activities in the area.

Fig. 1. Looking for the mosque in the virtual Afghan village

When the squad enters the village, they see three children playing along the road. While the squad passes by/possibly greets the children, the children come closer, attempt to touch the weapons, and beg for chewing gum and candy. A local woman appears from a house on the other side, shouts angrily at the children, and waves them away. The squad approaches the local woman to inquire about the whereabouts of the village chieftain (Fig. 2). After talking to her, the soldiers continue on the road, looking for the village mosque. There are some characteristic features distinguishing the mosque from ordinary houses (Fig. 1). The squad needs to wait outside and greet the chieftain and his two men appearing from the mosque. If the squad greets the chieftain properly, he might invite them to his house. While passing by a house, the squad observes a crying woman, visibly injured. After helping the woman, the squad arrives at the chieftain's compound. They enter his reception room where the squad and the chieftain are to discuss the security situation in the area.

There are several possible paths to the village chieftain, depending on the players' preferences but also on their abilities to choose an optimal course of action for each situation. If the soldiers give chewing gum to the children in the beginning of the role-play (Example 1), it might upset the local woman. Furthermore, if they talk to the local woman in the next scene (Example 2) in a way she perceives as disrespectful, she would be less inclined to share information about the whereabouts of the village chieftain and the position of the mosque where he is most likely to be since it is Friday prayer time (Examples 3 and 4). Consequently, the squad must spend more time locating the mosque, probably contacting the home base/ 'game master' for the assistance. If the soldiers fail to observe the cultural codes treating the locals in an impolite and inappropriate manner, the chieftain might get upset and unwilling to provide information about Taliban activities (Example 5).

Fig. 2. A male and a female soldier talking to a local woman (Example 2)

3.1   Example 1: Dealing with Children

In this example, three children play along the road. While the squad passes by, the children come closer, attempt to touch the weapons, beg for chewing gum and candy. A woman appears from a house on the other side, shouts angrily at the children and waves them away. The learning sub-goals for this example are T1: Identifying possible threats + T3: Securing an area + T4: Keeping the civilians outside danger + S3: Dealing with children + L1: Basic polite phrases in local language. In this scene, the soldiers need to react to and reflect on the following cues:

1. Children touching weapons are in the way => potentially dangerous situation for the civilians?
2. Woman shouts angrily => locals dislike the contact between the soldiers and the children
3. Children play freely => says something about the security situation?

Based on the cues, there are different possible responses the soldiers could choose, with corresponding outcomes, from 'optimal' course of action to typical mistakes, as summarized below:

1. The soldiers give candy and chewing gum to the children (dropping a 'candy' object from SL inventory) => the children keep nagging, the woman might get more angry (shouting more, gesticulating) => another round attempting to resolve the situation ('worst case/mistake')
2. The soldiers give nothing to the children, yell at them => the children get disappointed, are no longer in the way, but the woman might get offended, the relations to the locals might worsen => to the next scene, where the woman will be less inclined to answer any questions

3. The soldiers give nothing to the children, try to avoid direct contact, waving friend-ly to them, stay calm, say some general phrases/ask them to step aside => the children stop nagging, nobody gets offended => to the next scene ('best case/appropriate reaction')

3.2   Example 2: Conversation with a Local Woman

In this example, the squad approaches a local woman (who appears from her house to wave away the children in the previous example) to inquire about the whereabouts of the village chieftain. The learning goals for this scene are composed of the following sub-goals: G3: Verbal contact with local women (Table 1) + S1: Polite greeting + L1: Basic polite phrases in local language + L2: Interaction between the interpreter, the locals, and the squad. The soldiers need to react to and reflect on the following cues in this scene:

1. A local woman who has potentially useful information, her age and social status
2. Whether the woman is alone in the house
3. Whether the woman is neutral or unfriendly minded towards the Norwegians (after their interactions with local children)

Possible responses the soldiers could choose and corresponding outcomes are summa-rized below:

1. One of the male soldiers approaches the woman (in the worst case, with a direct contact between the avatars) and greets her => the woman, especially if she is young, hides in the house, expresses fear, provides no information => another round with a female soldier attempting to resolve the situation/contacting the game master/'home base' for help ('worst case/mistake')
2. Male soldiers follow the woman into the house to talk with her without any of her family present => the woman might feel dishonored or protests => another round with a female soldier attempting to resolve the situation/contacting the game mas-ter/'home base' for help ('worst case/mistake')
3. One of the male soldiers greets the woman without approaching => the woman (especially if she is older) answers that the village chieftain is in the mosque but does not show where the mosque is, goes back to the house => to the next scene
4. A female soldier/interpreter approaches the woman, possibly enters the house, starts asking questions => the woman perceives the greeting as not polite enough/is angry after what happened in the previous scene/misunderstands what is said by the interpreter, answers that the village chieftain is in the mosque but does not show where the mosque is, goes back to the house => to the next scene
5. A female soldier/interpreter approaches the woman, possibly enters the house, greets her politely, starts asking questions => the woman answers that the village chieftain is in the mosque and shows the way there => to the next scene ('best case/appropriate reaction').

Table 1. Gender-related learning goals with associated cues, appropriate reactions, typical/possible mistakes and typical responses in case of mistake

Learning goals	Cues from the environment	Appropriate reactions	Typical/possible mistakes	Typical responses in case of mistake
G1. Close contact with local women	• A local woman asks for/needs (medical) assistance (e.g. her clothes are bloody) • Presence / absence of other family members	• Female soldier approaches the woman, talks to her and provides necessary assistance	• Male soldier approaches the woman, talks to her and in the worst case touches her while attempting to provide assistance • Male soldier enters the woman's house while no other family members are present	• The woman gets upset/hostile • Negative reactions from the locals
G2. Female soldiers on a house visit	• Female soldier enters a house with several local men present	• Seating herself in the back, with her legs together	• Taking a seat too close to the men • Sitting in a 'tailor' position	• Negative reactions from the hosts
G3. Verbal contact with local women	• Meeting a local woman during patrolling	• Female soldier greets the woman	• Male soldier greets the woman • Male soldier enters the woman's house while no other family members are present	• The woman gets upset, does not answer, turns away • Negative reactions from the locals

Table 2. Religion-related learning goals with associated cues, appropriate reactions, typical/possible mistakes and typical responses in case of mistake

Learning goals	Cues from the environment	Appropriate reaction	Typical/possible mistake	Typical response in case of mistake
R1. Correct behavior during a prayer	• A man (men) praying	• Showing respect, not disturbing, waiting until the prayer is over	• Disturbing a praying man with questions	• The praying man/men might get upset
R2. Food during Ramadan	• Being offered refreshments during Ramadan	• Declining politely, finally accepting some tea/water if the host repeatedly insists	• Accepting food right away	• Upset locals, but probably no visible response
R3. Recognizing a mosque, correct behavior in/outside the mosque	• Building with minbar, dome, minarets, possibly audible prayer calls	• No going inside and disrupting the prayer unless emergency • Respectful behavior (taking off shoes, silence)	• Failing to recognize the mosque, behaving without due respect • Entering / disturbing during prayer time • Entering without taking off shoes	• Offended worshippers, mullahs, locals in general

3.3   Example 3: Looking for the Mosque

In this example, the soldiers follow the way, looking for the village mosque. There are some characteristic features that distinguish the mosque from ordinary houses. The learning sub-goals in this example are: T1: Identifying possible threats + T2: Interaction within the squad/home base + R3: Recognizing a mosque, correct behavior in/outside the mosque (see Table 2). The cues to react to and reflect on are given below:

1. A prominent building with a minbar, dome and possibly minarets => a mosque
2. Hearing a prayer call from a building => most probably a mosque
3. Cues/'intel' from the 'home base' about the location of the mosque => combining with the external characteristics/cues from the environment => identifying the mosque
4. Cues for continuous evaluation of possible security threats (e.g. presence of women and children in the village, their behavior) = > renewed evaluation of the security situation

The possible courses of action the soldiers could take in this example are summarized below:

1. The soldiers do not manage to find the mosque based on the external characteristics (and possibly because of the missing info from the woman in Example 2) => asking the game master/'home base' for assistance and getting either concrete directions based on 'intel'/previous reconnoitering of the village or hints about typical characteristics of the mosque => finding the mosque from the combination of cues and proceeding to the next scene ('worst case/mistake')
2. The soldiers do not manage to find the mosque based on the external characteristics (and possibly because of the missing info from the woman in Example 2) => back to the previous scene for further questioning of the woman
3. The soldiers identify the mosque correctly from the external characteristics and/or information from the woman in Example 2 => to the next scene ('best case/appropriate reaction')

3.4   Example 4: Outside the Mosque

After locating the mosque, the squad is to wait outside and greet the village chieftain ('malik') and his two men appearing from the mosque. The learning sub-goals for this example are the following: S1: Polite greeting + T2: Interaction within the squad/home base + R1: Correct behavior during a prayer + R3: Recognizing a mosque, correct behavior in/outside the mosque (see Table 2) + L1: Basic polite phrases in local language + L2: Interaction between the interpreter, the locals and the squad. The cues to react to and reflect on are presented below:

1. Being outside the mosque + it is Friday, Ramadan and prayer time (cues from the mission order) => is basically a normal situation, respectful behavior is required
2. Identifying the status (and age) of those exiting the mosque based on external characteristics (a large turban worn by the village chieftain) and mutual avatar position => distinguishing between the village chief and his entourage.

Responses and possible outcomes in this example are as follows:

1. The soldiers enter the mosque during the prayer looking for the village chieftain, interrupt the prayer, do not take off their shoes => the village chief and other villagers get offended/irritated => another round, the game master will possibly need to interfere with hints and help ('worst case/mistake')
2. The soldiers recognize the status of the chieftain incorrectly and make some serious mistakes in the beginning => e.g. greeting the chieftain's men first and him afterwards, the chief is greeted by a female soldier => the chief is less accommodating => another round, the game master will possibly need to intervene with hints and help
3. The soldiers are waiting outside the mosque until the prayer is finished, recognize the status of the chieftain and his companions correctly when they come out and make the appropriate greetings in the correct order => the village chieftain is pleased and attentive, and invites them quickly to his compound => to the next scene, possibly following the village chieftain directly ('best case/appropriate reaction')

3.5   Example 5: In the Village Chieftain's Reception Room

In this example, the squad/squad leader and the village chieftain are having a conversation about the security situation in the village in the chieftain's reception room. During the conversation, the soldiers are offered food and water, and they need to decide whether to accept it or not, considering that it is Ramadan (Fig. 3).

Fig. 3. Conversation with the village chieftain

The learning goals in this scene can be summarized as follows: S1: Polite greeting + S4: House visit + T2: Interaction within the squad/home base + T3: Securing an area + G2: Female soldiers on a house visit + R2: Food during Ramadan (Table 2) + L1: Basic polite phrases in local language + L2: Interaction between the interpreter, the locals, and the squad. Correspondingly, the soldiers need to react to and reflect on the following cues:

1. Being served tea and cookies during Ramadan and in the middle of the day (mission order) => the locals do not eat or drink, eating is rude unless the host repeatedly insists
2. 'Hierarchy' of both the Afghans and Norwegians present, in terms of external features (large turban worn by the village chieftain), the Norwegian soldiers' uniform, gender and mutual position of avatars => determining who sits where in the room
3. Shoes, helmet, and sunglasses are not suitable inside the house => should be removed when entering.

Based on the cues, the responses and possible outcomes can be summarized as follows:

1. The soldiers do not take off shoes / helmet / weapons => perceived as rude by the Afghans, the conversation is slow, the squad does not get the necessary information => another round trying to improve the situation ('worst case/mistake')
2. The female soldier / interpreter sits too close to the village chieftain's place, or the Norwegian squad leader occupies the chieftain's place in the room => perceived as rude by the Afghans, the conversation is slow, the squad does not get the necessary information => another round trying to improve the situation ('worst case/mistake')
3. The soldiers accept the refreshments they are offered right away even though it is Ramadan => perceived as rude by the Afghans, the conversation is slow, the squad does not get the necessary information => another round trying to improve the situation ('worst case/mistake')
4. The interpreter fails to make the soldiers aware of their mistakes, and does nothing actively to rectify the situation => there are misunderstandings and confusion, the conversation is slow, the squad does not get the necessary information => another round trying to improve the situation
5. The squad leader goes straight to the point and starts asking questions about security situation in the village => the atmosphere might get tense, the conversation is slow, there is a need for more specific clarifying questions => another round to get necessary information
6. The interpreter speaks too little/unbalanced with one of the groups, or does not convey nuances correctly => there are misunderstandings and confusion between the two sides, in the worst case somebody gets insulted, and the conversation is slow, there is a need for additional clarifying questions => another round to get the necessary information
7. The squad/squad leader makes no serious mistakes, beginning with some polite 'small talk' and moving on to specific questions about the security situation, when offered refreshments first politely declines but finally takes some tea after the host repeatedly insists => the conversation goes as expected, the squad gets important information => the game master ends the game ('best case/appropriate reaction').

4   Implementation

The scenarios exemplified above provided requirements for the design and implementation of the virtual environment. As with the former, the focus during implementation was on low cost, short development time, and reusability.

The project scenario describes the main location for the educational simulation – the virtual environment of an Afghan village. At the same time, each mini-scenario required some additional specific content. The design and development of the environment went through several stages of implementation, following the description of the scenarios. The idea was to split the design of the environment into parts, which can be combined and reused. The environment consists of general content for creating the generally required context and atmosphere (such as landscape elements, animals, vehicles, parts of buildings, furniture, proper clothing for avatars, and relevant textures) and content designed for specific mini-scenarios (such as a mosque, a school building, a ball, a medical kit, a photo camera, a specific gun, and tableware).

First, the required objects had to be created or collected. Practically, some of the objects and avatar clothing have been acquired from the SL marketplace (a portal for trading virtual content) as well as searching free objects everywhere in SL. Many other VW platforms allow importing 3D models, which can be found in free online libraries. However, most of the specific artifacts required in the mini-scenarios were designed from scratch. They also usually need to be highly authentic.

Second, when the basic objects (or elements) were collected and platform is set up, building and co-locating the typical elements could be started. The basic elements could usually be reused in multiple places of the environment or joined in different combinations. These elements were later copied (sometimes slightly modified) and used in multiple places in the environment. After receiving feedback from the subject experts, some of them were modified or replaced.

5   Evaluation: Understanding Culture through Role-play and Perspective Taking

The study was organized as a one-day experiment conducted at the Norwegian Military Academy on November 25, 2011. It was preceded by a rehearsal session the week before. In addition, the participants received two-hour training in SL (moving avatar, communication, teleporting, and choosing objects from inventory).

Totally 14 cadets from the Norwegian Military Academy participated in the experiment, playing roles of the Norwegian soldiers in the simulation (Fig. 4). In addition, six students and two teachers from the Norwegian Defense Language and Intelligence School participated in the experiment. The former played the roles of the Afghan civilians or interpreters for the Norwegian squad, while the latter played the role of the Afghan civilians and provided input to the scenario development.

Fig. 4. Cadets at the Norwegian Military Academy exploring the virtual Afghan village

The role-play was organized in two rounds. In each of them, a group of the cadets / squad executed the mission, proceeding through the different scenes of the scenario (see section 3). In the first round, the squad leader had a previous field experience from Afghanistan. Totally three debrief sessions conducted by an expert in Afghan culture were integrated in the role-plays, following the milestones in the mission plus one between the two role-play rounds.

The data have been collected through observation of the role-play and screen-capture recording, pre- and post-questionnaires (with 14 respondents), and three in-depth interviews of selected participants following the completion of the role-play. We used commercial screen capture software (BSR screen recording) to record the two role-playing rounds. This program recorded everything taking place during the simulation in SL (relative to the position of the observer's camera), including sound and image. Parts of this recording provided the data on interaction between the soldiers and the 'Afghans'.

The data that are presented here are a limited set of the collected data (for space reasons), but selected on basis of being representative for all the data: we provide a summary of the quantitative data and four snapshots of the qualitative data. The former provides an overview, whereas the latter goes into depth on some critical issues, namely how the Norwegian soldiers acquire better understanding of Afghan culture by perspective taking through role-play. Each type complements the other and contributes to the empirical evidence for our claims.

The complete overview of the evaluation results is outside the scope of this paper. The evaluation results have been also presented in [14].

5.1   Summary of Quantitative Data

The questionnaire results indicate that the soldiers were generally positive to the use of a virtual world as a learning environment for training cultural awareness. It turned out some of the soldiers were not active in the simulation, which was reflected in their responses some of the questions (they did not take part in the action because they were securing the area which prevented them from overhearing the communication taking place in the village). There was a variation in the answers on what categories provide most impact. For example, when it comes to cross-cultural communication, the majority agreed that the knowledge of the local customs and proper treatment of women is important. The responses concerning tactics were spread across different categories, with a majority of answers being "neutral" and "agree". To some of the questions there were no significance changes from before to after test, which implies there were other sources for learning about it, ranging from previous theory studies, previous missions in Afghanistan, and most significantly, the debriefing sessions after the first round of role-play.

5.2   Qualitative Data Analysis

Proper perspective taking of key stakeholders is a prerequisite for the team to achieve its goals. It happens in stages, and more or less consciously. We show examples of this below, organized into four data analyses sections: 1) non-active participation, 2) communication with Afghan woman, 3) gender perspective, and 4) perspective taking as a dual process.

Data Excerpt 1: Non-active Participation. The first data excerpt (Table 3) is a comment by one of the soldiers during a debriefing; the soldier describes the experience of those who were securing the area for the other soldiers. She said she "will not get anything out of the conversation," and that she will "not learn anything." In order to be able to hear what others are saying in SL, they need to be near in proximity, i.e. where the action is. In real military operations, this is compensated by radio communication. As this was not supported here, the gaming and learning experiences diminished for these participants. It points out that learning experience in SL requires active participation, which is a characteristic of sociocultural and constructivist learning environments.

Table 3. Debriefing session: Non-active participation

Solder:	The first thing I think of in terms of pure gaming purposes. It is fair enough that you need to secure the area, but I will not get anything out of the conversation so that I will not learn anything. And then it is just sitting and looking at the screen well okay what happens now? Unless I zoom in and seek information, but then I stop doing what I am supposed to do.
Project leader:	Yes, quite right. Good point, good point. And that is something we found out really fast huh. This does not function as the radio communication in the field. This is a function you lose. You have to be near people to hear and communicate, so it is quite right

Data Excerpt 2: Communication with Afghan Woman. The squad leaders mostly determined how communication with the Afghans developed, but the interpreters were in a unique position of being able to communicate with the Afghans directly. In Table 4, a squad leader asked the interpreter about the impression interpreter got from a woman they just talked to (in Example 2) and how to act towards people who pray in the mosque.

Table 4. Discussion within the Squad after Talking to the Afghan Woman

Squad leader:	Interpreter, I need to talk with you.
Interpreter	Yes
Squad leader:	What impression did you have of the lady? [...] Would she talk? Is this a Pashtun city?
Interpreter	She seems to be like that... She spoke Dari. She was shy and when we came in she asked the children to pull away and that this was dangerous. So I think it is useful to talk a little bit longer with those we meet [...] To show that we are not a threat
Squad leader:	Yes, but it sounds fine. What do you recommend about the mosque now? I suggest that we stand here and wait until they come out.
Interpreter	Agree
Squad leader:	Now we just wait here until they come out

This excerpt shows that soldiers had to take into account the cultural and religious point of view of the Afghans. They also needed to use the knowledge they already had of this area of deployment to solve various situations they encountered. Communication was essential to both the Afghans and the Norwegian soldiers in order to understand each other's perspectives.

An important point illustrated by this excerpt is the Gender Perspective (see also Excerpt 3). Gender perspective is a special form of perspective taking. In the role-play, the soldiers were confronted with gender-related challenges in several situations: in communication with men, women, and children. The Afghan woman in the scenario reacts differently depending on whether a woman or a man tries to talk to her.

By gaining an insight into how the villagers perceive the soldiers, it would be easier for the squad leader to understand the Afghan perspective and adapt communication in accordance with their reactions. In the situation depicted here, the squad leader gets the information that it is useful to spend more time talking with the local people they meet, so that people in the village feel safe around the soldiers and understand that they are there to help and not a threat.

Data Excerpt 3: Gender Perspective. The following excerpt illustrates how the soldiers can learn more about the people they meet in Afghanistan by considering the gender perspective during communication. The soldiers in the squad talk to an injured Afghan woman. She damaged her head when she fell from the roof of her house and needs medical assistance. The female soldier in the squad talks to the woman, using a female interpreter (Table 5).

Table 5. Gender Perspective

Female soldier:	Do you want us to bandage your wound? We can do that for you.
Interpreter (Afghan woman):	Thanks a lot, but it must be a woman who bandages me
Female soldier:	It is OK. I will help her with your head.
Female soldier:	Squad leader, I am going to use my medical kit to bandage her head. She wants a woman to help her.
Squad leader:	Received. When you are finished, tell her there is nothing more we can do, we don't have a doctor with us. Thank her politely and withdraw from the building, so that we can proceed to our primary meeting, over.

Data Excerpt 4: Perspective Taking as Dual Process. This excerpt from the reflection round after the debrief shows how the soldiers based on the knowledge they already have on cross-cultural communication reflect on how to deal with the Afghans in the village. The soldiers emphasize the importance of a dual process, i.e. as they show understanding and respect for Afghan culture, they expect the same in return form the Afghans (Table 6).

Table 6. After debrief Session: Perspective Taking as a Dual Process

Solder 1:	So we talk a lot about us respecting the Afghans, respecting the culture and being humble. But one must not forget that we represent a culture, too [...] And the Afghans are also aware of that. If you are humbled by the people you talk to, it can give them a bad opinion of you. It is important that you dare to stand up for what you represent as well [...] it is about pushing the Afghans a little bit and because [...] they have a slightly different agenda than we have. We do not have the time they have [...] so you have to push a bit [...].
Solder 2:	It's a very big difference between being humble and being weak

During the reflection rounds after the role-play, the soldiers reflected on the perspective taking process and the importance of a dual process when bridging Norwegian and Afghan cultures.

Perspective taking is central ability of communication. It happens in stages, and more or less consciously. First, one must find the means of communicating, next be aware if its usefulness, then how it is exercised in practice, and eventually find a balance that serves both parties, as they have different goals. Proper perspective taking of key stakeholders in complex situation (e.g., international diplomacy, war time negotiation) is a prerequisite for all parties to reach their goals. These excerpts show stages of perspective taking as part of an online learning environment by users who are cadets and interpreters of the Norwegian Armed Forces.

5.3   Summary of Results

The interview data (not shown) provided further indications that the soldier' understanding of cross-cultural issues improved over the course of the experiment. One of the female participants noted: *"I got very much out of it during a very short time"*, *"plenty of aha-experiences"*. She also reported a high level of immersion in her role. Another, male participant believed that: *"This (system) can provide several possibilities in a deployment environment to increase understanding among troops preparing for international operations"*.

The questionnaire data give tentative evidence of an increased understanding of the cultural and religious aspects. At the same time, some of the soldiers disagreed that the experience in SL was suitable for correct evaluation of the threat situation due to the lack of 'crowd feeling,' which could possibly indicate an ambush, and some did not feel part of the experiment as they were outside the range of communication. The cadets have been generally positive to the use of 3D cyberworlds for training cultural awareness. Overall, they reported that the simulation in SL has been a user-friendly, motivating, and fun experience. At the same time, the participants identified a number of limitations, especially, a limited selection of avatar gestures and body language that complicated expression and perception of certain cultural and social aspects.

6   Discussion

We believe that in this project we have demonstrated the potentials of 3D cyberworlds for teaching cultural awareness and inter-cultural communication by role-play, providing recommendations for creating flexible low-cost simulations, both in the military and civilian context, with a focus on resource reuse.

Our experience shows that this approach has several advantages:

- Virtual simulation provides a safe environment for exploration and experimentation, where the participants playing the roles of e.g., 'Norwegians' and 'Afghans' could improve their understanding of each other's cultural representations before critical encounters in real life, something that is especially important in a military context and generally in conflict areas all over the world.
- Virtual simulations provide possibilities for creating representations of cultural artifacts that may serve as boundary objects through virtual settings, objects, avatars, and scenario modules. These boundary objects created opportunities for perspective taking as the 'Norwegians' learned some aspects of 'Afghan' culture through the role play, such as learning how to commutate with woman without offending, proper procedure for initiating dialogue with village inhabitants of unequal stature, identifying a mosque and procedures for waiting.

However, the majority of currently available 3D cyberworlds have a number of limitations for supporting virtual simulation, something that was also identified during the evaluation of the CAMO project:

- The limited graphical possibilities of SL, especially in terms of body language, might lead to misinterpretations and oversimplified models of real cultural interactions.
- 3D cyberworlds such as SL require high bandwidth, making it complicated to use in developing countries. However, if used as a part of training program of a well-equipped educational facility prior to deployment, this problem is less critical.
- We identified two limitations of role-plays. First, by abstracting away significant features of the real situation, learning opportunities will be missed (threat authenticity, contextual information, etc.). Second, for optimal application of perspective taking, both parties should learn the other's position. Our scenarios focused more on Norwegians learning from Afghans (Afghan culture) than on Afghans learning Norwegian culture.

At the same time, we believe that the methodology could be easily extended and adjusted for non-military use in conflict areas as also mentioned in Introduction, for example, for embassy workers, non-governmental organizations workers (e.g., Red Cross), medical workers and journalists. Extending and adjusting from military to civilian use might have the following implications for scenario methodology:

- Exchanging existing tactical learning goals with safety learning goals, with similar triggers and responses. For example, in the learning goal "Identifying possible threats", encountering an empty village would indicate a possible ambush to civilians as well (such as Red Cross employees), the difference would be in a more passive appropriate response (e.g., hiding, not entering the village) as opposed to reconnoitering by the military.
- Gender, socializing, religion, and language learning goals could be used without any (or major) alterations.
- The mini-scenarios can be re-arranged and used as building blocks for different types of general scenarios, more relevant for civilians, for example Red Cross working in a refugee camp or journalists working in conflict areas.
- While a number of elements could be reused across areas and situations (such as learning goals related to Islam), for better credibility and realism it is important to take local nuances into account, such as Shia/Sunni Islam and different local customs (e.g., Dari vs. Pashtun village), with corresponding variations in learning goals. In order to systematize these differences, it is necessary to create a repository with appropriate metadata and annotations possibilities.

In addition, we identified the following implications for technology design and reusable design elements:

- Most of the 3D environment elements are reusable. For example, the same village can be used for simulating both military and purely civilian situations that can happen there.
- Most of the elements used for military simulations, such as the ones found in the village (houses, avatars, furniture, etc.) could be recombined to simulate other situations such as a refugee camp. At the same time, the library of objects should be further extended to encompass a greater variety of possible civilian situations, such as Red Cross or other humanitarian organizations in disaster and war-town areas.
- Similarly as for scenarios, a library of objects should be structured and systemized, including both generic and area-specific objects. These should be linked with the corresponding mini-scenarios and instantiated when the mini-scenario is used.

For flexible and effective development and extension of scenario and design elements base, a wiki-based approach could be most suitable. This will require establishing an open community for exchanging resources, something that was not quite feasible in a purely military context, but there are plenty of open communities for exchanging virtual resources in other domains with e.g., Second Life Community Resources portal.

7   Conclusions and Future Work

In this paper, we have reported the results of the CAMO project using 3D simulations for cultural awareness training in a military context, focusing specifically on scenario and design methodology for producing low-cost easy-to-use and reusable solutions.

We reported the results of an evaluation of a one-day trial of the resulting environment and the methodology. We consider the study presented in this paper a pilot one that will be followed up with a full-scale study to verify our tentative assumptions.

The methodology is an important outcome of the project and could be used further in connection with similar projects at the Norwegian Armed Forces. The authors are aware that the scripts developed using this methodology might provide an oversimplified representation of the reality. However, in accordance with the Naturalistic Decision Making approach [18,21], these scripts provide 'patterns' necessary for making decisions under critical conditions and a basis/skeleton for improvisation. This methodology could be developed further and reused for deployment in other countries than Afghanistan, but experiencing conflicts where peacekeeping troops are involved. Due to its modular structure, the methodology can be extended, reused, and adjusted in a flexible manner at the mini-scenario level to be applicable for civilian use as well, especially in neighboring countries with a complex security situation. This will constitute an important direction for the future work.

In addition, in order to address the identified limitations, the Afghan village is currently being enhanced with NPCs (Non-Playing Characters), representing Afghan villagers. The goal of this development is to provide a more realistic simulation of village life as well as a more nuanced representation of various threat situations. The NPCs exhibit different appearances (women in burka, men in traditional clothing) and behaviors (walking, sitting, talking), with planned interactive features, such as simple conversations and certain reactions to e.g., soldiers approaching. Apart from increased realism, the presence of NPCs will contribute to activating and engaging the players.

Acknowledgments. The authors would like to express their gratitude to all participants from the Norwegian Armed Forces, to Øystein Ramseng from Ytre Venstre who helped to organize the design the study, and to Ingvill Thomassen from Department of Education, University of Oslo, who helped to collect and organize the empirical data.

References

1. Bruner, J.S.: The Culture of Education. Harvard University Press, Cambridge (1996)
2. Papert, S., Harel, I. (eds.): Constructionism: research reports and essays 1985 - 1990 by the Epistemology and Learning Research Group. Ablex Publishing Corporation, Norwood (1991)
3. Star, S.L.: The Structure of Ill-Structured Solutions: Boundary Objects and Heterogeneous Distributed Problem Solving. In: Distributed Artificial Intelligence, vol. II. Morgan Kaufmann Publishers Inc., San Mateo (1989)
4. Fischer, G.: External and shareable artifacts as opportunities for social creativity in communities of interest. In: Gero, J.S., Maher, M.L. (eds.) 5th International Conference on Computational and Cognitive Models of Creative Design, Heron Island, Australia, December 9-13, pp. 67–89. University of Sydney (2001)
5. Gillespie, A.: Games and the Development of Perspective Taking. Human Development 49(2), 87–92 (2006)

6. Cannon-Bowers, J.A., Bowers, C.A.: Synthetic learning environments: On developing a science of simulation, games and virtual worlds for training. In: Kozlowski, S.W.J., Salas, E. (eds.) Learning, Training, and Development in Organizations, pp. 229–261. Taylor & Francis, New York (2010)

7. Sant, T.: Performance in Second Life: some possibilities for learning and teaching. In: Molka-Danielsen, J., Deutschmann, M. (eds.) Learning and Teaching in the Virtual World of Second Life, pp. 145–166. Tapir Academic Press, Trondheim (2009)

8. Connolly, T.M., Boyle, E.A., MacArthur, E., Hainey, T., Boyle, J.M.: A systematic literature review of empirical evidence on computer games and serious games. Computers & Education 59(2), 661–686 (2012)

9. Warburton, S.: Second Life in higher education: Assessing the potential for and the barriers to deploying virtual worlds in learning and teaching. British Journal of Educational Technology 40(3), 414–426 (2009)

10. Johnson, W.L.: A Simulation-Based Approach to training Operational Cultural Competence. In: Anderssen, R.S., Braddock, R.D., Newham, L.T.H. (eds.) International Congress on Modelling and Simulation, MODSIM (2009)

11. Zielke, M.A.: The First Person Cultural Trainer Whitepaper (2011), http://www.utdallas.edu/~maz031000/res/FPCT_White_Paper.pdf

12. Surface, E.A., Dierdorff, E.C., Watson, A.M.: Special Operations Language Training Software Measurement of Effectiveness Study: Tactical Iraqi Study Final Report. Special Operations Forces Language Office, Tampa, FL, USA (2007)

13. Singer, M.J., Knerr, B.W.: Evaluation of a Game-Based Simulation During Distributed Exercises. U.S. Army Research Institute for the Behavioral and Social Sciences, Research Report 1931 (2010)

14. Prasolova-Førland, E., Fominykh, M., Darisiro, R., Mørch, A.I.: Training Cultural Awareness in Military Operations in a Virtual Afghan Village: A Methodology for Scenario Development. In: 46th Hawaii International Conference on System Sciences (HICSS), Wailea, HI, USA, January 7-10, pp. 903–912. IEEE (2013)

15. Salmoni, B.A., Holmes-Eber, P.: Operational Culture for the Warfighter: Principles and Applications. Marine Corps University Press, Quantico (2008)

16. McDonald, D.P., McGuire, G., Johnston, J., Selmeski, B., Abbe, A.: Developing and managing cross-cultural competence within the Department of Defense: Recommendations for learning and assessment. Department of Equal Opportunity Management Institute (2008)

17. Caird-Daley, A., Dawson, B., Ciereszko, R., Osborne, B., Parker, I.: Training decision making using serious games: Requirements analysis for decision making training. Human Factors Integration Defence Technology Centre, UK, HFIDTC/2/WP4.6.2/1 (2009)

18. Hartog, C.: Scenario design for serious gaming: guiding principles for the design of scenarios and curricula in military Job Oriented Training. TNO Defense, Security & Safety (2009)

19. Holo, T., Andreassen, M.D.: Culture astray: A review of Norwegian military's focus on cultural understanding. Norsk Utenrikspolitisk Institutt (NUPI), Oslo, Norway (2010)

20. Phillips, J.: Decision-centered MOUT training for small unit leaders. U.S. Army Research Institute for the Behavioral and Social Sciences, Fort Benning, GA, USA (2001)

21. Klein, G.: Sources of Power, How People Make Decisions. The MIT Press, Cambridge (1999)

Collision-Free Navigation with Extended Terrain Maps

Andrei Sherstyuk[1] and Kiyoshi Kiyokawa[2]

[1] University of Hawaii, USA
andreis@hawaii.edu
[2] University of Osaka, Japan
kiyo@ime.cmc.osaka-u.ac.jp

Abstract. In virtual environments, navigation is one of the most fundamental tasks that requires timely collision detection and collision avoidance mechanisms [1]. It was shown that when navigation is constrained to moving on a terrain surface, the problem of collision detection can be reduced from 3D to 2D case, by rasterizing all 3D objects that constitute travel obstacles and encoding them into a terrain elevation image map, using a dedicated color [2]. The original algorithm was developed for static Virtual Reality (VR) scenes explored by a single user, immersed into the scene with a head mounted display and navigating by continuous steering.

The new improved system, presented in this article, is capable of processing collisions for various types of virtual travelers, ranging from immersed VR users to autonomous virtual agents, in dynamically changing environments with moving obstacles. Implementation details of the new system are presented, with a number of case studies and a discussion of future work.

Keywords: virtual travel, collision avoidance, mobile agents.

1 Introduction

Terrain maps have been used for landscape generation in virtual worlds for nearly three decades now [3]. A survey of recent advances on terrain synthesis may be found in [4]. Presently, generating terrain data from height-field images has become a standard practice in building virtual worlds: this method is fast, convenient and provides 3D artists plenty of tools to make the virtual environment visually appealing and realistically looking.

One of the most attractive features of terrain image maps is that they allow instantaneous mapping between all points on the scene and the physical elevation of any entity that is constrained to the surface of the terrain. One of the most common uses for that mapping is real-time positioning of moving objects. For every virtual traveler moving on a 3D terrain, its elevation may be obtained immediately, at the fixed cost of accessing the corresponding pixel value from the terrain image map.

M.L. Gavrilova et al. (Eds.): Trans. on Comput. Sci. XXIII, LNCS 8490, pp. 139–156, 2014.
© Springer-Verlag Berlin Heidelberg 2014

In order to provide high precision in elevation computations, terrain image files typically store data with 16 bits per color channel. To maintain compatibility with popular image editors, these images store three channels per pixel: red, green and blue, although only one channel is needed for real-time updates of the traveler's elevation. Thus, 66% of the memory reserved for terrain image map asset remains unused at game-time. Given the fact that standard terrain image maps for many online worlds are 2K x 2K size (for example, Blue Mars Online [5] and SimCity [6]), the amount of allocated but unused memory is about 16 MB per scene. There is growing demand from the developers community to make these maps even larger. In addition, if the 3D scene contains objects on the terrain surface that constitute travel obstacles, the corresponding pixels on the map become inaccessible by virtual travelers, which increases the amount of wasted memory even more.

To make a better use of terrain maps for navigation purposes, it was suggested to encode the geometry footprint of all static obstacles to the map off-line and then use the map for collision detection, in real-time [2]. This approach was developed for and proved to work well in immersive Virtual Reality (VR) applications [7], [8], with a static environment and a single traveler, exploring the scene in first-person view mode.

This article presents a number of extensions of the original algorithm. Specifically, the new system allows processing of multiple travelers of various kinds, moving in dynamic scenes with moving obstacles.

2 Related Work

Reliable collision avoidance requires, in general, detecting and processing collisions between every traveling object and all other objects on the scene. In large dynamic environments populated by freely-moving multiple travelers, the problem may become demanding computationally, calling for various optimization techniques. For a review of general algorithms for collision detection, please see [9] and [10].

Processing collisions during navigation received much attention both from academic and industry communities, due to growing popularity of massively multiplayer online games and increased interest in crowd simulation. The algorithm developed by Sakr and Sudama [11] exemplifies research efforts in gaming industry, aiming to provide collision-free travel environment for hundreds and thousands avatars flying freely in 3D space. Their method is based on a simple hierarchy of bounding spheres and fast analytical solution for detecting path/object intersection for avatars moving along linear or curvilinear paths. Methods developed by crowd simulation community [12], [13], [14] typically employ more rigorous models, that account for inter-agents interaction forces. Such algorithms yield more realistic behavior of large crowds and may also run in real-time. For a detailed survey of existing navigation control algorithms, the readers are referred to Curtis et al [15].

In many cases, the focus of research is placed on creating meaningful collision responses, aiming to optimize the global traffic in crowded scenes and make the overall simulation visually believable. For that purpose, movement is often confined onto a single 2D plane and the moving objects are modeled as disks, in order to minimize efforts on collision detection [14], [15].

The goal of the proposed work is to optimize and generalize the collision detection process itself, when the travelers are moving on an arbitrary 3D surface, colliding with 3D obstacles of arbitrary shapes. It is considered a priority to make the collision detection process as general as possible, in order to make it applicable to a wide variety of traveling objects. The traveling object may be an autonomous agent, driven by an in-built set of rules and animations, or it may be a user-controlled avatar, which is free to change its path at will, at any time. A bouncing ball is yet another example of a traveling object which needs to detect and resolve collisions with the environment. In all cases, pending collisions will be detected using our unified collision detection algorithm.

Collision responses, on the contrary, must be computed individually for each kind of traveler. For example, a user-controlled avatar may be naturally brought to a full stop to avoid a collision, assuming that the user will take active control over further movements. An autonomous traveling object, on the contrary, should be deflected from the obstacle automatically, resuming its motion in a new direction.

3   Contribution

In the previous work [2] [16], it was suggested to use a dedicated color value (for example, red) to mark all possible static obstacles in the terrain map, making these pixels distinct from all other monochrome pixels in the map. The proximity to a colliding obstacle is determined in real-time by counting the number of red pixels in the vicinity of the traveler. In this article, the original algorithm is significantly extended, as summarized below.

1. The proposed system is able to navigate autonomous traveling agents, such as non-playable characters, which became popular in online virtual worlds. These characters typically have limited pre-programmed behavior and can not make complex travel decisions on their own, unlike user-driven avatars. In the new system, their travel paths can be adjusted automatically in the presence of obstacles.
2. The collision detection algorithm, developed for static obstacles [2], is extended to handle moving objects as well. For that purpose, the terrain map is constantly updated, reflecting current positions of all colliding objects. As the result, travelers become aware of each others presence and are able to avoid mutual collisions.
3. Finally, the new system provides means for detecting collisions between travelers that are moving freely in 3D over the terrain surface. This is the major improvement over the original system, which was able to handle only ground travelers.

The remainder of the article is organized as follows. In Section 4, the process of creating modified terrain maps is explained. Sections 5 and 6 provide detailed description of the new algorithms for collision detection and avoidance. Section 7 presents three case studies, followed by a discussion of extensions and limitations, in Section 8.

4   Generating Extended Terrain Maps

The 3D environment described below was designed for a clinical VR system installed at Tripler Army Medical Center in Honolulu, Hawaii, for research on chronic pain control and biofeedback [7]. Later, this system was updated and then used at JABSOM School of Medicine, University of Hawaii, for teaching medical students and first responders triage techniques and life saving procedures [8]. Users were immersed into the environment with a stereo head mounted display, navigating on uneven terrain with multiple obstacles, using hand-steering travel technique.

Fig. 1. An aerial view of the 3D environment, showing a small sandy island with various rock formations, stylized Stone Age dwellings, and palm trees. The scene was sound-scaped with the ocean, nature and other prerecorded sounds, localized in 3D. This environment was used for teaching triage skills in VR.

The 3D scene is shown in Figure 1. It depicts a small sandy island with two oval-shaped stone houses and massive stone gates. In all training scenarios, users were required to travel actively, searching for virtual patients. These virtual patients were were hidden inside the buildings and other hard to find areas. The house walls and gate pillars were considered as obstacles during travel. In addition, immersed users were not allowed to travel too deep into the water. Small or thin objects, such as trunks of palm trees, beach umbrellas and small rock debris were ignored during travel.

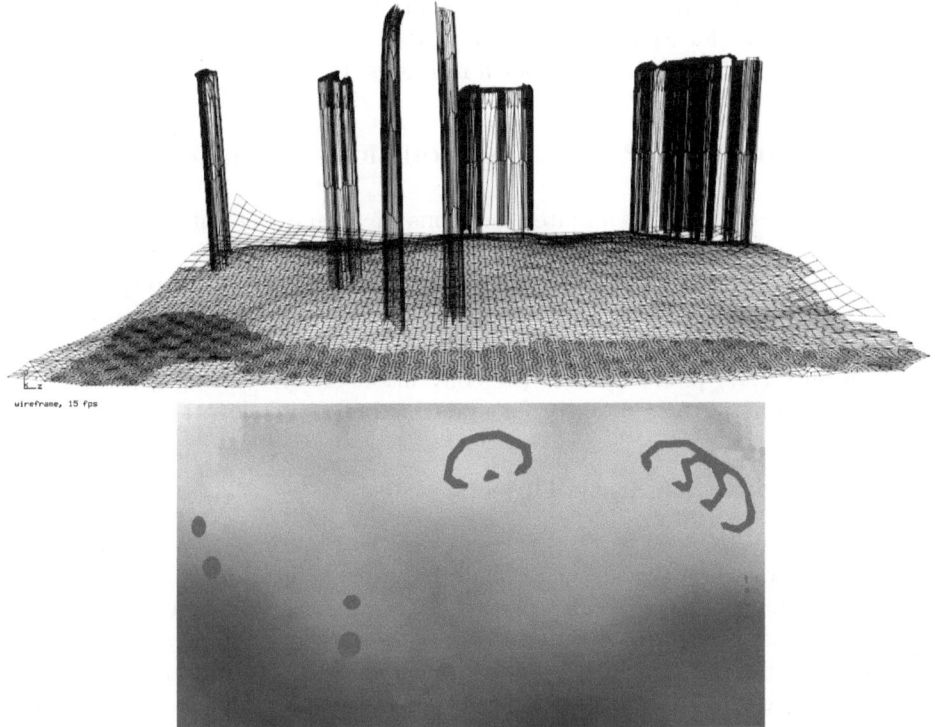

Fig. 2. Creating navigation terrain map from 3D scene data. Top: all colliding objects are placed into terrain mesh. Bottom: resulting terrain map with embedded colliding objects, painted in red.

For this environment, an extended terrain image map with embedded static obstacles was created using the following steps:

1. Using Maya 3D authoring tool, all 3D models of obstacle objects were placed on the beach surface, including houses and the stone gates. The palm trees and both beach umbrellas were excluded as insignificant;
2. Non-colliding parts of obstacle objects, such as house roofs and gate tops, were removed;
3. All vertices of remaining colliding parts were moved up in Y-direction, to mark them as seeds of the future no-travel zones (see Figure 2, top). The 3D mesh of polygons was then converted into a terrain raster image, with all colliding vertices saved as red pixels with (1 0 0) RGB values. The seed red pixels were propagated outwards, in order to form continuous no-travel zones.
4. To reduce the noise around borders, the image map was hand-touched in Photoshop.

The resulting terrain map image is shown in Figure 2, bottom. The red zones match exactly the locations and geometry of all static obstacles: the gate pillars and the walls of the two houses, shown in Figure 1.

5   Detecting and Processing Collisions with Terrain Maps

During travel, the system updates locations of all moving entities, by adding incremental displacements on the (X, Z) plane, accordingly to their current velocities. The vertical displacements are computed using bilinear interpolation of height values obtained from $(i, j), (i + 1, j), (j + 1, j + 1), (i, j + 1)$ pixels, where (i, j) are pixel coordinates on the terrain map, corresponding to the traveler's location on (X, Z) plane. This is the conventional way of using terrain maps, treating them as a static resource for updating travelers' elevation.

5.1   Collisions with Static Objects

As explained in previous section, the extended terrain map now contains areas that are prohibited for travel, such as building walls and tall rocks (see Figure 2). These pixels have pure red RGB values (1 0 0), which makes them easy to detect at run-time for collision detecting purpose.

The basic step of the collision detection process involves computing the value of "danger level" (D). This value reflects the density of red pixels in the vicinity of the traveler, sampled over a disk area, as shown in Algorithm 1. The *radius* parameter defines the size of the search area, in pixels. For $radius = 2$, 21 pixels are tested for being red, so the granularity of $D(radius = 2)$ is $1/21$, as shown in the illustration to Algorithm 1. The danger level ranges from $D = 0$ (no red pixels found, travel is unrestricted), to $D = 1$ (maximum danger, travel is impossible). It is useful to set a collision detection threshold T to be less than 1 (a good value is $T = 0.5$). While D is still below threshold, collision avoidance procedures should be taken. When D reaches the threshold, collision is detected and collision response procedures are applied. The danger level is updated each time when the traveler moves into a new pixel on the map.

The described collision detection system is based on the fact that the geometry layouts of all travel obstacles are embedded into the terrain map. For static obstacles, this can be easily done off-line, when the scene resources are created (see Section 4). The collision detection system that used "pure red" pixels with RGB values (1 0 0) for encoding static obstacles, was successfully tested in immersive VR settings [2], with a single traveler. Next, we explain how this basic algorithm can be extended to handle collisions between multiple *moving* obstacles, including travelers' avatars.

Algorithm 1. Basic collision detection for static obstacles, based on danger level D. In this example, the traveler is moving from point A to B to C and is approaching one of the gate pillars shown in Figures 1 and 2. D values are: $D_A = 0$ (the traveler moves freely), $D_B = 5/21$ (below threshold T=0.5: collision pending), $D_C = 14/21$ (above threshold T=0.5: collision detected).

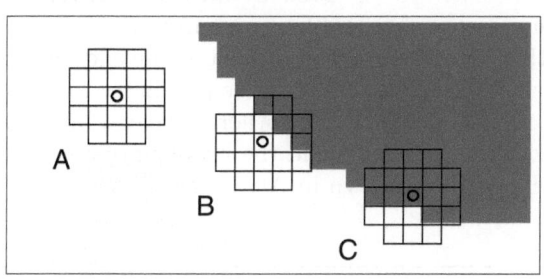

```
01: procedure process_collisions(Object self, Image map)
02:     Position P ← get_new_position(self)
03:     Pixel pixel ← position_to_pixel(P, map)
04:     float D ← danger_level(pixel, map, radius = 2)
05:     if D = 0 then
06:         // point A: no pending collisions
07:     else if D ≤ THRESHOLD then
08:         // point B: collision pending
09:         apply_collision_avoidance()
10:     else
11:         // point C: collision detected
12:         apply_collision_response()
13:     end if
14: end procedure
```

```
01: procedure float danger_level(Image map, Pixel point, int radius)
02:     N_red ← 0
03:     N_total ← 0
04:     for all pixels p : ||p − point|| ≤ radius do
05:         N_total ← N_total + 1
06:         Color RGB ← get_pixel_value(map, p)
07:         if R = 1 and G = 0 and B = 0 then
08:             N_red ← N_red + 1
09:         end if
10:     end for
11:     danger_level ← N_red/N_total
12:     return danger_level
13: end procedure
```

5.2   Collisions with Moving Objects

In order to detect and process collisions in dynamic scenes, the terrain map is continuously updated by adding and removing RGB values (1 0 0) to all pixels that are occupied by each moving object (traveler, for short, although the object of interest may be any moving entity). Each time a traveler moves on the scene, its 2D pixel footprint on the map is updated, using the current location and size of its bounding box, projected onto (XY)-plane. Thus, each traveler leaves a trace of red pixels that are observed by all other travelers, during collision detection. Travelers remove their old footprint from the map in the beginning of their *update()* method and add a new footprint at the end. Footprints of multiple travelers may overlap, when they are in close proximity to each other. However, each traveler can only see footprints of other travelers, but never its own. This way, all moving objects naturally avoid the problem of detecting false collisions with themselves. The code is shown in Algorithm 2.

Algorithm 2. Detecting and processing collisions between moving objects. The algorithm is implemented as part of the update() method of moving objects, executed at each time-step of the main simulation loop. The functions for collision avoidance (line 12) and collision response (lines 15-16) are instantiated for a test case of autonomous agents that will be discussed in the next section.

```
01: procedure update_traveler(Object self, Image map)
02:     remove_pixel_footprint(map, self.P_old, self.Box_old)
03:     Position P ← get_new_position(self)
04:     BoundingBox Box ← get_bounding_box(self)
05:     Pixel pixel ← position_to_pixel(P, map)
06:     float D ← danger_level(pixel, map, radius = 2)
07:     if D = 0 then
08:         // no pending collisions: update 'safe' position
09:         self.P_safe ← P
10:     else if D ≤ THRESHOLD then
11:         // collision avoidance: change speed
12:         update_speed(self, D)
13:     else
14:         // collision response: move to saved position and bounce
15:         set_position(self.P_safe)
16:         reverse_direction(self)
17:     end if
18:     self.P_old ← P
19:     self.Box_old ← Box
20:     // update its footprint on the map
21:     add_pixel_footprint(map, P, Box)
22: end procedure
```

Adding and removing pixel footprints to the map is a safe operation that does not destroy the original elevation data at affected pixels. When a traveler marks its presence at certain location, the red value (1 0 0) is added to all pixels that fall inside the bounding box of the traveler. When the travelers moves out, the same values are subtracted from these pixels and they can be safely used for elevation calculation again. Note, that when a terrain map is updated dynamically, the criterion of a pixel to be "red" changes from $R = 1, G = 0, B = 0$ (see Algorithm 1, procedure *danger_level()*, line 07), to simply $R \geq 1$. Visually, the temporarily occupied pixels have pink hue. Their color is restored to the original monochrome elevation values, when the current occupant moves away from that location.

5.3   Collisions with Objects, Moving Freely in 3D

One of the most interesting features of the described system is that it may be further enhanced to process collisions for travelers that are *not* restricted to remain on the terrain during travel. Recall, that each traveler updates its pixel footprint on the scene, marking zones prohibited for travel for all other travelers. As described, these pixels are treated as no-travel boxes on (X, Z) plane, that have infinite height in Y dimension. Now we encode the Y position of the traveler into the map, using the remaining available blue color channel (the green channel still holds the original elevation data for this pixel). Effectively, each pixel in the footprint turns into a voxel, storing the updated position of the traveler in full (XYZ) space. The X and Z coordinate of the traveler are stored implicitly as the (i, j) indices of the corresponding pixel. The Y-value temporarily resides in the blue channel of that pixel.

As for ground travel, the collision detection between freely flying entities happens at the fixed cost of sampling the "voxelized" terrain image map and reading color channels, that indicate presence and elevation of moving obstacles. Needless to say that vertical bounds of all static objects in the environment, such as building tops, also can be encoded into voxelized 2D map, and used in real time for processing collisions in 3D space.

6   Collision Avoidance and Response Mechanisms

The presented algorithm of detecting pending collisions is very general and can be applied to various situations where travel is involved. On the contrary, collision avoidance and collision response mechanisms may require fine tuning for each particular type of virtual traveler and each type of travel technique. In this section, an adaptive speed control will be presented, which is suitable for immersed first-person human travelers and autonomous moving agents.

The speed control mechanism prevents travelers from moving deeper into red zones, by monitoring the values of danger level D and changing their speed accordingly. When values of D are increasing, the speed is reduced. Eventually, when D reaches the threshold level, the traveler is stopped and relocated to the last safe location, where D has zero value. In such locations, the speed values are unconstrained. If the danger level remains unchanged during travel, the speed neither changes. If the danger level decreases, the speed is restored to its original value. In other words, the speed control mechanism makes it easier for travelers to move outside of dangerous areas where obstacles are present, rather than going deeper inside. The speed control code is shown in Algorithm 3, where S_0 is the desired speed and S is the speed value after adjustments. This code is referenced in Algorithm 2, line 12.

Algorithm 3. Speed control mechanism checks the current value of danger level D and, if it increases, reduces the speed (line 11). In critical cases, when the danger level reaches threshold value, the traveler comes to a full stop (line 08).

```
01: procedure update_speed(Object self, float D)
02:     float factor
03:     if  D = 0 then
04:         // zero danger: no obstacles in sight, full speed
05:         factor ← 1
06:     else if  D ≥ THRESHOLD then
07:         // collision detected: full stop
08:         factor ← 0
09:     else if  D > self.D_previous then
10:         // danger level increases: getting closer to obstacle, slow down
11:         factor ← (1 − D)²
12:     else
13:         // danger level decreases: moving outside red zone, full speed
14:         factor ← 1
15:     end if
16:     // adjust speed and save current danger level
17:     self.S ← self.S_0 ∗ factor
18:     self.D_previous ← D
19: end procedure
```

Originally, the speed control mechanism was developed for medical VR systems [7] and [8]. It was evaluated experimentally [2] and was proven effective for preventing immersed human travelers from colliding with obstacles in the test scene shown in Figure 1.

The same mechanism was used to update speed of autonomous traveling agents, controlled by a simple set of pre-loaded animations and pre-programmed rules. The agents' 3D objects were modeled and rigged in Maya 3D authoring tool, using anatomically correct hierarchy of joints and stylized humanoid appearance. For their animation, real human motion datasets were used, produced with motion capture technique (MOCAP). The agents and their animations are shown in Figure 3. The live snapshot from the test scene is shown in Figure 4.

Unlike real human travelers who could freely steer away from obstacles, the autonomous agents needed additional pre-programmed behavior to help them avoid pending collisions. Sliding along the edge of an obstacle was implemented,

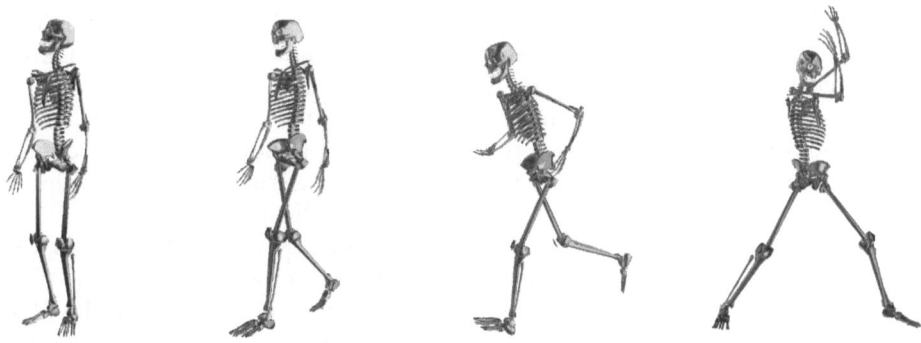

Fig. 3. Autonomous agents, animated with MOCAP data: idle, walking, jogging, fighting. Each animation yields pixel footprints of different shapes and sizes. The fighting animation sequence (right) was used for testing only, as it produced footprints with distinct elongated shapes.

by forcefully placing the agent to a new location, where the density of red pixels was minimal. This approach provided collision-free continuous travel, but it did not produce visually acceptable results for MOCAP-animated agents, due to severe foot sliding problem. Instead, a simpler solution was used: the agents were allowed to approach colliding objects as close as possible. When a collision was finally detected, the agents turned around and simply walked away from the obstacle. While the agents were still approaching an obstacle, their speed was reduced by decreasing the time increment in their simulation update loops. As the result, the agents were moving in slow-motion, which looked like a reasonable response to an upcoming collision and allowed to avoid problems related to foot sliding.

7   Implementation

The described system was implemented in the open source VR engine *Flatland*, developed at the Albuquerque High Performance Computing Center [17]. The system was evaluated on a Sony Vaio laptop running Ubuntu Linux, with 2.53 GHz Intel CPU and nVidia GeForce GT 230M graphics card.

Three scenarios were created for processing collisions with static, moving-on-terrain, and freely flying objects. These case studies are described next. The corresponding methodology and collision processing algorithms are discussed in detail in Sections 5.1, 5.2, and 5.3, respectively.

7.1   Collisions with Static Objects

For this case study, three autonomous agents were programmed to move continuously on the island test scene, rotating their walking, jogging and idle animations. Before each new animation was applied, the agents turned in-place for some angle, in order to randomize their travel paths and cover as much territory as possible. A live snapshot from the test scene is shown in Figure 4. Figure 5 shows agents' travel paths after 3 minutes of simulation time.

The collision response was implemented as a simple turn for 170 degrees at the collision point. This behavior resulted in multiple bounces within confined spaces and map corners. This was not an optimal but still a feasible solution to ensure deadlock-free travel, which was essential for this test.

To evaluate robustness of the collision processing mechanism, the agents were programmed to run their animations using very large time increments (in "fast-forward" mode), generating high-speed collision events. The agent with the white path was moving at double speed, gray path – triple speed, black path – quadruple speed. The simulation was allowed to run until nearly all locations on the map were visited by at least one agent. By that time, all gray-scale pixels on the map were covered by agents' trails. The red pixels, indicating locations of static obstacles, remained intact everywhere on the map. The agents successfully detected all collisions, including the high-speed events marked with dotted paths.

Fig. 4. Autonomous agents walking and running on the island scene, bouncing off the static obstacles, such as gate pillars. In the terrain map, these pillars appear as red ovals (see Figure 5).

7.2   Collisions with Moving Objects

In this series of tests, two agents were placed in front of each other, and set into a walking motion. Each agent detected an upcoming collision, stopped, turned and walked away in the opposite direction. The test was repeated multiple times, varying the agents' walking speed.

As explained in Section 5, the terrain map is updated by each agent in turn, by removing old and adding new red pixels. Thus, it was expected that the collision detection process, based on the current state of the map, should also depend on the order in which the agents are processed by the system. In other words, the first agent in the database could have an advantage over other agents and be the first to detect the pending collision.

It turned out that this asymmetry does not manifest itself easily, at least under the described conditions. The order of collision detection did not depend on the order of the agents in the database. Instead, the agent's moving speed proved to be the most important factor in breaking the symmetry. Regardless of the order of appearance, the agent with a higher speed consistently was one time-step ahead in detecting the collision, even with the adaptive speed control mechanism in effect, as described in Section 6.

The reason for this effect is that the fastest agent has higher chances to enter the other agent's footprint first, because its own updated footprint is not yet on the map at this moment. It is important to account for this feature when implementing collision responses. For example, if the agent who first detects the collision simply vanishes from the place of the event, all other agents will not have a chance to detect the collision that just happened, because the pixel footprint of the "impactor" will never appear in the vicinity of the event.

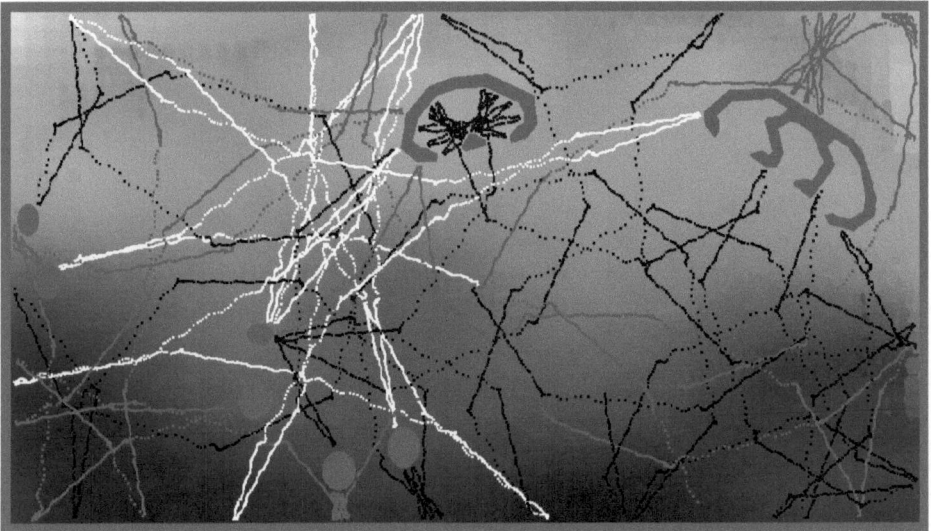

Fig. 5. Travel paths of three agents, moving on the island scene, captured at 3 minutes simulation time. Each agents marked its current location at every cycle of the simulation. Solid trails show paths where agents were walking slowly. Dotted paths correspond to fast moving agents. The paths are not perfectly straight, because all motions were recorded from real human actors.

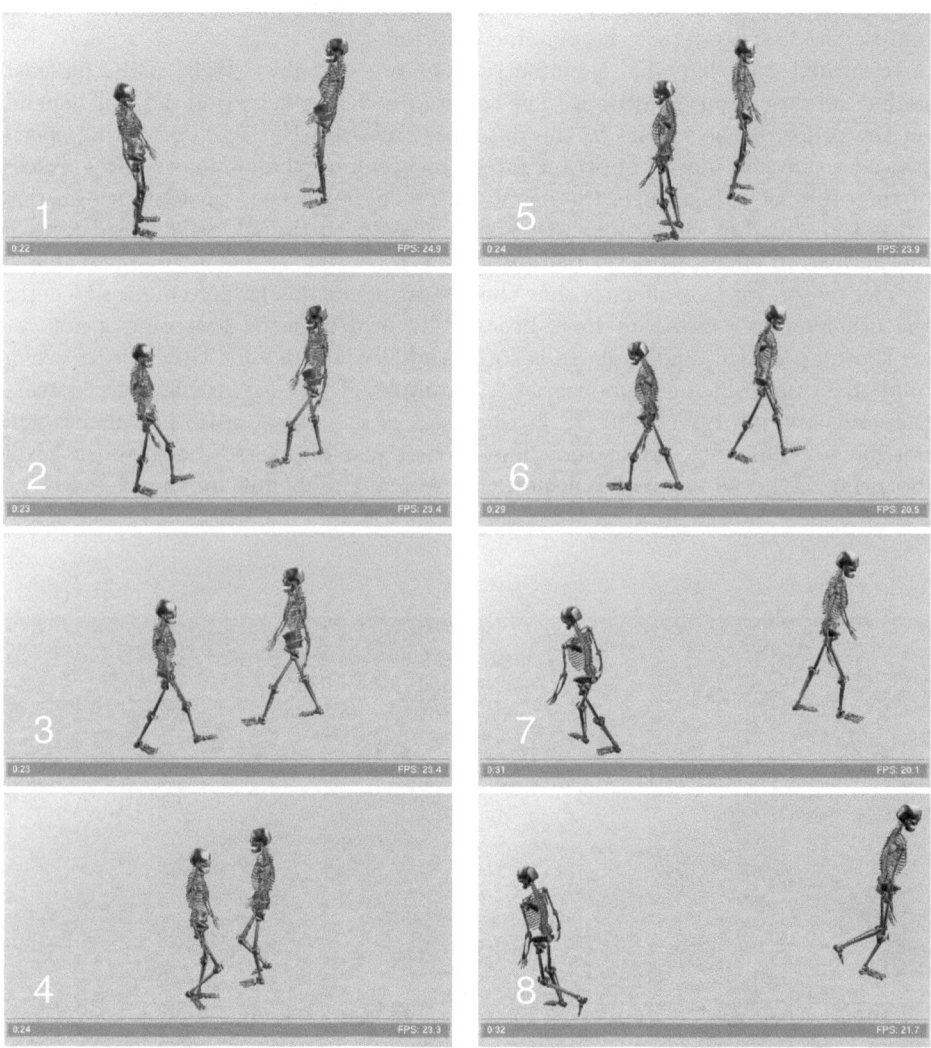

Fig. 6. Processing mutual collisions between moving objects. Two agents are standing in a "duel" position (1), walking towards each other (2-3). Both successfully detected the collision (4), turned around (5), and walked away (6-8).

Recall that for this particular test, the collision response was programmed as follows: freeze, turn, and walk away. The first step guarantees that the impactor's updated location will be reflected on the map and detected by other agents involved in this collision. Figure 6 presents one of the test cases, with both agents moving at the same speed. Their encounter was screen-captured at approximately 25 per second, selected frames are shown. Here, the responses from both agents are completely symmetrical.

The asymmetric nature of detecting collisions between moving agents has its own merits. For example, it allows to estimate the chances for every agent to be the first to detect the pending collision, by comparing their speeds. However, if fair treatment of agents is a priority, the symmetry may be restored by moving the footprint update functions (Algorithm 2, lines 02 and 20) outside the body of procedure *update_traveler*(), into a pre-processing loop over all agents. This will guarantee that all collisions will be detected by all involved agents simultaneously. However, additional efforts will be required for each agent to avoid colliding with their own red-pixel footprints. It seems that occasional breaks in symmetry, which are easy to mitigate as described above, is a small price for keeping the whole process as simple as presented in Algorithms 1, 2, and 3.

7.3   Collisions with Flying Objects

To test collisions between freely moving objects in 3D, two hand-animated seagulls were used, shown in Figure 7. Both seagulls ran the same sequence of motions: standing (1), walking (2-3), take off (4) and flying (5-10). While the birds were in contact with the ground (1-3), their elevation was set to the value from the terrain map. Once the birds were airborne, they were no longer subject to that restriction and were able to fly freely.

For this test, two birds were placed on the beach one after another, a few meters apart. Both birds were set into motion simultaneously, taking off from the beach and flying towards the ocean. The bird that was initially behind, was moving 1.5 times faster than the other. Very soon, the faster bird approached and collided the slower bird, as captured in Figure 7, second row. Both birds detected the collision event simultaneously, as indicated by the red high-light.

8   Discussion and Further Work

There are two known issues, that may be significantly improved.

First, as any sample-based technique, the proposed system is subject to potential under-sampling artifacts, which may become a problem when a traveler is moving at very high speed. In such cases, the traveler may "jump over" small red pixel areas in two consecutive time steps, without noticing. This is a well understood problem, that can be solved by making the size of the sample are speed-dependent. For example, the radius of the sample area (see Algorithm 2, line 06) can be dynamically set to the distance between the traveler's previous location $self.P_{old}$ and its current location $self.P$.

Fig. 7. Processing collisions between freely moving objects in 3D. Top row: after take-off, the seagull is flying above terrain at various heights, that need to be stored in one of the color channels of the pixel footprint. Second row: two seagulls, flying over the terrain at different speeds. The left seagull is approaching the one that is still ahead (6-7), both birds collide in the air, as indicated by red high-light (8-9); the faster bird is now ahead, no collisions detected at this time (10). Bottom: the travel paths, projected on terrain map.

Secondly, in the current implementation, encoding all colliding objects into a terrain image map does not preserve their identities. As the result, travelers have no information what kind of object they are colliding with. It is reasonable to suggest that collision response procedures should be object-specific, in order to diversify the travelers' behavior. However, this issue has a simple solution. In the basic method of generating collision maps, illustrated in Figure 2, all colliding objects are encoded with a single red color, using (1 0 0) RGB values. The green and blue channels remain available for using some predefined palette of colors, that can uniquely identify all colliding objects. For example, the small house in Figure 1 can appear on the collision map painted with yellow pixels (1 1 0), the larger house – magenta pixels (1 0 1), the pillars of the massive waterfront gate – brown pixels (1 0.25 0.25) and so forth. During collision detection, the identity of the object can be determined from the pixel color at that location.

9   Conclusions

The novel system was presented for providing collision-free travel for multiple moving entities in real-time, including first-person travelers in VR, human-controlled 3D avatars and autonomous traveling agents. The proposed collision detection algorithm is able to detect pending collisions at the fixed cost of reading pixel values from extended terrain map, which makes it independent of scene complexity, in case of static obstacles. For dynamic scenes, the cost of collision detection grows linearly with the number of potentially colliding objects.

The proposed approach makes an effective use of redundant parts of the memory allocated for storing the terrain elevation map. Thus, it does not require any additional storage. Several variations on collision avoidance and collision response were discussed and tested using the proposed framework. These algorithms are straightforward and can be easily incorporated into processing of various travel metaphors that provide continuous relocation on the virtual scene.

The underlying idea of employing unused values of the terrain image memory lends itself well to a number of useful extensions for real-time control of various parameters related to the present location of a traveler. For immersed users, these parameters may include lighting controls and sound intensity from spatially distributed sources. The scene may be sound-scaped or illuminated at very fine level of detail, localizing light and sound effects to the size of a single pixel on the scene map. Last but not least, most of such work can be done in Photoshop, by painting desired effects on the terrain map, rather than programming them. The latter extension deems to be a worthy topic for the future work.

References

1. Ruddle, R.A.: Navigation: Theoretical foundations and techniques for travel. In: IEEE Virtual Reality Conference, p. 311 (2005)
2. Sherstyuk, A., Treskunov, A.: Collision-free travel with terrain maps. In: Proceedings of the 8th International Conference on Virtual Reality Continuum and its Applications in Industry, pp. 175–178. ACM, New York (2009)

3. Miller, G.S.P.: The definition and rendering of terrain maps. In: Proceedings of the 13th Annual Conference on Computer Graphics and Interactive Techniques, SIGGRAPH 1986, pp. 39–48. ACM, New York (1986)
4. Zhou, H., Sun, J., Turk, G., Rehg, J.M.: Terrain synthesis from digital elevation models. IEEE Transactions on Visualization and Computer Graphics 13(4), 834–848 (2007)
5. Avatar Reality: Blue Mars Online Virtual World (2010), http://www.bluemars.com
6. Electronic Arts: Sim City (2013), http://www.simcity.com
7. Sherstyuk, A., Aschwanden, C., Saiki, S.: Affordable virtual environments: Building a virtual beach for clinical use. In: 13th Annual Medicine Meets Virtual Reality Conference. IOS Press (2005)
8. Vincent, D., Sherstyuk, A., Burgess, L., Connolly, K.: Teaching mass casualty triage skills using immersive three-dimensional Virtual Reality. Academic Emergency Medicine 15(11), 1160–1165 (2008)
9. Jiménez, P., Thomas, F., Torras, C.: 3d collision detection: A survey. Computers and Graphics 25, 269–285 (2000)
10. Akenine-Möller, T., Haines, E., Hoffman, N.: Real-Time Rendering, 3rd edn. A. K. Peters, Ltd., Natick (2008)
11. Sakr, Z., Sudama, C.: A curvilinear collision avoidance scheme for interactive 3d gaming environments. In: ACE 2008: Proceedings of the 2008 International Conference on Advances in Computer Entertainment Technology, pp. 130–133. ACM, New York (2008)
12. Sud, A., Gayle, R., Andersen, E., Guy, S., Lin, M., Manocha, D.: Real-time navigation of independent agents using adaptive roadmaps. In: Proceedings of the 2007 ACM Symposium on Virtual Reality Software and Technology, VRST 2007, pp. 99–106. ACM, New York (2007)
13. Sud, A., Andersen, E., Curtis, S., Lin, M., Manocha, D.: Real-time path planning for virtual agents in dynamic environments. In: ACM SIGGRAPH 2008 Classes, SIGGRAPH 2008, pp. 55:1–55:9. ACM, New York (2008)
14. Karamouzas, I., Overmars, M.: A velocity-based approach for simulating human collision avoidance. In: Safonova, A. (ed.) IVA 2010. LNCS (LNAI), vol. 6356, pp. 180–186. Springer, Heidelberg (2010)
15. Curtis, S., Snape, J., Manocha, D.: Way portals: efficient multi-agent navigation with line-segment goals. In: Proceedings of the ACM SIGGRAPH Symposium on Interactive 3D Graphics and Games, I3D 2012, pp. 15–22. ACM, New York (2012)
16. Sherstyuk, A., Kiyokawa, K.: Naviagtion maps for virtual travelers. In: Proceedings of the International Conference on Cyberworlds, Yokohama, Japan, pp. 175–178 (2013)
17. Flatland: The Homunculus Project at the Albuquerque High Performance Computing Center, AHPCC (2002), http://www.hpc.unm.edu/homunculus

Audio-Visual Art Performance System
Using Computer Video Output
Based on Component Video to Audio Signal Conversion

Yuichi Ito[1], Carl Stone[2], Masashi Yamada[2], and Shinya Miyazaki[2]

[1] Graduate School of Computer and Cognitive Sciences, Chukyo University, Japan
[2] School of Engineering, Chukyo University
Tokodachi 101, Toyota, Aichi. 470-0393, Japan
`yuichi.8445@gmail.com`,
`{carl,myamada,miyazaki}@sist.chukyo-u.ac.jp`
`http://www.chukyo-u.ac.jp/educate/secu/`

Abstract. This paper proposes a method for controlling video images during a performance using video signals in the audio domain, and applying an intentional misuse of video compression algorithms for artistic ends. A demonstration performance system using this representation method is also described. The system consists of hardware for converting a component video signal into an audio signal, and software for easy control of image to control the frequency, amplitude, rhythm, and wave shape. The proposed representation method seeks to create a unique relationship between video and audio signals, and shows a new perspective regarding the use of computational devices.

Keywords: Media Art, Audio-Visual Art, Live-Performance, Component Video Signal.

1 Introduction

In this paper, an expression technique and system for audio-visual art, along with a performance system using this technique, are proposed. While video usually employs sound as a supplemental aspect, audio-visual presentations generally build an equal relationship between the video and audio, and in fact, the expression of sound can often be the more important of the two. In general, a synchronized change in the video and audio content can create a sense of harmony and consistency in an audio-visual presentation [1][2][3]. From an aesthetic point of view, enhancing this harmony is a key component in increasing the value of such presentations [4].

To this end, we seek a new perspective for existing systems and equipment through the excavation of unknown, little known, or underappreciated device functions. In this way, an artistic presentation can lead viewers to discover an unexpected way to use such functions, and to reconsider or even change their points of view.

As a basic pre-digital example, electric guitar players in as early as the 1950s overdrove, and generally misused, their amplifiers to create new and richer tones

M.L. Gavrilova et al. (Eds.): Trans. on Comput. Sci. XXIII, LNCS 8490, pp. 157–177, 2014.

through distortion and feedback, which engineers had taken great pains to minimize in both the playback design and recording. Later, these techniques of misuse were encoded into so-called *stomp boxes* that allowed for the reproducibility and portability of such sounds. As a later example, hip-hop DJs have produced new and rich acoustic presentations by scratching vinyl records both literally and figuratively, and by using non-linear random access techniques with tone arms and magnetic cartridges. They have in essence made new musical instruments from a turntable. In the digital age, glitch art is created through the corruption of data, either intentionally or fortuitously, to produce digital or analog errors in service of a particular aesthetic.

There are generally two types of audio-visual presentations. One is simple video playback, and the other is a real-time performance, which we call audio-visual art. In the latter case, the tools or equipment used to generate sound function as musical instruments in service of the performance, and the combination of video, sound, and the execution of the performer is usually the complete expression of the work. As the goal of the present work, we seek to determine the value of the aforementioned synchronization of video and sound. From an aesthetic point of view regarding video presentations, both synchronization with sound and the display of images including specific information such as text can provide a strong message.

This paper describes our proposed production techniques of intentional misuse, the details of which will be a helpful archive for researchers and artists conducting similar works.

Since the 1960s, a variety of audio-visual presentations using electronic equipment have been produced, and we can see in them the application of performance techniques for modifying electronic devices in particular ways, including intentional misuse [5]. In recent years, circuit bending has become perhaps the most popular way of intentional misuse in that the artist or performer is able to directly access both audio and visual content by converting the circuits or network of electronic equipment used. As a proto-circuit bender, the artist Nam June Paik produced one of the first video synthesizers based on direct electro-magnetic modification of a video signal. David Tudor built handmade synthesizer-like units by attaching and constructing electronic audio signal networks during a performance, very often from scratch. These two artists have profoundly influenced many of today's younger artists.

In his book, *Circuit-Bending: Build Your Own Alien Instruments* [6], Reed Ghazala stated that classic instrumental sounds are conventional, and circuit-bending is required to destroy conventionality. In *Handmade Electronic Music*, Nicolas Collins introduced many production examples for instruments designed using circuit bending [7]. Ghazala also introduced many cases of this type of production.

In this paper, we propose a performance system that synchronizes video with sound, and a type of video expression using specific information from computer video output by converting component video into audio. In a traditional musical approach, rhythm, melody, and harmony are essential components when playing an instrument or creating music. Our proposed technique controls the pitch, volume, rhythm, and timbre by controlling the computer video output. In addition, we created a performance system using this technique. The proposed system consists of simple hardware allowing the input of video signals from the computer directly to a sound speaker, and performance software that allows us to modify videos so as to be able to control the pitch, volume, rhythm and timbre easily, producing a new way for applying computers as a musical instrument.

As stated above, we believe that the combination of audio and video makes for a strong presentation, which is the main reason for our selection and development of the proposed production technique. A strong presentation means increasing the transmission efficiency of the message in a particular work. In addition, our proposed production technique makes it possible to produce sound and video at the same time, with a very fast reaction rate and little latency, further strengthening the presentation.

Our personal aesthetic requirements in this case are as follows: real-time performance capability through the generation and control of video and sound simultaneously, the synchronicity of images and sound, and the use of concrete imagery (especially text) with a presentation that allows the audience to find a new and different perspective away from natural preconceptions regarding imagery, transition, shape, and form. While this paper documents our own adoption of the proposed system for the creation of a live performance, in conformance with our own particular aesthetics, we also believe that other applications are readily achievable, such as installation art, music videos, digital signage, and TV commercials.

In Section 3, we describe the hardware system used to convert a component video signal into audio, and the relationship between the video and the pitch, volume, rhythm, and timbre of the audio. Next, we describe the control of the computer video software and performance when applying the proposed system. We then verify the proposed performance technique and system through an evaluation from a performance competition.

This paper introduces a work created based on the proposed production techniques, and by describing the detail of the production method used, we hope that the current paper will serve as a helpful archive for researchers and other artists conducting similar works.

2 Precedents

We can classify different works applying circuit bending based on three points. The first point is whether the video and audio signals were directly converted, as direct conversion means a lower latency and increased sense of synchronicity. The second point is whether the video and audio, when created and controlled simultaneously, are controlled by a single set of data. When multiple datasets and performance gestures must be used, the performance can become extremely complicated. To reduce such complications, it is desirable to create and control the video and sound through a single operation to improve the accuracy of the musical instruments and the synchronization. The last point is whether, in creating a specific video expression such as a text display, we can achieve a sense of concreteness and a strong message. Of course, many various audio-visual art works and performances have been created. The production and presentation methods used in the precedents listed in this section are examples of intentional misuse.

The Breadboard Band[1] makes and modifies circuits on breadboards, which are typically used for the design and experiments of electric handicraft or built-in systems, all in real-time in the context of a live performance. They change the wiring of the breadboards extemporaneously without preparation or forethought, and create sound for a live performance. Craftwife + Kaseo +[2] conducts the circuit bending of toy dolls with electronic voices based on TV animation characters, and uses this technique during their live performances. In the case of Atsuhiro Ito's *Optron project*[3], we can see some examples of circuit-bending showing the relationship of sound and light in a simple manner. *Optron* is a self-built musical instrument made by amplifying the electromagnetic noise leaking from fluorescent light using a guitar pick up. The performer starts and stops the light, and uses the intermittence of the starter to create random noises and rhythms. Since this noise originates from a simple AC current, and has little variation on its own, the performer also modifies the sound output using pedal effecters. In this performance, we can see the simple result of hearing a sound when the fluorescent light is turned on or off. The visual itself is exceedingly simple. Carsten Nicolai's *telefunken*[4] is a work connecting the output of a CD player to the composite video input of a TV player, allowing the visualization of audio signals. When an audio signal is converted directly into video, the relationship between sound and image is clear. In this case, the sound from the CD is created first and the resultant video comes next. The concept behind this piece does not include a real-time presentation of sound and image simultaneously. In *Apeiron / Peras*[5], a live performance piece by Phillip Stearns, sound and images are generated simultaneously using a self-built audio-video synthesizer. The results are delicate abstract patterns without text or specific content.

While the value and quality of each of the above examples cannot be denied, for our particular aesthetic requirements, we found each case to be lacking in certain aspects.

* The Breadboard Band uses a computer as an intermediary between video and sound. Their imagery consists mostly of self-references and recursions because they shoot their own breadboard activities as they are being executed. They do not convert video and sound directly, and do not use a specific video expression such as a text display.
* Craftwife + Kaseo + also does not directly convert video and sound, and uses a computer as an intermediary, increasing the latency.

---

[1] The Breadboard Band Web: http://www.breadboardband.org/ (accessed 2013-11-11).

[2] Craftwife+Kaseo+: http://www.craftwife.com/kaseo/ (accessed 2013-11-11)

[3] Atsuhiro Ito: http://gotobai.net/ (accessed 2013-11-11).

[4] Carsten Nicolai: *telefunken*, http://www.carstennicolai.de/?c=works&w=telefunken (accessed 2013-11-11).

[5] Phillip Stearns: *Apeiron / Peras*, http://phillipstearns.wordpress.com/projects/apeiron-peras-2007-ongoing/ (accessed 2013-11-11).

Table 1. Classification of examples

	Both video signal and sound signal are converted directly	Generate and control video and sound simultaneously	Specific video expression (text and so on)
The Breadboard Band		✓	
Craftwife + Kaseo +		✓	✓
Optron	✓	✓	
telefunken	✓		
Apeiron | Peras	✓	✓	

* While *Optron*'s linking of visuals and sound is unmediated and well synchronized, allowing the audience to see their direct relationship, it does not provide a concrete video expression.
* The piece, *telefunken*, is essentially a static work based on pre-recorded audio material and does not represent a performance.
* Finally, *Apeiron / Peras* allows the audience to experience a direct relationship between imagery and sound, but like with *Optron*, the piece does not contain a concrete expression.

Table 1 classifies these examples based on the three points described above. Realized items are marked with a check. As Table 1 shows, in each of the examples, while various points are satisfied, none completes our personal aesthetic requirements as we previously outlined. In Sections 3 and 4, we describe a performance system that satisfies our aesthetic requirements and enables us to conduct a live performance.

3   Construction of Video-to-Audio Conversion System

The first step is to create a system for performing the proposed technique using computer video output based on converting a component video signal into audio. This system consists of hardware for signal conversion, and software for achieving the actual performance.

3.1   Examples of Video-to-Audio Signal Conversion

The process of converting video signals into audio has previously been explored. Ei Wada's Braun Tube Jazz Band[6] employed methods to convert video into audio and vice versa as part of the creative and experimental stages in preparing for a performance we could see the documentary film[7]. In the final performance, however, Ei Wada deviated from these strategies and instead used his body as a conductor of electromagnetic noise emitted from a CRT, highly amplified with a guitar amp,

---

[6] Bye Bye Broadcasting by Braun Tube Jazz Band / EI WADA Interview:
  http://youtu.be/Ouue59iY0Hs (accessed 2013-11-11).
[7] (Live) EI WADA - Braun Tube Jazz Band:
  http://www.nicovideo.jp/watch/sm11098276 (accessed 2013-11-11).

touching the display as a percussionist might do. Therefore, the order of conversion was video into body movement, and body movement into sound. The control of the pitch, volume, and rhythm depended on the performer's body movements. The imagery was fixed in advance, using pre-recorded videotape.

3.2   Different Types of Video Signals

In our system, we use a component video signal to separate the luminance (Y) and color difference, R and B (Cr, Cb), based on Y. Braun Tube Jazz Band employs a general composite video signal in which the luminance, chrominance, and sync information have been superimposed into a single signal using one of the coding standards. Y, Cr, and Cb signals are not propagated separately because the signals for a video display are superimposed. Another video signal, commonly known as analog S-video, is used, where Cr and Cb signals are superimposed but luminance Y is separated. The lack of separate Cr and Cb signals makes it difficult to convert an image into audio signals directly from the image information as displayed.

3.3   Constitution of the System Hardware

Here, we show the constitution of the system hardware and the procedure used for signal conversion (Fig. 1). First, we split the computer's video signal output using a video signal splitter. Next, we convert a VGA signal into component video signal Y, Cr, and Cb using a cable. We input one or more signals into an audio mixer or powered speaker. In this way, we can easily synchronize the sound according to changes in video output of a PC desktop. The display resolution is XGA (1,024 pixels × 768 pixels), and the horizontal scan frequency is 48.363 kHz. Of course, this is much higher than the human audible frequency range (maximum of 20 kHz). What listeners hear is the wave envelope of the connecting sound signal wave peaks (envelope waveform). After conversion, the same wave patterns are repeated, as shown in Fig. 2, which corresponds to the output images. The display resolution of this figure is XGA and the refresh rate is 60 Hz. The following shows how to characterize the sound elements using video.

3.4   Relationship between Video and Audio

As we stated in the previous section, examples of converting acoustic signals into video have been previously reported. Until the present study, however, how a video generates sound elements has not been sufficiently researched. Here, we show the relationship between the video and output sound of the proposed system from the perspective of pitch, volume, rhythm, and timbre for an audio-visual performance.

The component video signal format is strictly defined, and the flexibility is therefore limited. Nonetheless, we will describe what types of acoustic representations can be realized even under such limitations.

While we present several simple image and sound examples, users can create more complicated combinations of such techniques to develop greater richness and uniquely adapted approaches.

Pitch. In Fig. 3, horizontal white bands stand atop each other at certain intervals, and a luminance signal forms audible pulse waves with frequencies in inverse proportion to the width and interval (black bands) of these white bands. We call this the control interval. If a white band with a single pixel width requires a $1/48.363\,ms$ scan time, and the widths of the continuous white and black bands are n_w and n_b, the frequency of the luminance signal can be described through the following formula:

$$T_w + T_b = \frac{1}{48.363 \times 10^3}(n_w + n_b)$$

where T_w and T_b are the scan times of the white and black bands, respectively, and the the minimum period T_{min} is $2/48.363 \times 10^3 \approx 0.0414\,ms$. There is no signal during a screen refresh; thus, the white band display considers the screen refresh rate, control interval rate, and the number of white bands, allowing the optional control of the audio output frequencies.

Volume. The audio output volume reflects the amplitude of the luminance signal, where the amplitude follows the video luminance value. Fig. 4 (upper) shows a change in video signal luminance value from 0 to 255, recorded as an audio signal, and Fig. 4 (bottom) shows the change in volume. When the luminance changes, the audio volume output changes logarithmically. This dynamic range (256-step luminance) is not granular enough for a reasonable sound expression control. Fig. 2 shows the amplitude of the luminance signal changes based on the amount of white pixels on the scanning line. In Fig. 5, changes in white bandwidth produce changes in the width of the audible pulse wave, and with a 16 dB difference between a 1-pixel and 50-pixel white bandwidth, we have a sufficient dynamic range for an artistic sound expression.

Rhythm. A completely black image produces zero audio output (silence), and we can therefore insert black frames into white band frames repeatedly to create a rhythm.

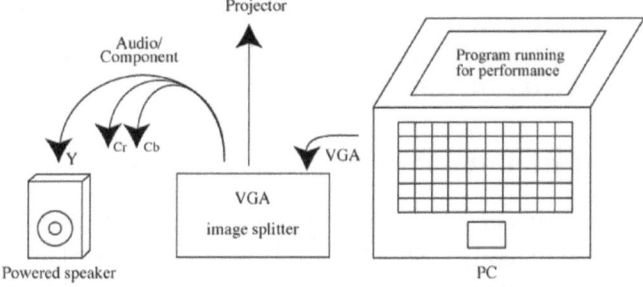

Fig. 1. Constitution of the system hardware

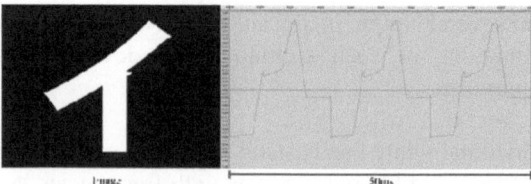

Fig. 2. A luminance signal waveform from the display of a Japanese character

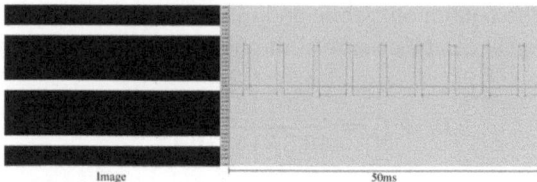

Fig. 3. Waveform of an arrangement with regular intervals of the horizontal white bands

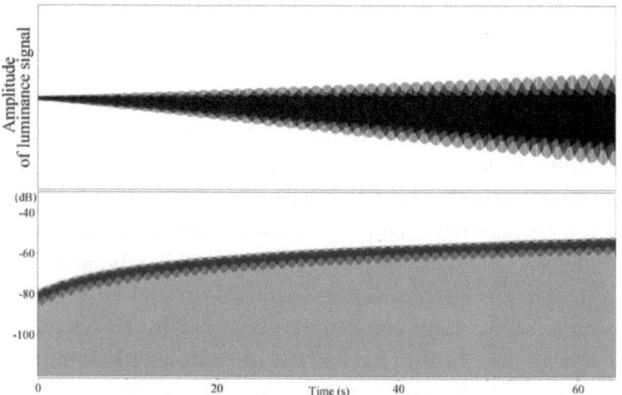

Fig. 4. Increase in luminance in 256 steps

Timbre. Regarding the timbre, the white square in the center of the screen shown in Fig. 6 indicates a 60 Hz directional wave. In the letter Q in Fig. 7, we can see a complicated change in the wave. Various kinds of timbre can therefore be generated by applying the proposed technique.

A video clip of a performance using a combination of these principles can be found at http://youtu.be/Ju-XuLm2Jw4 .

4   Development of the Performance Software

In the companion software used for generating a real-time performance, design functions are applied to easily control the video and performance based on the video-sound relationship mentioned in the previous section. The software utilizes two modules, each with its own performance goal. One is a white band video audio synthesizer used to confirm the proposed performance technique using white bands as a basic display function for audio control. The other is called a desktop display video processor, which allows a computer to be utilized as a musical instrument using standard video imagery and the output of a PC display, while offering various effects to users. We developed this performance software using Cycling '74 Max[8] (version 5.1.9). In addition, we used a datamoshing video to produce new sounds.

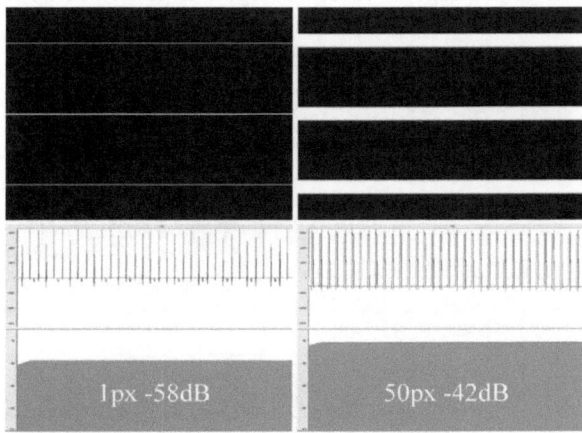

Fig. 5. Comparing the sound pressure of white bands: 1 px (L) and 50 px (R)

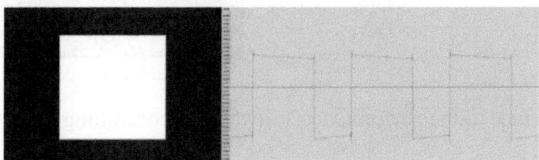

Fig. 6. A waveform when displaying a white rectangle

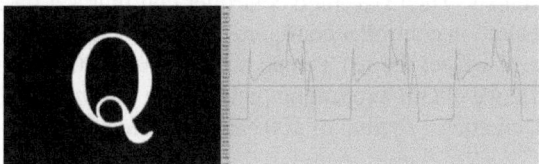

Fig. 7. A waveform when displaying the letter Q

4.1   White Band Video Audio Synthesizer

Based on continuous white band images, we generate various sounds by controlling the width, shape, and number of white bands[9]. Fig. 8 shows the interface of the white band video audio synthesizer and describes the main functions of this software.

---

[8] Cycling '74: Max, http://cycling74.com/products/max/ (accessed 2013-11-11).
[9] Yuichi Ito: *sas1080n*, http://youtu.be/Ju-XuLm2Jw4 (accessed 2013-11-11).

Starting and Stopping the Image and Sound Generation. Operating the (1) Audio On/Off and (2) metro On/Off controllers, the drawing of white bands on a black display, along with the sound, start and stop, respectively. As this program uses sound signals as one aspect of controlling a white band image, we can start the sound processing by operating the (1) Audio On/Off controller. In Max5, the use of periodic waveforms in the audio domain elevates the video display efficiency, and reduces the burden of PC video generation. A waveform signal is generated through sound processing and is used only to control the white bands, and not as audio output from the PC.

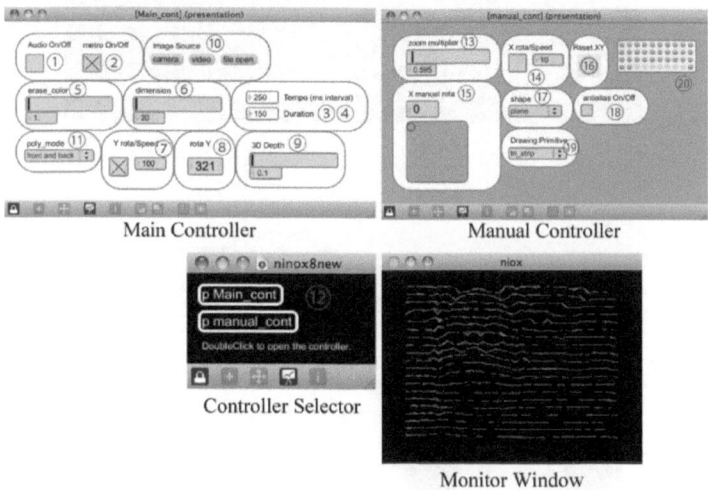

Fig. 8. Interface of the performance software for controlling white band video

Video Burst Control. According to the values of the (3) Tempo and (4) Duration controllers, we can insert black screen frames between the white band frames to generate white band images bursts. The (3) Tempo controller configures a flashing cycle of white bands, and the (4) Duration controller configures the duration of flashing white bands per cycle. For example, if we set the (3) Tempo controller to $500\ ms$ and the (4) Duration controller to $100\ ms$, we obtain a repeating pattern with $100\ ms$ of white bands and $400\ ms$ of black screen, creating a rhythm of 120 beats per minute (BPM).

Control Envelope Using a Fade. The control envelope creates images using a white band fade-out with a (5) erase_color setting of the fade-out time control. As the white band fades out, the video signal voltage decreases, gradually imposing amplitude envelopes on the waveform.

Control of the Number of White Bands and Interval. The (6) Dimension controller designates the number of white bands and draws them equally within a fixed range; as the value of the Dimension controller increases, the number of white bands does as well, and we therefore have smaller intervals between bands and higher pitch results, and vice versa.

Enhancing Video Expression Function. In addition to the numerical settings and audio signals used to control the generated white bands, we can also use a Web camera or desktop video as a control input. The rotation of the white band images is controlled by the (7) Y rota/Speed and (8) rota Y controllers. The 3D depth is achieved using the (9) 3D Depth controller, and the (10) Image Source controller designates the luminance value of the video or Web camera video signal, and corresponds to the z value (Fig. 9). Currently, if the number of bands exceeds 250, the burden placed on the PC increases and the image display becomes unacceptably discontinuous. Our software therefore limits the number of bands to within the range of 10–250. The resultant loss of pitch resolution needs to somehow be compensated for, and our unique solution is to use the (7) Y rota/Speed rotation controllers of the white bands on the screen centered to the horizontal axis, with a precise pitch change as a result. Selecting the display mode using the (11) poly mode controller, i.e., from a white band display to the choice of a wire frame, polygon, or texture display type, changes both the image and sound dynamically. Fig. 10 shows the difference in frequency spectrum between a wire frame drawing and the applied texture.

Fig. 9. The left-side image shows a white band reflecting the Web camera image on the right

More Precise Image Expression Function. We prepared a manual controller to make maximum use of the 3D expression of the drawn object. Double-clicking on the (12) manual cont sub-patcher invokes the controller. The controller makes it possible to change the size of the drawing object using the (13) zoom multiplier. The (14) X rota/Speed and (15) X manual rota are used to control the vertical axis centered rotation. The (16) Reset XY initializes the XY rotation position of the white bands or objects, and the (17) shape value changes the shape of the drawing object. As the name implies, the (18) anti-alias On/Off controller sets the anti-alias. The (19) Drawing Primitive controller allows the user to select between a variety of dots and line combinations. While the above controllers do not affect the sound too much, they have a large visual impact and help with the dynamism of the video presentation. It is also possible to store and recall the specific value combinations as presets, as shown in (20).

4.2   Desktop Display Video Processor

The desktop display video processor makes it possible to generate sound, and clearly expresses the computer's capability as an integrated audio-visual performance instrument. Fig. 11 shows the interface used, which is part of the desktop image display that is processed and designed to merge more or less seamlessly with any other elements that are part of the desktop image display. Showing the performance interface as part of the display seen by viewers further highlights the aspect of real-time performance control. The following are the main functions used for generating images and sound. Readers can see a performance by viewing the video at `http://youtu.be/oQElyfYkuFM`.

Lower-resolution Function. This function lowers the input desktop screen resolution and makes a block display resembling large bands of colors. As we mentioned in Section 3, when an image become a seemingly random arrangement of bands, we have an increased sense of pitch value when compared to the original screen image. Fig. 12 shows the differences in waveform between a normal desktop screen and a processed screen.

Image Feedback Function. The image feedback introduced at a sub-optimal resolution will produce interesting visual artifacts similar to an error and block noise. Such feedback generates errors and displays an effect similar to block noise. Fig. 13 shows an example of applying this effect.

OS Command Script Execution Function. The right side of the interface window allows us to make macro changes to the PC video display by controlling the system level commands, such as changing the Finder window size, changing the text size, putting the display zoom under program control, and automating changes to the Finder display parameters continually.

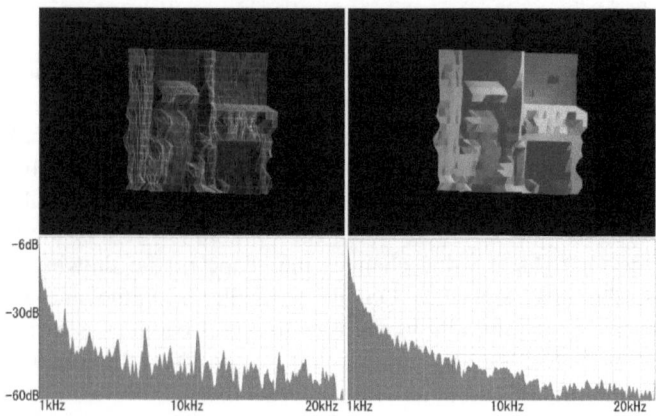

Fig. 10. Difference in frequency spectrum based on the display mode

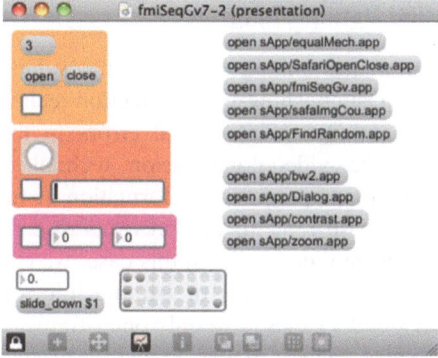

Fig. 11. Interface of the performance software used for processing a desktop image

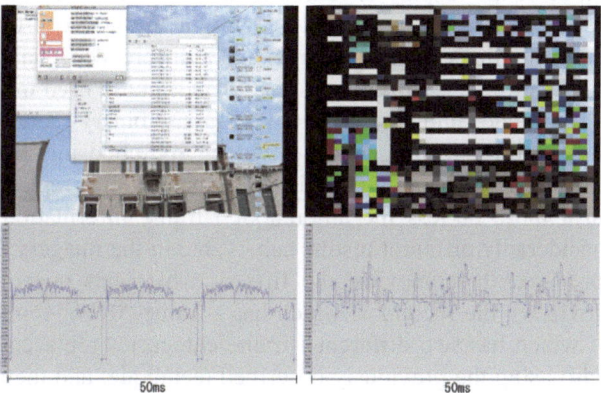

Fig. 12. Difference in waveforms between a low-resolution blocky desktop display (R) and a normal display (L)

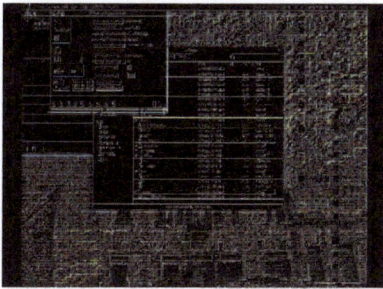

Fig. 13. An error video generated using feedback video

4.3   Experiments Using Datamoshing

Our aim is to produce new and unique sounds using a datamoshing video and the hardware described herein. Datamoshing is a production technique for creating unique video representations by introducing intentional errors in the motion compensation inter-frame prediction of the video-compression technology used. Our concrete approach is to disable important prediction information (I-frames) during the video playback of an MP4 file. Please refer to our previous research for additional details regarding the datamoshing technique [8][9]. In this case, we chose the use of MP4 files because they offer a variety of categories of I-frame information, which makes our control easier. In comparison, AVI files have only one I-frame category, "0000 01b0."

In this experiment, a video camera makes an analog capture of a computer display while playing back a video. Analog capture by a camera is the preferred method (compared to screen capture software) for minimizing the latency. The component video signal output of the display is routed as analog audio information to the line input of the video camera. In addition, to highlight the stereo effect, we assign a luminance signal (Y) to the left audio channel and a difference signal (Cb) to the right audio channel for recording. A difference signal (Cr) is not in used in this experiment. When replacing I-frame numbers with "0000" as binary data, we apply the fundamental datamoshing technique to a video. By choosing between I-frames "01b6," "01b0," "01b3," or any combination thereof for replacement, we can essentially control more or less the amount of I-frame information that is deleted overall, with considerably different results achievable in the imagery. For comparison purposes, we prepared three movies, the first of which has no editing of I-frame information (Movie A), the second of which has I-frame "01b6" replaced (Movie B), and the third of which has two different I-frame categories replaced (Movie C). We captured the audio using the previously described technique, and then examined it on an online audio editor.

The sound from Movie A has a gradual change in both timbre and volume. The sudden entrance of a noise image in Movie B introduces what sounds subjectively like a poor audio connection contact. The sound of Movie C has drastic volume changes when visual noise appears. The rate of image change in Movie C can also result in increases in audio amplitude. Although comparatively subtle, Movie B has sounds with a digital error characteristic that do not appear in Movie A.

Figs. 14 through 16 show one-second excerpts from each Movie (A, B, and C), and images captured at every 10 frames, along with the audio waveform.

Figs. 14 and 15 show captured images and an audio waveform of Movies A and B, respectively. We can clearly see changes to the audio waveform between the two. Likewise, we can see larger differences in both the images and sound when comparing Movie A with Movie C (Fig. 16). By mapping the resultant changes, we can place the audio under compositional control using datamoshing. We found that we can produce a piece that has a strong relationship between the sound and video, and with a unique sound quality. We can therefore consider the application of datamoshing for creating new sounds a valuable addition to the pallet of an electronic music composer.

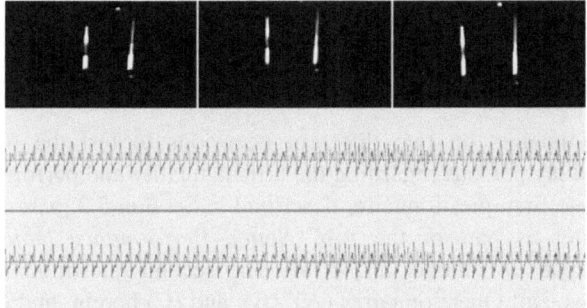

Fig. 14. Images and sound of Movie A

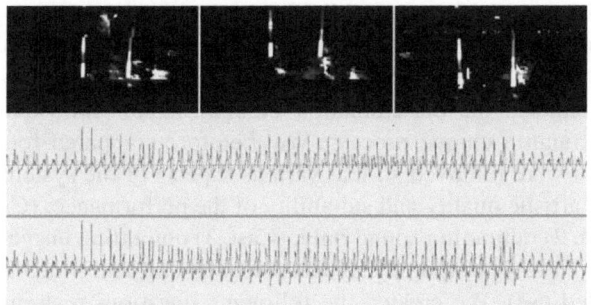

Fig. 15. Images and sound of Movie B

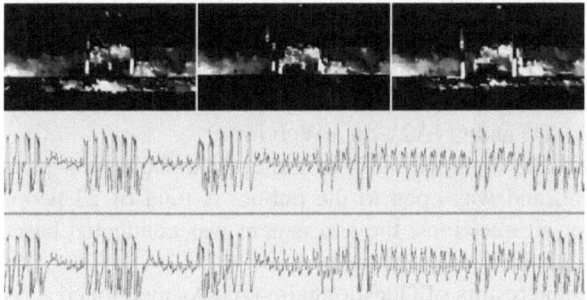

Fig. 16. Images and sound of Movie C

However, this series of operations for applying the datamoshing of MP4 files has thus far not been realized in real-time using the software described in this paper. We strongly believe in the benefits of a real-time audio-visual performance and strive to build a method that will make such a performance achievable in the near future. The movie created through this experiment can be seen at `http://youtu.be/4_BFeHcq550`.

5   Evaluation and Study

5.1   Evaluation through Questionnaires

We used questionnaires on two different occasions to test the opinions of both professionals and lay persons regarding the artistic quality and performance suitability of our system. The first questionnaire, described in Section 5.2, was developed by the Aichi Arts Center as part of the *AAC Sound Performance Dojo Competition*[10], Nagoya City, Japan on January 21, 2011. The second questionnaire was a set of surveys, which we call Questionnaires (A), (B), and (C) herein, and can be described as follows.

Questionnaire (A) was regarding the artistic quality and the suitability of the performance achieved. To test the public reaction to the system, we gave a series of performances and uploaded them onto the Web in video form. We then made them available and sought the audience response through a set of questions in Web form.

Our system features the dissemination of both sound and video generated and synchronized through a unique process. We therefore compared four cases, the key features of which were removed so that various aspects of the system could be tested to determine the artistic quality and suitability of the performance: (Case 1) outputting video only, (Case 2) outputting sound only, (Case 3) outputting unsynchronized sound and video, and (Case 4) outputting synchronized sound and video (i.e., unmodified from our intended use). We created the following questions regarding each case: Q (A1) Is the work interesting? Q (A2) Would you be interested in creating a performance using this system? Q (A3) Do you feel that a computer can be used as a musical instrument? In addition, we asked the following questions for cases 3 and 4: Q (A4) Do you feel a sense of unity between the sound and video? Furthermore, we introduced The Breadboard Band, Craftwife + Kaseo +, *Optron*, *telefunken*, and *Apeiron / Peras*, cited in Section 2, through Web-based movies, and asked the same two questions, Q (A1) and Q (A2), on a Web form.

The production and administration of the questionnaire took place in a university wide environment, and was open to the public. A total of 23 people completed the questionnaire. For all questions, the assessment was conducted based on five grades, from which we took the average grade.

Table 2 shows the results of Questionnaire (A). As mentioned, Case 4 in Table 2-A shows that, when all features are fully used, our system ranks consistently highest when compared to situations in which certain features are not present. Table 2-B shows the additional performance evaluations of the other artists. *Optron* was ranked the same as our full-featured system. In addition, The Breadboard Band ranked .1 point higher that our system for Q (A1), and the same as our system for Q (A2).

Questionnaire (B) was regarding the operation of our proposed system. To test the operation of our system in the hands of other users, we invited the participation of 25

---

[10] AAC Sound Performance Dojo secretariat:
http://www.aac.pref.aichi.jp/bunjyo/jishyu/dojo/index.html
(accessed 2013-11-11).

university students familiar with the Max/MSP programming environment, and with a stated interest in sound art performance and techniques for sound design and production. We described our system and presented a video showing the operation of the white band video audio synthesizer and desktop display video processor. We then installed the system in our laboratory, conducted a demonstration, and invited participants to the experiment and asked them questions about the system's functionality and usability. We then queried them through Questionnaire (B) as follows: Q (B1) Evaluate the ease of image manipulation. Q (B2) Evaluate the ease of audio manipulation. Q (B3) Evaluate the overall ease of use and enjoyability. We also included a section where the respondents were invited to include additional comments. Table 3 shows the results of questionnaire (B).

With Q (B1) and Q (B2) being about the usability of the system, we can recognize from the responses that, while image manipulation of the system was generally considered to be easy, the audio manipulation was more problematic to some of the users, and we therefore deem this aspect of our interface to require further improvement. The overall ease and enjoyability, while ranking high, drew helpful comments and suggestions regarding system improvements. The suggestions ranged from simplifying the button and display design, to providing better human interface cues (for example, by pre-displaying images or shapes that can be selected by the user). Some respondents felt some difficulty in seeing the relationship between the input and output, such as being able to anticipate which button or parameter would lead to which type of video and sound. On the other hand, a significant number of respondents found the design to be sufficiently simple and easy to understand. The consensus was that, while the system is not 100% intuitive, once the rather gentle learning curve is sufficiently overcome, the system will prove to be easy to operate.

Table 2. Results of Questionnaire (A)

A	Q (A1)	Q (A2)	Q (A3)	Q (A4)	B	Q (A1)	Q (A2)
Case 1	2.5	2.3	1.4	-	The Breadboard Band	4.3	3.9
Case 2	2.8	2.5	2.6	-	Craftwife + Kaseo +	3.8	3.3
Case 3	3.5	3.4	3.3	2.8	*Optron*	4.2	3.9
Case 4	4.2	3.9	3.8	4.6	*telefunken*	3.4	2.8
					*Apeiron	Peras*	3.2	3.2

Table 3. Results of Questionnaire (B)

Q (B1)	Q (B2)	Q (B3)
4.3	3.7	4.5

In Questionnaire (C), we collected subjective comments regarding the perceived difference with other systems, especially in regard to the artistic quality and suitability of the performance that is achievable. We also collected suggestions regarding new uses of the proposed system and points that need improvement. Question (C1) queried the respondents about their impressions of the piece achieved using the proposed system, points to be improved, and suggestions for alternative uses. Question (C2) asked the respondents to subjectively list what they considered as the good and bad points of our system.

In Question (C1), we obtained the following impressions regarding our system.

* I think the idea is simple but interesting.
* It could be more immersive.
* I feel the uniqueness of generating sound directly from video in real-time.
* The fact that the sounds change based on the video deployment is interesting.
* I could feel the versatility of the system as an instrument for producing sound using only video signals.
* By watching your performance, it became possible to sense the sound output visually.
* It seems difficult to control what kind of sound is emitted based on the video used.

We obtained some additional suggestions, including the following.

* To break down a form of musical instruments, show an intentionally playing rather than somehow sounding.
* Changing the sound characteristics by applying an audio filter to the generated sound could be an interesting addition.
* I hope to see this system applied on different platforms (e.g., Raspberry PI or tablet PC).
* Using different video standards, such as Thunderbolt and HDMI, for variation could be an interesting addition.
* I am interested in the possibility of visualization through the application of sound.

We received various suggestions along these lines, including comments related to the performance style. We also received suggestions regarding the scalability of the video signal. From these suggestions, we believe that the proposed system was sufficiently validated, and there is potential to extend it to various performance styles.

For Question (C2), we received the following objective opinions based on a comparison with other systems.

* It is hard to imagine controlling the system as a musical instrument.
* In terms of creating works with a harmony (synchronicity) between sound and video, I felt your system was superior to *Apeiron / Peras*.
* The system achieved a feeling of 3D.
* The sound and video are synchronized, making your system easier to understand in terms of development.
* I'm missing the spread of sound in your system.
* If we do not know the process well, it can be confusing to differentiate from other audio-visual performances.
* I thought the impact of your video was better than in the other works.
* It is possible to achieve a performance at a smaller scale and lower cost compared to other systems, which I think is a good point.
* It was difficult to match the performance and operation because it was difficult to see what the player was doing in comparison with the other types of systems.

5.2   Performance Evaluation Using the Desktop Display Video Processor

We presented the proposed desktop display video processor at the *AAC Sound Performance Dojo Competition*, Nagoya City, Japan on January 21, 2011. The performance emphasized our concept of the computer as a musical instrument, and utilized processed MacOS desktop images and controlled sound. The most important aspect of this work was to create a performance using a computer as a musical instrument, and to obtain the display information necessary to create a clear relationship between the computer and audio output.

Performance Constitution. We used the desktop display video processor, and projected the real-time processed PC desktop display onto the center of a screen placed above the stage area. The CamTwist[11] software package was used to input the desktop screen as data to our software. The equipment and settings were similar to those shown in Fig. 1. We inserted an audio mixer between a VGA splitter and the speakers for control of the volume and placement in the stereo field. For the component video signal cables, three RCA connectors were connected to the mixer. When connected, we assigned the audio represented by the luminance to the center of the stereo field, and the two color difference signals to the L and R channels, respectively. Intermittently muting the luminance channel during the performance promoted a greater sense of stereo differentiation.

The first part of the performance consisted of the performer inputting a text explaining the process of the piece onto the PC display and thus into the projected video. The text itself began to be modified by the described process, and the form and content were therefore referentially joined. In this way, the audience could recognize the performance process, the synchronization of image and sound, and the artist's aesthetic view. In the second part of the performance, the performer played freely without providing any text explanation, while still using the desktop display video processor function, creating sounds using the PC desktop display to create dynamic changes in sound.

Evaluation of the Competition. The judges of *AAC Sound Performance Dojo* are respected artists and professionals in the field of sound art and sound performance. After the submissions were initially screened, pieces that were deemed to be excellent and showed the possibility of future growth were selected. The selected pieces were performed in front of the judges, and a live audience was drawn from the general public. The judges voted for the merit awards, and the audience voted for the audience awards.

There were 21 applicants in 2011, the year we entered our system into the competition. Four proposals were selected including our own. After the selection of the artists, the contestants had access to the judges' comments, suggestions, and criticisms for a six-week period. After the six weeks, the final performance was held in front of a live audience. Our piece was selected by both the judges and the audience as the first runner-up. A questionnaire was distributed to the audience as a part of the

---

[11] AllocInit: CamTwist, http://CamTwistStudio.com/ (accessed 2013-11-11).

event, and the comments received were mainly complementary and often enthusiastic, including remarks such as "playing sound using a PC screen is a novel method of expression" and "the performance was executed simply and without decoration, and was very interesting."

5.3   Video Performance by Other Artists Using Our System

We wanted to test the efficacy of our system in the hands of other professional artists who were not involved in its development. We asked Vokoi[12], an independent Japanese artist who specializes in real-time visual performance, to use our system. Fig. 17 shows images the artist used to make sounds, including changes in pitch. Our proposed system is not intended simply for our private use, but was designed in such a way that it can be utilized and exploited by other artists as well. It facilitates a special type of audio-visual artwork, and makes communication between artists and their audiences possible by finding interesting connections between audio and video information.

Fig. 17. Video images used by Vokoi

6   Conclusion

In this paper, we proposed an expression technique for achieving an audio-visual performance, and a method for converting a component video signal into sound in keeping with our general artistic inspiration and aesthetic sensibilities. In addition, we built a system consisting of both hardware and two types of performance software for generating and controlling video and sound based on this approach, and applied this system to an audio-visual performance at the *AAC Sound Performance Dojo 2011* competition. The performance and underlying system used to achieve it were both positively evaluated by the judges as excellent, showing the possibility of future growth. Furthermore, the performance itself gained an excellent evaluation from the audience based on a questionnaire.

As future work, we plan to develop additional formats and new strategies for applying techniques such as an intentional misuse of signal information in real-time, and develop a higher accuracy in the operation of a computer as a musical instrument.

---

[12] ARch project: http://www.arch-project.com/ (accessed 2013-11-11).

Acknowledgments. We thank the judges of the Secretariat of *AAC Sound Performance Dojo* for their high evaluation of our work. In addition, we give thanks to Masahiro Ura (Institute for Advanced Studies in Artificial Intelligence, Chukyo University), whose comments and suggestions were invaluable throughout the course of our study.

References

1. Iwamiya, S.: The Interaction Between Auditory and Visual Processing when Listening to Music via Audio-visual Media. Journal of the Acoustical Society of Japan 48(3), 146–153 (1992)
2. Iwamiya, S.: The Effect of the Matching of Sound and Video on the Interaction Between Auditory and Visual Processing in Communication via Audio-visual Media. Journal of the Acoustical Society of Japan 48(9), 649–657 (1992)
3. Sugano, Y.: Effects of Synchronization Between Musical Rhythm and Visual Motion on the Congruency of Music and Motion Picture. Journal of Music Perception and Cognition 5, 1–10 (1999)
4. Iwamiya, S., Seki, M., Yoshikawa, K., Takada, M.: Congruency Between Sound Effects and Switching Patterns of Images. The Japanese Journal of Ergonomics 39(6), 292–299 (2003)
5. Ghazala, R.: Circuit-Bending: Build Your Own Alien Instruments. Wiley Publishing, Inc. (2005)
6. Collins, N.: Handmade Electronic Music. Routledge (2006)
7. Kubota, A.: Bending Culture. IPSJ SIG technical reports, EC, Entertainment Computing 2006(39), 45–46 (2006)
8. Ito, Y., Stone, C., Yamada, M., Miyazaki, S.: Datamoshing Technique for Video Production, The Society for Art and Science. In: Proc. of NICOGRAPH International 2013, CD-ROM, pp. 60–71 (2013)
9. Ito, Y., Stone, C., Yamada, M., Miyazaki, S.: A Technique for Real-time Datamoshing Using Web Camera Input. The Journal of The Institute of Image Information and Television Engineers 67(11), J413–J416 (2013)

Experiments for Emotion Estimation from Biological Signals and Its Application

Masaki Omata, Daisuke Kanuka, and Xiaoyang Mao

Interdisciplinary Graduate School of Medicine and Engineering,
University of Yamanashi,
Kofu, Japan
{masakio,g10mk014,mao}@yamanashi.ac.jp

Abstract. This paper describes elementary experiments for a technique to estimate the emotion of a user from the biological signals of user's central nervous system, such as cerebral blood flow and brain wave. The proposed technique uses multiple regression analysis in providing a high resolution measure to the emotional valence, which could not be realized with the existing methods based on peripheral nervous system. To demonstrate the effectiveness of the proposed emotion estimation technique in emotion based interaction, we also implemented an emotional painting tool that dynamically adapts the colors of brush and the outline of canvas to the estimated emotion of the user by recording biological signals and analyzing them in real time. The tool allows users to create original images that reflect their emotion.

Keywords: emotion estimation, biological signals, brain wave, hemoencephalography, emotional painting tool.

1   Introduction

There have been many studies in recent years about affective interfaces which use user's emotion as a new interaction modality. In addition to providing traditional user interface functions, affective interfaces aims to achieve more smooth communication between human and computer by making computer being aware of user's emotion. One of the research challenges in the field is how to recognize and classify emotions. Some studies use a user's voice to recognize the user's emotion [1], while others interpret emotions from the user's facial expressions [2]. However, such recognition techniques require users to intentionally input the information about their emotions by modulating their voices or moving their facial muscles. It usually thus adds extra cognitive load to users and may fail to give an objective measure to the true status of users' emotion.

This paper proposes a technique for estimating users' emotion using biological signals from their central nervous system such as brain waves and cerebral blood flow (CBF), as well as autonomic nervous system signals such as pulse waves and electrodermal activity. To deal with emotion computationally, Russell's 2D emotion model [3] has been well used. It describes the affective space

M.L. Gavrilova et al. (Eds.): Trans. on Comput. Sci. XXIII, LNCS 8490, pp. 178–198, 2014.
© Springer-Verlag Berlin Heidelberg 2014

by two dimensions: emotional valence, indicating the hedonic value (positive vs. negative), and arousal, indicating the emotional intensity (see figure 1). Biological signal based emotion estimation systems of previous studies have succeeded in estimating arousal level. However, to the best of our knowledge, providing a high resolution measure to the emotional valence remains to be a challenging topic. Especially, it has been difficult to estimate positive valence from user's biological data. Therefore, the main contribution of this paper is to present a higher-accuracy regression model to estimate emotional valence from negative to positive. This paper describes an experimental study of using multiple regression analysis for measuring the emotional valence from biological signals.

We begin our study by conducting some experiments investigating the relations between the subjects' various biological signals and the emotional index of images when the subjects are presented with the images from International Affective Picture System (IAPS) [4]. The reasons why we used the pictures are that the pictures had been evaluated with emotional valence and arousal as standard indexes in other studies. We run three different regression analysis models and found that Multivariate Adaptive Regression Spline (MARS) model has a contribution rate as high as 0.66 for describing the relations between the emotional valence and the biological signal of brain waves and cerebral blood flow. To validate the effectiveness of using the proposed emotion estimation technique for emotion based interaction, we implemented an interactive painting tool which dynamically adapts the colors of brush and the outline of canvas to the estimated emotion of the user.

The remainder of the paper is organized as follows: Section 2 briefly introduce the existing emotion estimation technologies based on biological signals. Section 3, 4 and 5 describes the biological signals we analyzed, the experiment upon which the multiple regression based technique is developed and the experiments for investigating the relation between users' emotion and drawing parameters. Section 6 presents the emotional painting tool as its application.

2   Related Work

Mandryk et al. [5] proposed a method for estimating the emotional states of game players by analyzing their galvanic skin response, electrocardiograms, and facial electromyograms. Jones et al. [6] proposed an automatic emotion detection system using a neural network with an 11-dimensional feature vector computed from blood volume pulse (BVP), skin conductance (SC), and respiration measurements. Their experiment shows that the degradability of emotion is not uniform along the valence axis. Similarly, Kim et al. [7] categorize emotions into nine different states within the framework of emotionally intelligent contents. While it is relatively easy to distinguish a negative state from a neutral state, distinguishing a positive state from a neutral state is usually difficult. Recently Wu et al. [8] proposed to use a support vector machine to classify psychophysiological responses in estimating arousal levels.

Cano et al. [9] suggest that the P300 event-related brain potential has larger amplitudes at frontal areas for positive images, compared to negative or neutral

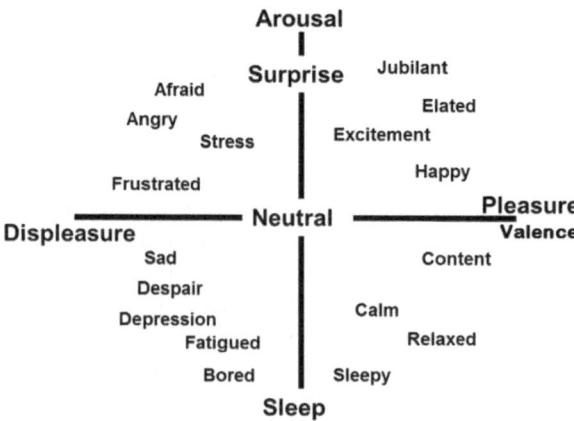

Fig. 1. Russell's arousal-valence 2D emotion model [3]

color images. The P300 is a features of brain waves at around 300 (300) ms in positive (P) electric potential. Murugappan et al. [10] summarize human emotion recognition through different sets of electroencephalogram (EEG) channels using discrete wavelet transforms while their subjects watch emotional video clips. Their experimental results indicate that one of the proposed features has a maximum average classification rate of 83.26 %. Yuen et al. [11] developed a back-propagation neural network to classify five types of emotions, with an overall classification rate of 95 %. Bos [12] suggests a classification procedure for recognizing emotions from brain signals measured with the Brainquiry EEG device. During the experiment, the best performances for arousal were for the power of beta waves at F3 and F4, which are measurement points of electrode on scalp. Mikhail et al. propose an approach that analyzes highly contaminated EEG data produced by a new emotion elicitation technique [13]. They achieved an average accuracy of 51 % for joy, 53 % for anger, 58 % for fear, and 61 % for sadness. Peter explored correlates between physiological patterns and emotions experienced by subjects [14]. He analyzed a multivariate Pearson Correlation of valence, arousal, electro-dermal activity, heart rate, pupil diameter and skin temperature. The all of the correlations among them are under 0.4.

The difference between the abovementioned studies and ours is that we integrate the biological signals of the central and autonomic nervous systems and develop a regression model for the continuous estimation of emotion. Most of the above mentioned studies recognize emotions either by a few levels (for example, unpleasant, neutral and pleasant) or status (for example, disgust, happy, surprise, and fear, neutral), while our model aims to estimate continuous levels in higher accuracy.

3   Biological Signals

This section introduces the biological signals analyzed in our experiments.

3.1 Central Nervous System

brain Waves. Electroencephalogram are detected on the scalp as neuronal electric fluctuations in the brain and are classified by frequency: theta (4-8 Hz), alpha (8-13 Hz), and beta (13-30 Hz). Alpha waves are detected when a person is relaxed and beta waves are detected when a person is concentrating. Additionally, event-related potentials (ERP) are detected as transient electric fluctuations due to an internal event. We recorded these data by using EEG-Z and EEG-Z3 sensors (Thought Technology Ltd.), classifying frequencies and calculating the power of each frequency band. Figure 2a shows such electrodes on a subject's forehead.

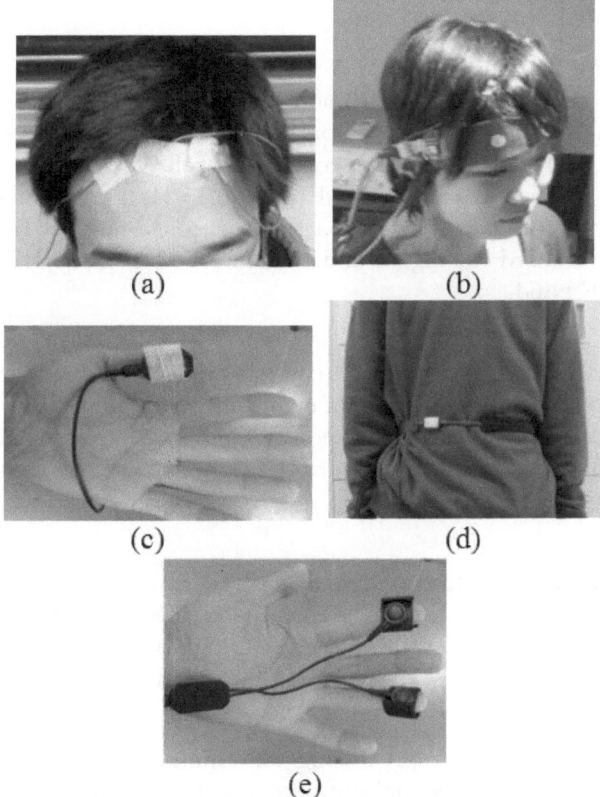

Fig. 2. Sensors to record biological signals. (a) EEG electrodes on a forehead, (b) a bandanna-type HEG sensor on a forehead, (c) a BVP sensor on a finger, (d) a belt-type respiration sensor and (e) a pair of SC electrodes on a hand

hemoencephalography (HEG). The level of oxygenated hemoglobin increases during brain activation. We therefore measure the CBF, the volume flow rate of oxygenated hemoglobin, obtained 2 cm subcutaneously at the forehead, by measuring the absorptive power of near-infrared and red light. For this we use a near-infrared headband (MediTECH Electronic GmbH; see figure 2b) to measure hemoencephalography (HEG) ratios, defined as the fractions of red light to near-infra red light, a measure of blood oxygenation. We use the HEG ratio calculated by the equation

$$HEG = \frac{RED}{IR} 200 \qquad (1)$$

where RED is the absorptive power of red light about oxygenated hemoglobin and unoxygenated hemoglobin, IR is the absorptive power of red light about oxygenated hemoglobin and unoxygenated hemoglobin.

3.2   Peripheral Nervous System

Blood Volume Pulse (BVP). A pulse wave is an index of the coarctation and angiectasis of peripheral blood vessels. The frequency characteristics of such waves reflect the tone of sympathetic and parasympathetic nerves. The high-frequency, or HF (0.15-0.4 Hz), component reflects the tone of sympathetic nerves, while the low-frequency, or LF (0.04-0.15 Hz), component reflects the tone of both types of nerves. We use a BVP sensor (Thought Technology Ltd.; see figure 2c) to record the signal and calculate power of the HF band and the power of the LF band.

Respiration. Respiratory movement consists of inspiration and expiration. The respiration rate (RESP) is an index of emotion, with an increase indicating tension and a decrease indicating relaxation. We use a respiration sensor (Thought Technology Ltd.; see figure 2d) to record the respiratory movement and calculate respiration rate from them.

Skin Conductance (SC). A hand's SC reflects conduction changes due to the eccrine sweat between two fingers. The value of the sensor increases when the subject is in an excitatory state or a stressful situation. We use an SC sensor (Thought Technology Ltd.; see figure 2e) that measures it in micro-Siemens.

Preprocessing. As the preprocessing for eliminating individual differences among users, the biological signal data are standardized by the equation

$$Z = \frac{X - \mu}{\sigma} \qquad (2)$$

where X is the raw data when stimulus are presented, μ and σ are the mean and standard deviation in neutral state. Equation (2) is used to calculate the indexes of Electroencephalogram, HEG ratios, and SC. The indexes of the respiration rate and pulse rate are calculated using the relative ratios of the experimental and neutral values.

4   Experiment 1: Emotional Images and Biological Signals

Our hypothesis is that biological signals of central nervous system lead to a high accuracy continuous model to estimate emotional valence ranging from positive to negative. We, therefore, first investigated the relations between subject's biological signals of central nervous system and the subjective emotional indexes (valence and arousal) when the images from International Affective Picture System (IAPS) [4] are presented. After measuring the signals, we run three regression analysis models and adopted the one with the highest contribution rate.

4.1   Environment

Figure 3 shows our experimental setting. A 17-inch (1280 x1024 pixel) monitor in front of a subject is used to display an image as a visual stimulus. We use the oddball paradigm for the experiment. The oddball task is to react to a target stimulus that is low occurrence rate amongst common stimuli. The subject, therefore, presses a button when a target image is presented. We use the 10-20 system to place both the HEG sensors and EEG electrodes. The 10-20 system is an internationally method to describe and apply the location of scalp electrodes. Each site has a letter that consists of an alphabet character(s) such as F, T, C, p and O with a numeric character. One HEG sensor is placed at Fp2 and two electrodes are placed at F3 and F4.

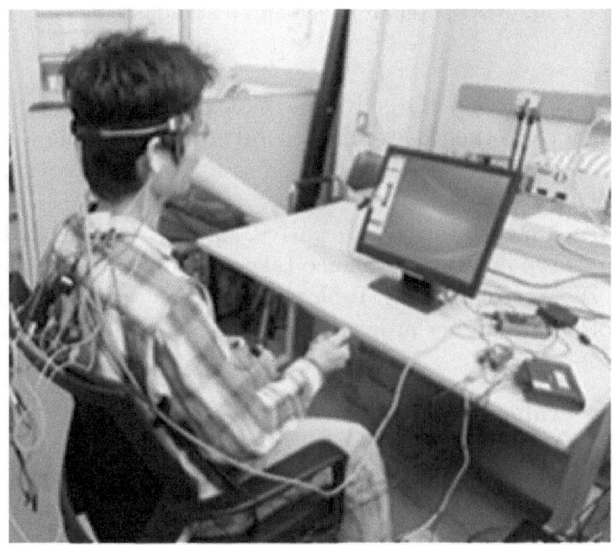

Fig. 3. An experimental setting

A total of 12 subjects (10 males and two females), 21 to 23 years old, participated in the experiment. The number of the subjects is determined by referring
to other studies [9] [11] [12].

4.2   Task

The subject carries out an oddball task that requires pressing a button when
a target image is displayed. There are three types of visual stimulus: a target
image, a standard image, and an interval image. The interval image is simply a
black point over a white background (figure 4a) and is displayed for 4 seconds
between the other images. The standard image is a checkered pattern (figure 4b)
and the target images are taken from IAPS and depict emotional scenes. The
standard image and the target image are each displayed for 1 second. The ratio
of the frequency of the target image to that of the standard image is 3 to 7.

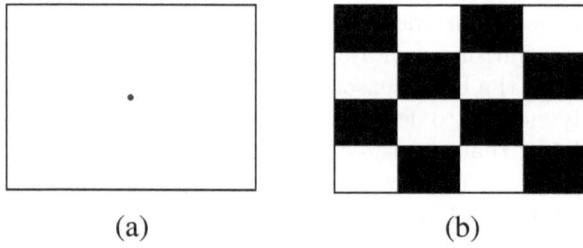

(a)   (b)

Fig. 4. An interval image and a standard image

Before starting the task, the subjects' biological signals are recorded for 1
minute while they close their eyes in a neutral state. After the task, the subject
fills out a nine-step Likert scale questionnaire about the emotional valences of
the target images.

We used three images, positive, negative, and neutral, from IAPS, each of
which has a nine-step emotional valence Likert scale and a nine-step emotional
arousal Likert scale as shown in Table 1. A higher valence value indicates a
positive emotion and a higher arousal value indicates high arousal.

Table 1. Experimental pictures from IAPS [4]

IAPS number (description)	Valence (SD)	Arousal (SD)
1440 (seal)	8.19 (1.53)	4.61 (2.54)
2780 (actor)	4.77 (1.76)	4.86 (2.05)
2900 (crying boy)	2.45 (1.42)	5.09 (2.15)

4.3   Results

Figure 5 shows the boxplot of the result of the questionnaire on valence. There is a significant difference ($p < 0.001$) between the valence score of image No. 1440 and that of the other two images, which means No. 1440 has a higher valence than the other two.

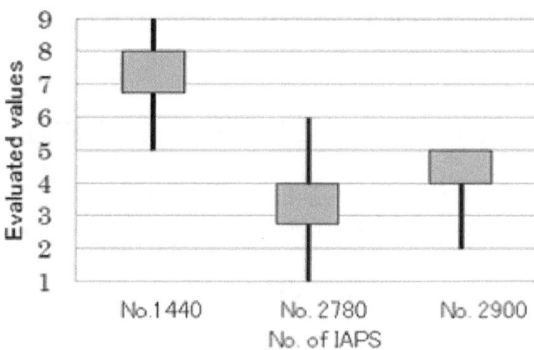

Fig. 5. Evaluated values of emotional valences of the pictures

We conducted three types of multiple regression analyses: stepwise, logistic and Multivariate Adaptive Regression Spline (MARS) [15], with the emotional valence as an objective variable and the biological indexes as explanatory variables. The contribution ratios of the stepwise, logistic, and MARS methods are 0.49, 0.64, and 0.66, respectively. The MARS method is the highest ratio among them, and the ratio means that the method can steplessly estimate a value of valence with 0.66 contribution ratio. Therefore, the method can explain the relation between valence and biological indexes more accurately than the related works described in Section 2.

The relation between the evaluated emotional valence and biological indexes by using MARS method is as follows:

$$
V = C
\begin{pmatrix}
((\alpha_2(F4) + 0.09 \\
-0.09 - \alpha_2(F4) \\
\theta(F4) - 0.15) \\
0.15 - \theta(F4) \\
\theta(F3) - 0.07 \\
HEG(Fp2) + 0.50 \\
-0.50 - HEG(Fp2) \\
P300(F4) * (0.15 - \theta(F4)) \\
(0.86 - \alpha_1(F4)) * (\alpha_2(F4) + 0.09) \\
(-0.09 - \alpha_2(F4)) * (\beta(F4) + 0.39) \\
(-0.09 - \alpha_2(F4)) * (-0.59 - \theta(F4)) \\
(-0.09 - \alpha_2(F4)) * (HEG(Fp2) + 0.39) \\
(-0.09 - \alpha_2(F4)) * (-0.39 - HEG(Fp2)) \\
(\theta(F3) - 0.07) * (0.06 - HEG(Fp2)))
\end{pmatrix}
+ 5.75 \qquad (3)
$$

where C is a matrix of the standardized coefficient. Table 2 shows the regression coefficients of the physiological indexes. The values indicate that the HEG, alpha2, and alpha2 indexes have high coefficients. The experiment showed that the difference of emotional images invokes the difference of biological signals. HEG, alpha1, and alpha2 signals are especially important in estimating a subject's emotional valences. Therefore, the results support our hypothesis that biological signals of central nervous system lead to a high accuracy continuous estimation model.

5   Elements of Drawing and Biological Signals

Following the results of the experiment 1, we found that there are relations between biological signals of central nervous system and emotional valence when presented with IAPS pictures. We further conducted two experiments to investigate the relations between viewer's biological signals and the different visual elements of pictures so as to associate the biological signals with the emotions of these visual elements. Finally with the results of these two experiments, we develop a drawing tool which can automatically adapting the drawing parameters to the emotion of users.

Table 2. The regression coefficients of the relational model (MARS) between the emotions and the physiological indexes

Explanatory variable	regression coefficient
$\alpha_2(F4) + 0.09$	2.60
$-0.09 - \alpha_2(F4)$	-7.85
$\theta(F4) - 0.15$	-0.55
$0.15 - \theta(F4)$	4.03
$\theta(F3) - 0.07$	-4.78
$HEG(Fp2) + 0.50$	-0.83
$-0.50 - HEG(Fp2)$	-10.87
$P300(F4) * (0.15 - \theta(F4))$	2.16
$(0.86 - \alpha_1(F4)) * (\alpha_2(F4) + 0.09)$	-2.77
$(-0.09 - \alpha_2(F4)) * (\beta(F4) + 0.39)$	9.96
$(-0.09 - \alpha_2(F4)) * (-0.59 - \theta(F4))$	14.03
$(-0.09 - \alpha_2(F4)) * (HEG(Fp2) + 0.39)$	2.66
$(-0.09 - \alpha_2(F4)) * (-0.39 - HEG(Fp2))$	11.21
$(\theta(F3) - 0.07) * (0.06 - HEG(Fp2))$	7.24

5.1   Experiment 2: Colors and Line Width and Biological Signals

We investigated the relations between viewer's biological signals and differences of basic elements of drawing when filtered images from IAPS are presented. We generated line images from two kinds of IAPS pictures (see Table 3) by detecting edges of the pictures and changing the color (orange or blue) of the edges and

Table 3. Experimental pictures from IAPS [4]

IAPS number (description)	Valence (SD)	Arousal (SD)
1590 (horse)	7.24 (1.45)	4.80 (2.10)
6570 (suicide)	2.19 (1.76)	6.24(2.16)

Fig. 6. The pictures used as stimulus in the experiment

the line width (thick or thin) of the edges. Therefore, our hypothesis is that the shape and color of edges affect biological signals of central nervous system in spite of the same content of the pictures.

Procedure. The experimental task is an oddball task similar to that of experiment 1. Viewers are presented with the eight pictures. The experimental factors are content of a picture (pleasure and displeasure), drawing color (orange and blue) and line width (thick or thin). Figure 6 shows the eight types of the pictures.

Each viewer looks at each of the eight pictures as a target stimulus in the oddball task. Recorded biological signals are EEG on F3 (10-20 system), F4 (10-20 system) and Fz (10-20 system) and HEG on Fp2 (10-20 system). Eight viewers (7 males and 1 female, from 21 to 24 years old) participated in the experiment. The number of the subjects is determined by referring to other studies [11] [12].

Result. We analyzed the data with a three-way ANOVA. There is significantly deferent between the average of HEG ratio when the orange pictures were presented and the average of HEG ratio when the blue pictures were presented ($p < 0.05$) as the main effect of the two types of the colors. The average of HEG ratio of the blue pictures is significantly higher than that of the orange is.

We also found that there is first-order interaction about the average power of the theta brain waves (F3) between the content factor and the color factor and between the color factor and the width factor ($p < 0.05$) (see figure 7). The results of sub-effect tests about the interaction show that there is a simple main

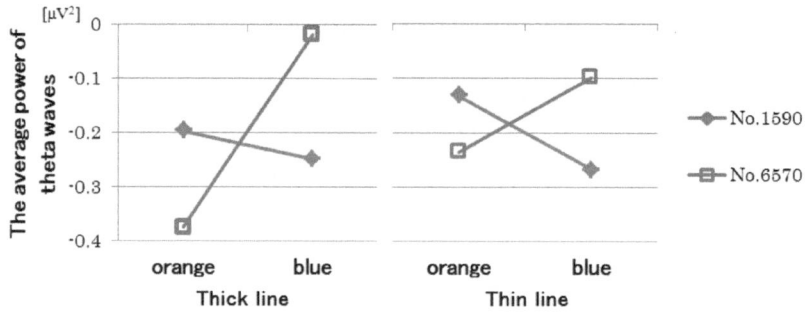

Fig. 7. The average power of theta brain waves when each picture was presented

effect between the orange and the blue of the displeased pictures ($p < 0.001$), there is a simple main effect between the blue pleased pictures and the blue displeased pictures ($p < 0.05$) and there is a simple main effect between the orange thick line and the blue thick line ($p < 0.001$). The results indicate that the power of theta waves when the blue displeased pictures were presented is significantly higher than that when the orange displeased pictures were presented is. Moreover, the results also indicate that the power of theta waves when the blue displeased pictures were presented is significantly higher than that when the blue pleased pictures were presented is. Therefore, we found that the results support the results of experiment 1, which show that power of theta brain waves negatively correlated with the value of valence.

The results of the experiment show relationships among colors, valence and biological signals. The results support our hypothesis about colors and line width. Additionally, the results support the results of Plutchik et al. [16] and Pan et al. [17], which showed that blue color represents displeasure and orange color represents pleasure.

5.2   Experiment 3: Colors and Shapes and Biological Signals

We investigate relations between viewer's biological data and painting elements: colors of brush, color and shape of a canvas. Our hypothesis of the experiment is that drawing color, background color and shape of canvas affect viewers' emotional valence, emotional arousal and biological signals even when the contents of the pictures remain unchanged.

Procedure. The experimental task is an oddball task similar to that of experiment 1. As the visual stimuli, viewers are presented with eight pictures in different drawing parameters. The pictures are line drawings generated from a single image evaluated as neutral in IAPS study [4]. The experimental factors are drawing color (red, green, blue, and yellow), background color (white and black) and shape of a canvas (rounded and cuspate). The reason why we focus on shape of a canvas is that existing studies have shown there are strong relationships between shapes and emotions [18] [19] [20]. Figure 8 shows the eight types of pictures based on L8 orthogonal array and the factors. Each viewer looks at each of them as a target stimulus in the oddball task. After that, they answered the value of nine-step emotional valence Likert scale and the value of nine-step emotional arousal Likert scale of each picture.

Recorded biological signals are EEG, HEG of central nervous system RESP, BVP and SC of peripheral nervous system. The reason why we recorded the multiple signals of both nervous systems is that we wanted to investigate which types of signals, either of peripheral nervous system or central nervous systems, reflect the valence or arousal more. The laterality index between F3 and F4 of the EEG is defined as an explanatory variable based on following expression [9].

$$LI_k = \frac{P_k(F3) - P_k(F4)}{P_k(F3) + P_k(F4)} \tag{4}$$

where P is the spectral power value. The reason why we used the biological signals of peripheral nervous system is that the signals are related to emotional arousal [21].

Eight viewers (7 males and 1 female, from 21 to 24 years old) participated in the experiment.

Result. Figure 9 shows the boxplots of the evaluated values about emotional valence and emotional arousal of the pictures. The figure shows that valence was little evoked by the pictures and that arousal was evoked more than the valence. We analyzed the evaluated values by ANOVA. As the results, there is significant difference about valence between white background and black background ($p < 0.01$). It means that the white background evoked positive valence than the black background. There is significant difference about arousal among drawing colors ($p < 0.01$). By conducting multiple comparisons, the results show that the red and yellow evoked arousal more than the green and blue. Moreover, there is significant difference between rounded and cuspate about arousal. It means that the shape of cuspate canvas evoked arousal more than the shape of rounded canvas.

After the statistical test, we analyzed the data with regression analysis in order to model the relationship between shape of a canvas and biological data as well as the relationship between viewers' arousal and their biological data. The objective variables are the experimental factors: brush color (red, green, blue and yellow) in optical wavelength, canvas color of either 0(white) or 1(black), and canvas shape of either 0(rounded) or 1(cuspate). The explanatory variables are biological signals. We used a logistic regression model and the contribution ratio about the relation between biological data and brush color is 0.26, biological data and canvas color is 0.27, biological data and canvas shape is 0.42. Expression (5) indicates the logistic regression model between the biological data and canvas shape.

Fig. 8. The pictures used as stimulus in the experiment

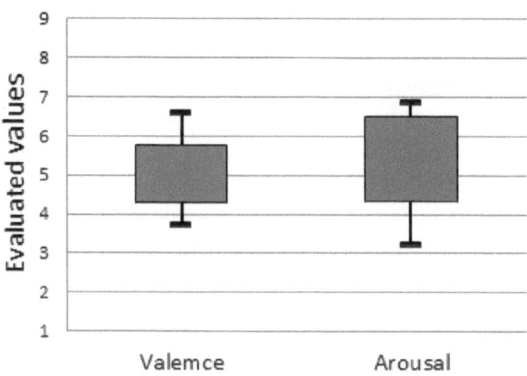

Fig. 9. Evaluated values of emotional valence and arousal of the pictures

$$FO = \cfrac{1}{1 + exp\left[-C\begin{pmatrix} Comp7 \\ Comp8 \\ Comp12 \\ Comp16 \\ Comp18 \end{pmatrix}\right]} \tag{5}$$

where FO is either 0 or 1 and C is the matrix of standardized coefficients. Table 4 shows a principal component score graph of the expression (5). As is obvious from the table, the 18th principal component is larger than the others. The table and the expression mean that the value of $\alpha_2(F3)$ was high when the viewers looked at the rounded canvases. They also mean that the amplitude of pulses is higher when the viewers looked at the cuspate canvases compared with the case when they looked at the rounded canvases.

Table 4. Principal component scores

	7th	8th	12th	16th	18th
$P300(Fz)$	-0.048	-0.165	0.096	0.298	-0.084
$\theta(F3)$	0.071	-0.031	-0.030	0.053	-0.076
$\alpha_1(F3)$	0.096	-0.019	-0.025	0.047	-0.052
$\alpha_2(F3)$	0.099	0.021	-0.048	0.261	0.676
$\alpha_3(F3)$	-0.061	0.036	0.152	-0.040	0.274
$\beta(F3)$	0.252	0.194	-0.335	-0.033	-0.086
$\theta(F4)$	0.011	-0.057	-0.029	-0.197	-0.185
$\alpha_1(F4)$	-0.032	-0.067	-0.088	-0.349	-0.398
$\alpha_2(F4)$	-0.010	-0.079	-0.054	-0.252	0.114
$\alpha_3(F4)$	0.111	-0.021	0.086	0.602	-0.370
$\beta(F4)$	0.173	0.118	-0.155	0.277	-0.004
$HEG(Fp2)$	-0.217	-0.033	0.385	-0.126	0.219
$Resp$	0.149	0.014	0.060	-0.251	-0.016
BVP	-0.146	-0.041	-0.322	0.041	0.021
SC	0.413	-0.057	0.137	-0.244	0.112
HF	0.746	-0.162	0.031	-0.027	0.034
LF/HF	-0.055	0.323	-0.317	0.035	0.081
LI_θ	0.084	0.665	0.177	-0.070	-0.069
LI_{α_1}	-0.039	0.240	-0.246	-0.133	0.059
LI_{α_2}	-0.112	0.032	0.330	0.033	-0.128
LI_{α_3}	0.011	0.474	0.075	0.052	-0.036
LI_β	0.133	0.195	0.472	0.022	-0.067

The contributing ratio of a logistic regression model between evaluated values about arousal and biological data after conducting principal component analysis is 0.75 in a condition of white background. The logistic regression model between the biological data and evaluated emotional arousal is given as.

$$AR = \cfrac{1}{1 + exp\left[-E\begin{bmatrix}\begin{pmatrix}Comp1\\Comp3\\Comp7\\Comp10\\Comp13\\Comp15\\Comp16\\Comp17\end{pmatrix}\end{bmatrix}\right]} \tag{6}$$

where AR is emotional arousal and E is the matrix of standardized coefficients. Table 5 shows a principal component score graph of the expression (6). As is obvious from the table, the 17th principal component is larger than the others. Moreover, because the signs of the principal component score of the BVP are similar to the signs of the coefficients, we found that the number of pulses from BVP increases when the user's arousal is high.

Table 5. Principal component scores

	1st	3rd	7th	10th	13th	15th	16th	17th
$HEG(Fp2)$	-0.053	0.073	-0.342	-0.076	0.205	0.042	-0.057	-0.100
$P300(Fz)$	-0.187	0.156	0.295	-0.574	-0.254	-0.164	0.262	0.121
$\theta(F3)$	-0.052	0.346	0.095	-0.086	0.071	0.382	-0.384	-0.110
$\alpha_1(F3)$	-0.349	0.059	-0.08	-0.019	-0.194	-0.272	-0.226	-0.222
$\alpha_2(F3)$	-0.346	0.062	-0.134	0.139	-0.144	-0.121	0.043	-0.223
$\alpha_3(F3)$	-0.344	0.076	-0.097	0.134	0.263	0.161	-0.322	-0.021
$\beta(F3)$	-0.261	-0.202	0.060	-0.173	0.044	0.196	-0.046	0.027
$\theta(F4)$	-0.075	0.049	-0.129	-0.058	-0.260	0.315	-0.026	0.195
$\alpha_1(F4)$	-0.355	0.052	-0.069	-0.009	-0.232	-0.198	-0.197	-0.108
$\alpha_2(F4)$	-0.348	0.072	-0.060	0.242	-0.111	-0.047	0.501	0.046
$\alpha_3(F4)$	-0.338	0.032	-0.092	0.256	0.156	0.307	0.278	0.172
$\beta(F4)$	-0.242	0.062	-0.102	-0.297	0.096	0.159	-0.047	0.490
$Resp$	-0.126	-0.292	0.314	-0.183	-0.166	0.274	-0.139	-0.443
BVP	-0.156	0.096	0.392	-0.106	0.193	-0.101	0.010	0.097
SC	0.136	0.211	-0.411	-0.106	-0.392	0.155	0.149	-0.213
HF	0.060	-0.192	-0.496	-0.455	0.068	-0.071	-0.039	0.013
LF/HF	-0.023	0.222	-0.045	-0.244	0.309	-0.160	0.050	-0.004
LI_θ	0.120	0.194	0.038	0.177	-0.238	-0.158	-0.304	0.306
LI_{α_1}	-0.017	0.270	-0.105	0.013	0.029	-0.219	-0.211	0.132
LI_{α_2}	0.088	0.280	0.123	0.077	-0.386	0.161	-0.078	0.199
LI_{α_3}	0.128	0.377	0.035	-0.102	0.070	0.363	0.210	-0.227
LI_β	-0.033	-0.472	-0.065	0.015	-0.235	0.198	-0.124	0.291

We found that there is a strong relationship among shape, emotion and bio-logical signals because of the high contribution ratio. Omata et al and Lockyer et al. obtained a similar result in their studies [18] [20]. On the other hand, regarding the color, we found it is necessary to user stronger stimulus because of the low contribution ratio among colors, emotion and biological signals.

6   Emotional Painting Tool

Figure 10 illustrates the concept of the emotional painting system. Emotional painting is realized by looping through the following 3 steps:

1. The Sensing step collects the biological data of the user with the sensors attached to the user.
2. The analysis step applies multiple regression model to the biological data to estimate the emotion status of the user.
3. The mapping step maps the emotion status to the drawing parameters, such as the color of brush and the shape of canvas.

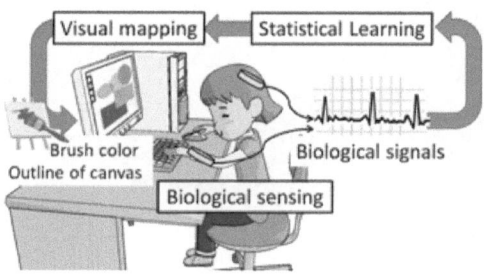

Fig. 10. A conceptual diagram of Emotional Painting System

The proposed painting tool allows a user to understand his/her own emotion through the feedback loop, and adapt the content of the drawing to the change of emotion. By building an emotional feedback loop into a creative tool or a self-expression tool, we expect to intensify emotion and stimulate creativity and imagination of users.

We have implemented two prototyping systems. One allows a user to doodle on a screen directly with the color of the brush adapted to the emotion of the user in real time (see figure 11). The other further provides the user a canvas with its shape and background color adapted to the emotion in addition to the brush color (see figure 12).

The first prototype system allows a user to automatically reflect valence and arousal of emotion to value and saturation of a brush color by estimating user's emotion from user's physiological data and tracking the position of the brush with a 3 dimensional tracker, which a user uses for doodle painting. The measuring data are electromyography (EMG) on angulus oris and glabella for estimating valence and SC for estimating arousal. The estimated valence values are mapped to brightness of a drawing color and the estimated arousal values are mapped to saturation of the color.

The second prototype system presents three canvases on the screen. The line styles of the drawings on the 3 canvases are the same, but the colors are all different (see figure 13). The left one is the original canvas on which the user can select a brush color through a color dialog box and paint interactively using a stylus pen. The upper right one is the emotional canvas on which the brush color as well as the color and shape of the canvas itself changes dynamically along with user's emotions estimated from biological signals. The lower right one is a transitional canvas with a shape similar to that of emotional canvas and the color is a fusion of the original one and emotional one.

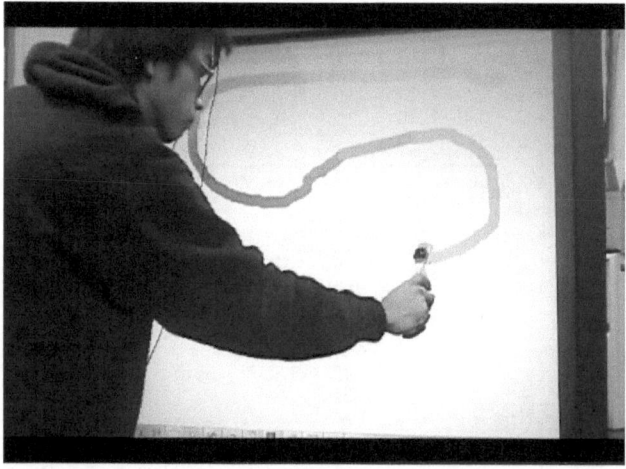

Fig. 11. Using the first prototype of the emotional painting tool

EEG, HEG ratio, BVP and SC of the user are recorded for estimating user's emotions of the prototypes. After the user wears the sensors, the data are recorded for 1 minute with the user being at rest in order to memorize the data of the neutral state as baseline to estimate changes. After that, the user can start drawing on the original canvas. The system records the data from the sensors, estimates user's emotion every 30 seconds by using logistic regression model and changes the color of the brush and the shape canvas accordingly.

The brush colors of the emotional canvas are determined by emotional valence and emotional arousal of the user. The valence is calculated by the MARS model by expression (3) described in chapter 4. The arousal is calculated by the logistic regression model by expression (6) described in chapter 5. With the valence value

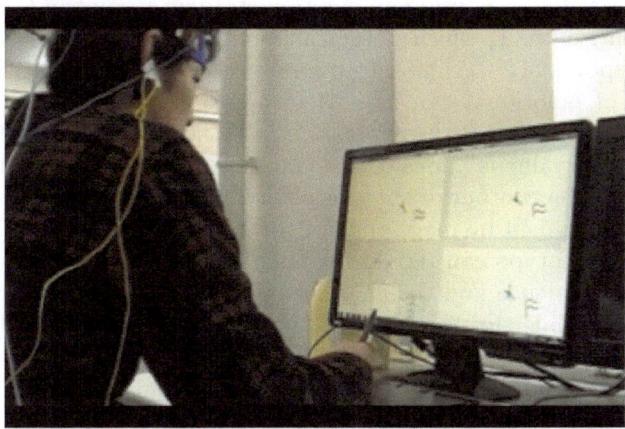

Fig. 12. Using the second prototype of the emotional painting tool

Fig. 13. The screen of the second prototype

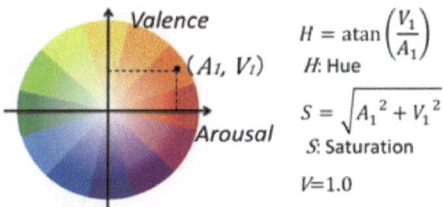

$$H = \operatorname{atan}\left(\frac{V_1}{A_1}\right)$$

H: Hue

$$S = \sqrt{{A_1}^2 + {V_1}^2}$$

S: Saturation

V=1.0

Fig. 14. Mapping between color and emotion space

and the arousal value, we obtain an emotion state as a point in the 2D emotion space shown in Figure 1, which is then mapped to a color based on the color-emotion correspondence [17] as shown in figure 14.

The shape of emotional canvas is determined by expression (5) described above. When the F value of the expression is 0, the canvas is standardly square shaped. When the value is above 0, the shape becomes more cuspate. When the value is under 0, the contour of the canvas becomes sin waves. The frequency of the waves is determined by magnitude of the arousal.

The second prototype can record the time series variation of user's emotion (the value of the valence and the value of the arousal) and user's drawing data every 30 seconds while the user is drawing a picture with it. Therefore, the user can confirm the series of his/her emotion and reflect them by him/herself after finishing drawing. The system can also express the time series variation of user's drawing by representing scene-by-scene cutoff animation. Therefore, the user and viewers can see not only a finished picture but also the time series variation of drawing it and the series of the drawer's emotions for self-expression.

One drawback of current prototypes is that users are forced to wear some wired sensors, which can actually affect the emotion of users. Therefore, we are planning to use wireless sensors instead of the wired sensors for the next prototype.

7   Concluding Remarks

We have proposed a technique using multiple repression analysis based on elementary experiments to estimate user emotion from biological signals. The effectiveness of the proposed method in emotion based interaction is demonstrated through its application to an interactive emotional painting tool. Drawing and painting are one of the most effective forms of self-expression and communication. People draw when thinking about a new idea, paint when being moved by a beautiful scene, and doodle when get frustrated. From an art work, we can read one's mood, emotion or even personality. Allowing users to easily express their emotion in their works without the necessity of low level parameter controlling would benefit many applications.

As a future work, we are going to conduct usability testing about the consistency between user's real emotion and the estimated one. Moreover, we are going to increase accuracy of the estimation methods by repeatedly conducting the same experiments with more subjects.

Acknowledgement. This work was supported by Grant-in-Aid for Scientific Research (C) (23500326).

References

1. Mitsuyoshi, S., Ren, F., Tanaka, Y., Kuroiwa, S.: Non-verbal voice emotion analysis system. International Journal of Innovative Computing, Information and Control 12(4), 819–830 (2006)

2. Shugrina, M., Betke, M., Collomosse, J.: Empathic painting: interactive stylization through observed emotional state. In: Proceedings of the 4th International Symposium on Non-Photorealistic Animation and Rendering, NPAR 2006, pp. 87–96. ACM, New York (2006)
3. Russell, J.: A circumplex model of affect. Journal of Personality and Social Psychology 39(6), 1161–1178 (1980)
4. Lang, P.J., Bradley, M.M., Cuthbert, B.N.: International affective picture system (iaps): Technical manual and affective ratings. Technical report, University of Florida (1999)
5. Mandryk, R.L., Atkins, M.S., Inkpen, K.M.: A continuous and objective evaluation of emotional experience with interactive play environments. In: Proceedings of the SIGCHI Conference on Human Factors in Computing Systems, CHI 2006, pp. 1027–1036. ACM, New York (2006)
6. Jones, C.M., Troen, T.: Biometric valence and arousal recognition. In: Proceedings of the 19th Australasian Conference on Computer-Human Interaction: Entertaining User Interfaces, OZCHI 2007, pp. 191–194. ACM, New York (2007)
7. Kim, M., Park, K.S., Kim, D., Cho, Y.: Emotional intelligent contents: Expressing user's own emotion within contents. In: Anacleto, J.C., Fels, S., Graham, N., Kapralos, B., Saif El-Nasr, M., Stanley, K. (eds.) ICEC 2011. LNCS, vol. 6972, pp. 391–394. Springer, Heidelberg (2011)
8. Wu, D., Courtney, C.G., Lance, B.J., Narayanan, S.S., Dawson, M.E., Oie, K.S., Parsons, T.D.: Optimal arousal identification and classification for affective computing using physiological signals: Virtual reality stroop task. IEEE Transactions on Affective Computing 1(2), 109–118 (2010)
9. Cano, M.E., Class, Q.A., Polich, J.: Affective valence, stimulus attributes, and p300: Color vs. black/white and normal vs. scrambled images. International Journal of Psychophysiology 71(1), 17–24 (2009) (Electrophysiology of Affect and Cognition)
10. Murugappan, M.: Classification of human emotion from EEG using discrete wavelet transform. Journal of Biomedical Science and Engineering 03(04), 390–396 (2010)
11. Yuen, C.T., San, W.S., Seong, T.C., Rizon, M.: Classification of human emotions from eeg signals using statistical features and neural network. International Journal of Integrated Engineering 1(3), 71–79 (2011)
12. Bos, D.O.: Eeg-based emotion recognition the influence of visual and auditory stimuli (2006)
13. Mikhail, M., El-Ayat, K., El Kaliouby, R., Coan, J., Allen, J.J.B.: Emotion detection using noisy eeg data. In: Proceedings of the 1st Augmented Human International Conference, AH 2010, vol. 7, pp. 7:1–7:7. ACM, New York (2010)
14. Pan, J.: Physiological sensing for affective computing. PhD Thesis, University of Rostock (2011)
15. Friedman, J.H.: Multivariate Adaptive Regression Splines. The Annals of Statistics 19(1), 1–67 (1991)
16. Plutchik, R.: The emotions. University Press of Americas (1991)
17. Pan, J.: An analytic study on the color expression of opposed feeling-images. The Color Science Association of Japan 23(4), 232–239 (1999)
18. Omata, M., Naito, Y., Imamiya, A.: Design and evaluation of an online chat system using speech balloons changed by user's biomedical signals. Human Interface Society 10(2), 179–189 (2008)

19. Isbister, K., Höök, K., Sharp, M., Laaksolahti, J.: The sensual evaluation instrument: developing an affective evaluation tool. In: Proceedings of the SIGCHI Conference on Human Factors in Computing Systems, CHI 2006, pp. 1163–1172. ACM, New York (2006)
20. Lockyer, M., Bartram, L., Riecke, B.E.: Simple motion textures for ambient affect. In: Proceedings of the International Symposium on Computational Aesthetics in Graphics, Visualization, and Imaging, CAe 2011, pp. 89–96. ACM, New York (2011)
21. Moriwaki, K., Omata, M., Kanuka, D., Mao, X., Imamiya, A.: A design of visual effects for affecting user arousal by measuring user's physiological data. The Institute of Image Electronics Engineers of Japan 40(5), 768–777 (2011)

Real-Time Subject-Dependent EEG-Based Emotion Recognition Algorithm

Yisi Liu and Olga Sourina

Fraunhofer IDM@NTU, Nanyang Technological University
Singapore
{LIUYS,EOSourina}@ntu.edu.sg

Abstract. In this paper, we proposed a real-time subject-dependent EEG-based emotion recognition algorithm and tested it on experiments' databases and the benchmark database DEAP. The algorithm consists of two parts: feature extraction and data classification with Support Vector Machine (SVM). Use of a Fractal Dimension feature in combination with statistical and Higher Order Crossings (HOC) features gave results with the best accuracy and with adequate computational time. The features were calculated from EEG using a sliding window. The proposed algorithm can recognize up to 8 emotions such as happy, surprised, satisfied, protected, angry, frightened, unconcerned, and sad using 4 electrodes in real time. Two experiments with audio and visual stimuli were implemented, and the Emotiv EPOC device was used to collect EEG data.

Keywords: emotion recognition, EEG, emotion recognition algorithms, Emotiv EPOC, Valence-Arousal-Dominance model.

1   Introduction

Recently, the EEG devices became wireless, more portable, wearable and easy to use, thus more research can be done on real-time emotion recognition algorithms. Emotion recognition algorithms can be subject-dependent and subject-independent. Subject-dependent algorithms have a better accuracy than subject-independent algorithms but the system training session for each individual user should be designed and implemented in the subject-dependent algorithms.

In this paper, we proposed and implemented a real-time subject-dependent algorithm based on the Valence-Arousal-Dominance (VAD) emotion model. A combination of features including Fractal Dimension (FD) was used because FD values reflect nonlinearity of EEG signals. Fractal Dimension analysis is a suitable approach for analyzing nonlinear systems and can be used in real-time EEG signal processing [4,72]. Early works show that Fractal Dimension can reflect changes in EEG signals [58], and Fractal Dimension is varied for different mental tasks [48]. In [63,66], music was used as a stimulus to elicit emotions, and Fractal Dimension was applied for the analysis of the EEG signal. In [5], it was demonstrated that the difference between positive and negative emotions can be discovered by estimating the dimensional complexity of the signal. Recent supporting evidence such as [23] and [24] shows that Fractal Dimension can reflect

M.L. Gavrilova et al. (Eds.): Trans. on Comput. Sci. XXIII, LNCS 8490, pp. 199–223, 2014.
© Springer-Verlag Berlin Heidelberg 2014

the activity of the sensorimotor cortex. More supporting evidence to successful use of Fractal Dimension in EEG analysis in different applications is described in [48,58,63,66]. These works show that Fractal Dimension based EEG analysis is a potentially promising approach in EEG-based emotion recognition.

Our hypothesis is that the feeling of changes can be noticed from EEG as fractal dimension changes. In 2008, we started to use fractal dimension to recognize positive and negative emotions from EEG [63]. In 2010, we proposed to use Higuchi algorithm for fractal feature extraction for real-time emotion recognition. We calculated subject dependent thresholds of emotions recognition, and we visualized emotions in real time on a virtual avatar [43,44]. At the same year, [33] and [26] also confirmed that Higuchi fractal dimension can be used in EEG-based emotion recognition algorithms. In 2011, we studied the fractal dimension methods such as box-counting and Higuchi using mono fractal signals generated by Brownian and Weierstrass functions [73] and in [64] both algorithms were applied to recognize high/low arousal and positive/negative valence [64]. In [46], two affective EEG databases were presented; two experiments were conducted to set up the databases. Audio and visual stimuli were used to evoke emotions during the experiments. In [46] and this work, we proposed to use a FD feature to improve emotion recognition algorithm accuracy. The algorithm consists of two parts: feature extraction and classification with the Support Vector Machine (SVM) classifier. Use of a Fractal Dimension feature in combination with statistical and Higher Order Crossings (HOC) features gave the results with the best accuracy and with adequate computational time. The features' values were calculated from EEG using a sliding window.

In the VAD model, the emotions are described as follows: a "satisfied" emotion is defined as a positive/ low arousal/ high dominance emotion, a "happy" emotion is defined as a positive/ high arousal/ high dominance emotion, a "surprised" emotion is defined as a positive/ high arousal/ low dominance emotion, a "protected" emotion is defined as a positive/ low arousal/ low dominance emotion, a "sad" emotion is defined as a negative/ low arousal/ low dominance emotion, a "unconcerned" emotion is defined as a negative/ low arousal/ high dominance emotion, a "angry" emotion is defined as a negative/ high arousal/ high dominance emotion and a "frightened" emotion is defined as a negative/high arousal/low dominance emotion [51], etc. The proposed algorithm should be tested on the EEG databases labeled with emotions where emotions were induced by visual, audio, and combined (music video) stimuli, and the best combination of features should be proposed. In this paper, 2 series of experiments on emotion induction with audio stimuli and with visual stimuli were designed and implemented based on the Valence-Arousal-Dominance emotion model. The sounds were chosen to induce happy, surprised, satisfied, protected, angry, frightened, unconcerned, and sad emotions from International Affective Digitized Sounds (IADS) [13], and the visual stimuli were chosen from International Affective Picture System (IAPS) database [41]. The data were collected from 14 subjects in Experiment 1 and 16 subjects in Experiment 2. The questionnaire and Self-Assessment Manikin (SAM) [12] technique were applied. Two databases with

EEG data labeled with 8 emotions were created. Recently, the DEAP benchmark database that used music video stimuli for emotion induction became available [35]. The proposed algorithm was tested on the benchmark DEAP database and on our own two experiments' databases.

The paper is organized as follows. In Section 2, emotion classification models, and EEG-based emotion recognition algorithms are reviewed. Mathematical models of the channel choice algorithm, statistical features, Higher Order Crossings (HOC), Fractal Dimension (FD) algorithm and the Support Vector Machine classifier that were used for feature extraction and classification are introduced in Section 3. In Section 4, the proposed and implemented experiments are given. The affective EEG database DEAP is also briefly described. A real-time subject-dependent algorithm is described in Section 5. The algorithm results and discussion are given in Section 6. Finally, Section 7 concludes the paper.

2 Background

2.1 Emotion Classification Models

The most widely used approach to represent emotion is the bipolar model with valence and arousal dimensions proposed by Russell [60]. In this model, valence dimension ranges from "negative" to "positive", and arousal dimension ranges from "not aroused" to "excited". The 2-Dimensional (2D) model can locate the discrete emotion labels in its space [50], and it could define emotions which are even without discrete emotion labels. However, emotion of fear and anger cannot be differed if they were defined by the 2D model as they both have the same high arousal and negative valence level values.

In order to get a comprehensive description of emotions, Mehrabian and Russell proposed 3-Dimensional (3D) Pleasure (Valence)-Arousal-Dominance (PAD) model in [51] and [52]. "Pleasure-displeasure" dimension of the model equals to the valence dimension mentioned above, evaluating the pleasure level of the emotion. "Arousal-non-arousal" dimension is equivalent to the arousal dimension, referring to the alertness of an emotion. "Dominance-submissiveness" dimension is a newly extended dimension, which is also named as a control dimension of emotion [51,52]. It ranges from a feeling of being in control during an emotional experience to a feeling of being controlled by the emotion [10]. It makes the dimensional model more complete. With the Dominance dimension, more emotion labels can be located in the 3D space. For example, happiness and surprise are both emotions with positive valence and high arousal, and it can be differentiated by their dominance level since happiness is with high dominance, whereas surprise is with low dominance [51].

In our work, we use the 3-dimensional emotion classification model.

2.2 EEG-Based Emotion Recognition Algorithms

The EEG-based emotion recognition algorithms are different on their dependence on subjects during the recognition and they can be implemented in either a subject-dependent or a subject-independent way. The advantage of subject-dependent recognition is that a higher accuracy can be achieved since the classification is catered for each individual, but the disadvantage is that every time a classifier is needed to be trained for a new subject.

[15,29,42,43,61,74] are examples of subject-dependent algorithms. In [42,43] and [61], the discrete emotion model was used. Four emotions such as joy, anger, sadness, and pleasure were recognized in [42] with 32 channels and an averaged accuracy of 82.29% using the differential asymmetry of hemispheric EEG power spectra and SVM as a classifier. In [43], 6 emotions such as pleasure, satisfaction, happiness, sadness, frustration, and fear were recognized with the proposed subject-dependent algorithm. Three emotional reactions including "pleasant", "neutral" and "unpleasant" were recognized in [61] with 4 channels, and the average accuracy is 66.7%. In [15,29,74], the dimensional emotion model was used. Positive and negative emotional states based on the valence dimension in the 2D emotional model were recognized in [74], and the accuracy obtained was 73% using 3 channels. [15] recognized positive and negative states with 4 channels and obtained an accuracy of 57.04%. [29] recognized positive/ negative valence states with the best mean accuracy of 83.1%, and strong/calm arousal states with the best mean accuracy of 66.51% using 32 channels.

[8,16,62,70] are examples of subject-independent algorithms. [16,62,70] employed the discrete emotion model. By using the powers of different frequency bands of EEG signals as features, [16] got maximum 56% accuracy for 3 emotional states such as boredom, engagement, and anxiety detection. By using the statistical features and SVM, five emotions such as joy, anger, sadness, fear and relaxation were recognized with accuracy 41.7% in [70]. Although [8] can achieve an average accuracy of 94.27% across five emotions, 256 channels were compulsory in the recognition. [62] used the dimensional emotion model, and it obtained accuracies of 62.1% and 50.5% for detecting 3 levels of arousal and valence respectively, and 32 channels were needed in the algorithm.

In [56], both subject-dependent and subject-independent algorithms were proposed. 4 channels were used in the recognition. In the subject-dependent case of [56], the accuracy ranges from 70% to 100%, and in the subject-independent case, the accuracy drops by 10% to 20%. It is important to notice that in the reviewed works, the reported accuracy was calculated on their own datasets.

All the above-mentioned works show that the accuracy of the subject-dependent algorithms is generally higher than subject-independent algorithms. Thus, we developed a subject-dependent algorithm in our work. The number of emotions that is possible to recognize and the number of the electrodes that is used are very important for the algorithms comparison. For example, although the accuracy that was obtained in [42] is higher than in [74], 32 channels were needed in [42] compared with 3 channels used in [74]. Besides that, if the algorithm is developed for real-time applications, the time needed for features extraction and the number of channels used should be minimized. If more electrodes are used, the comfort level of the user who wears the device decreases as well. Thus, our main objective is to propose an algorithm performing with adequate accuracy in real-time applications.

3   Method

3.1   The Fisher Discriminant Ratio

The Fisher Discriminant Ratio (FDR) is a classical approach that is used to select channels [7,19,40]. The output of FDR is a score corresponding to each channel. The selection of channels will follow the rank of their FDR scores. The formula of FDR value calculation is as follows:

$$FDR(p) = \frac{\sum_{i=1}^{C} \sum_{j=1}^{C} (\mu_p^i - \mu_p^j)^2}{\sum_{i=1}^{C} (\sigma_p^i)^2}. \tag{1}$$

where C is the number of classes, p is the channel index, μ_p^i is the mean value of the feature from the pth channel for the ith class, and σ_p^i is the standard deviation of the feature from the pth channel for the ith class [34].

3.2   Statistical, Higher Order Crossings and Fractal Dimension Feature Extraction

Although the EEG signal is nonlinear [38,39], little has been done to investigate its nonlinear nature when emotion recognition research is conducted. Linear analysis such as Fourier Transform only preserves the power spectrum in the signal, but destroys the spike-wave structure [67].

In this work, we proposed to use Fractal Dimension feature in combination with statistical features [57], Higher Order Crossings (HOC) [32,55] to improve emotion recognition accuracy. Statistical and HOC features were used as they gave the highest emotion recognition accuracy as it was described in [55,57,70]. In this work, the Higuchi algorithm [25] was proposed to be used for FD values calculation. The algorithm gave better accuracy than other FD algorithms as it was shown in [73]. Details of these algorithms are given as below.

Statistical Features

1. The means of the raw signals

$$\mu_X = \frac{1}{N} \sum_{n=1}^{N} X(n). \tag{2}$$

2. The standard deviations of the raw signals

$$\sigma_X = \sqrt{\frac{1}{N} \sum_{n=1}^{N} (X(n) - \mu_X)^2}. \tag{3}$$

3. The means of the absolute values of the first differences of the raw signals

$$\delta_X = \frac{1}{N-1} \sum_{n=1}^{N-1} |X(n+1) - X(n)|. \tag{4}$$

4. The means of the absolute values of the first differences of the normalized signals

$$\overline{\delta_X} = \frac{1}{N-1} \sum_{n=1}^{N-1} |\overline{X}(n+1) - \overline{X}(n)| = \frac{\delta_X}{\sigma_X}. \tag{5}$$

5. The means of the absolute values of the second differences of the raw signals

$$\gamma_X = \frac{1}{N-2} \sum_{n=1}^{N-2} |X(n+2) - X(n)|. \tag{6}$$

6. The means of the absolute values of the second differences of the normalized signals

$$\overline{\gamma_X} = \frac{1}{N-2} \sum_{n=1}^{N-2} |\overline{X}(n+2) - \overline{X}(n)| = \frac{\gamma_X}{\sigma_X}. \tag{7}$$

Thus, the feature vector composed is

$$\boldsymbol{FV_{Statistical}} = [\mu_X, \sigma_X, \delta_X, \overline{\delta_X}, \gamma_X, \overline{\gamma_X}]. \tag{8}$$

HOC-Based Features. The algorithm of HOC is given as follows.
The input data is a finite zero-mean series $\{X_n\}, n = 1, ..., N$.
First, a sequence of filters are applied on the input data

$$\nabla^{k-1} X_n \equiv \sum_{j=1}^{k} \frac{(k-1)!}{(j-1)!(k-j)!} (-1)^{(j-1)} X_{n-j+1}. \tag{9}$$

where ∇^{k-1} denotes a sequence of filters, when $k = 1$, it becomes the identity filter.

Then the number of zero-crossings associated with a particular filter is counted. To get the counts of zero-crossings,

$$Z_n(K) = \begin{cases} 1 & if \nabla^{k-1} X_n \geq 0 \\ 0 & if \nabla^{k-1} X_n < 0 \end{cases} \tag{10}$$

is used and

$$D_k = \sum_{n=2}^{N} [Z_n(k) - Z_{n-1}(k)]^2. \tag{11}$$

represents the number of zero crossings.
As a result, the feature vector [55] is constructed as

$$\boldsymbol{FV_{HOC}} = [D_1, D_2, ..., D_k]. \tag{12}$$

Higuchi Algorithm. Let $X(1), X(2), \ldots, X(N)$ be a finite set of time series samples. Then, the newly constructed time series is

$$X_t^m : X(m), X(m+t), \ldots, X\left(m + \left[\frac{N-m}{t}\right] \cdot t\right). \tag{13}$$

where $m = 1, 2, \ldots, t$ is the initial time and t is the interval time [25].

For example, if $t = 3$ and $N = 100$, the newly constructed time series are:
$X_3^1 : X(1), X(4), \ldots, X(100), X_3^2 : X(2), X(5), \ldots, X(98),$
$X_3^3 : X(3), X(6), \ldots, X(99).$
t sets of $L_m(t)$ are calculated by

$$L_m(t) = \frac{\left\{\left(\sum_{i=1}^{\left[\frac{N-m}{t}\right]} |X(m+it) - X(m+(i-1)\cdot t)|\right) \frac{N-1}{\left[\frac{N-m}{t}\right] \cdot t}\right\}}{t}. \tag{14}$$

$\langle L(t)\rangle$ denotes the average value of $L_m(t)$, and one relationship exists

$$\langle L(t)\rangle \propto t^{-dim_H}. \tag{15}$$

Then, the fractal dimension dim_H could be obtained by logarithmic plotting between different t(ranging from 1 to t_{max}) and its associated $\langle L(t)\rangle$ [25].

$$dim_H = \frac{\ln \langle L(t)\rangle}{-\ln t}. \tag{16}$$

Thus, the feature vector composed is

$$\boldsymbol{FV_{FD(Higuchi)}} = [dim_H]. \tag{17}$$

3.3   Support Vector Machine Classifier

The goal of SVM method is to find a hyperplane of high dimensional space which can be used for classification [18]. SVM is a powerful classifier. It projects low dimension features into higher dimension using kernel functions which can solve the inseparable cases [53]. There are different types of kernel functions used in implemented classifiers. The polynomial kernel used in our work is defined as follows [17]:

$$K(x \cdot z) = (gamma \cdot x^T \cdot z + coef)^d. \tag{18}$$

where $x, z \in R^n$, $gamma$, and $coef$ are the kernel parameters, d denotes the order of the polynomial kernel and T is the transpose operation. More information on SVM classifiers can be found in [18].

4   Experiment

We designed and carried out two experiments with audio and visual external stimuli to collect EEG data based on the Valence-Arousal-Dominance emotion model. The obtained EEG data with different emotional labels were used to test the proposed algorithm.

4.1   Stimuli

In Experiment 1, sound clips selected from the International Affective Digitized Sounds (IADS) database [13] that follows the Valence-Arousal-Dominance emotion model were used to induce emotions. The choice of sound clips is based on their Valence, Arousal and Dominance level rating in the IADS database. The experiment is composed of 8 sessions, and 5 clips targeting one emotion were played in each session. The details of stimuli used to target emotions in each session are given in Table 1.

In Experiment 2, we elicited emotions with visual stimuli selected from International Affective Picture System (IAPS) database [41].The experiment was also composed of 8 sessions, and 4 pictures targeting one emotion were shown in each session. The details of stimuli targeting emotions in each session are given in Table 2.

Table 1. Stimuli used in Experiment 1

Session No.	Targeted States	Stimuli No.
Session1	Positive/ Low arousal/ Low dominance (PLL)	170, 262, 368, 602, 698
Session2	Positive/ Low arousal/ High dominance(PLH)	171, 172, 377, 809, 812
Session3	Positive/ High arousal/ Low dominance (PHL)	114, 152, 360, 410, 425
Session4	Positive/ High arousal/ High dominance (PHH)	367, 716, 717, 815, 817
Session5	Negative/ Low arousal/ Low dominance (NLL)	250, 252, 627, 702, 723
Session6	Negative/ Low arousal/ High dominance (NLH)	246, 358, 700, 720, 728
Session7	Negative/ High arousal/ Low dominance (NHL)	277, 279, 285, 286, 424
Session8	Negative/ High arousal/ High dominance (NHH)	116, 243, 280, 380, 423

Table 2. Stimuli used in Experiment 2

Session No.	Targeted States	Stimuli No.
Session1	Positive/ Low arousal/ Low dominance (PLL)	7632, 5890, 5982, 7497
Session2	Positive/ Low arousal/ High dominance(PLH)	5000, 1604, 2370, 5760
Session3	Positive/ High arousal/ Low dominance (PHL)	5260, 1650, 8400, 849
Session4	Positive/ High arousal/ High dominance (PHH)	5626, 8034, 8501, 8200
Session5	Negative/ Low arousal/ Low dominance (NLL)	2682, 2753, 9010, 9220
Session6	Negative/ Low arousal/ High dominance (NLH)	2280, 7224, 2810, 9832
Session7	Negative/ High arousal/ Low dominance (NHL)	6230, 6350, 9410, 9940
Session8	Negative/ High arousal/ High dominance (NHH)	2458, 3550.2, 2130, 7360

4.2   Subjects

In Experiment 1, there are a total of 14 (9 females and 5 males) subjects participating in the experiment. In Experiment 2, there are a total of 16 (9 females and 7 males) subjects participating in the experiment. All of them are university students and staff whose age ranged around 20 to 35 years old and without auditory deficit or any history of mental illness.

4.3   Procedure

After a participant was invited to a project room, the experiment protocol and the usage of a self-assessment questionnaire were explained to him/her. The subjects needed to complete the questionnaire after the exposure to the audio/visual stimuli. The Self-Assessment Manikin (SAM) technique [12] was employed which used the 3D model with valence, arousal and dominance dimensions and nine levels indicating the intensity in all dimensions. In the questionnaire, the subjects were also asked to describe their feelings in any words including the emotions like happy, surprised, satisfied, protected, angry, frightened, unconcerned, sad or any other emotions they feel. The experiments were done with one subject at each time. The audio experiment was conducted following the standard procedure for emotion induction with audio stimuli [22,42]. Therefore, in Experiment 1, the participants were asked to close their eyes to avoid artifacts and to be focused on hearing. In Experiment 2, the subjects were asked to avoid making movement except working on the keyboard.

The design of each session in Experiment 1 is as follows.

1. A silent period is given to the participant to calm down (12 seconds).
2. The subject is exposed to the sound stimuli (5clips x 6 seconds/clip=30 seconds).
3. The subject completes the self-assessment questionnaire.

In summary, each session lasted 42 seconds plus the self-assessment time.

The construction of each session in Experiment 2 is as follows.

1. A black screen is shown to the participant (3 seconds).
2. A white cross in the center of the screen is given to inform the subject that visual stimuli will be shown (4 seconds).
3. The subject is exposed to the pictures (4 pictures x 10 seconds/clip=40 seconds).
4. The black screen is shown to the participant again (3 seconds).
5. The subject completes the self-assessment questionnaire.

In summary, each session lasted 50 seconds plus the self-assessment time.

4.4   EEG Recording

In this work, we used Emotiv [2] device with 14 electrodes located at AF3, F7, F3, FC5, T7, P7, O1, O2, P8, T8, FC6, F4, F8, AF4 and these locations are standardized by the American Electroencephalographic Society [3] (plus CMS/DRL as references) for both Experiment 1 and 2. The technical parameters of the device are given as follows: bandwidth - 0.2-45Hz, digital notch filters at 50Hz and 60Hz; A/D converter with 16 bits resolution and sampling rate of 128Hz. The data are transferred via a wireless receiver. Recently, Emotiv devices have become popular for research [54,59]. The reliability and validity of the EEG data collected by Emotiv device was done in [21,68]. EEG data recorded from standard EEG device and Emotiv were compared, and the results showed that the

Emotiv device could be used as the standard EEG device in real-time applications where fewer electrodes were needed [68] and it is creditable to be used in applications such as games [21].

4.5 Analysis of Self-assessment Questionnaire

Even though the stimuli were selected with targeted emotional states, we found out from the self-report questionnaire records that some emotions were not confirmed by the subjects. Our analysis was based on the questionnaire which gave us the recorded participants' feelings. We did not consider the data from the cases when the targeted emotion was not induced according to the self-assessment questionnaire record.

Since the aim of this work is to develop an algorithm to detect up to 8 emotions defined by combinations of high/low arousal levels, positive/negative valence levels, and high/low dominance levels, and in the benchmark DEAP database (described in Section 4.6) and two experiments' databases the self-assessment questionnaire has 9 levels rating in each emotional dimension, the level 5 was used as the thresholds to identify high and low values at each dimensional level as shown in Table 3. Here, 5 is considered as an intermediate level which does not belong to neither a high nor a low state, thus the data with rating 5 were not used in the following processing. For example, if the targeted emotion is Positive/Low arousal/Low dominance, then the subject's data will be considered compatible with the targeted emotion if the subject's rating for valence dimension is larger than 5, the rating for arousal dimension is lower than 5, and the rating for dominance level is lower than 5.

Table 3. The conditions of different states in the analysis of self-assessment questionnaire

Emotional Dimension	Targeted States	Conditions
Valence Dimension	Positive	Valence rating> 5
	Negative	Valence rating< 5
Arousal Dimension	High	Arousal rating> 5
	Low	Arousal rating< 5
Dominance Dimension	High	Dominance rating> 5
	Low	Dominance rating< 5

4.6 Affective EEG Database DEAP

Since EEG-based emotion analysis is attracting more and more attention, the DEAP database labeled with emotions was established and published [35]. It has a relatively large amount of subjects (32 subjects) who participated in the data collection. The stimuli to elicit emotions used in the experiment are 40 one-minute long music videos. In the DEAP database, a Biosemi ActiveTwo device with 32 EEG channels [1] was used for the data recording, which could give a more comprehensive understanding of brain activity.

There are a number of datasets available in the DEAP database. Here, we used the dataset after preprocessing [36]. The sampling rate of the original recorded data is 512 Hz, and the set of preprocessed data are down sampled to 128 Hz. The artifacts such as EOG were removed from the DEAP EEG data during the preprocessing. As suggested by the developers of DEAP, this dataset is well-suited to those who want to test their own algorithms. Thus, in our work, we used this dataset to validate the algorithm. More details about the DEAP database can be found in [35] and [36].

5   Implementation

5.1   Fractal Features

In this work, the FD values were proposed to be used as features to improve the accuracy of emotion recognition from EEG signals. To calculate one FD value per finite set of time series samples, the Higuchi algorithm described in Section 3.2 was implemented and validated on the standard mono fractal signal generated by the Weierstrass function where the theoretical FD values were known in advance [49]. The size of the finite set N defines the size of the window in our emotion recognition algorithm. Fig. 1 shows the result of the calculation of FD values of the signals generated by the Weierstrass function with different window sizes. As it is seen from the graph, the FD values calculated with the window size equal to 512 samples are more close to the theoretical values. Thus, in our algorithm, the size of the window of 512 samples was chosen. For each window size N, we used different t_{max} values ranging from 8 to 64 in (15)-(16) to compute the FD values. With $N = 512$, the value of t_{max} was set to 32 since it has the lowest error rate as shown in Fig. 2.

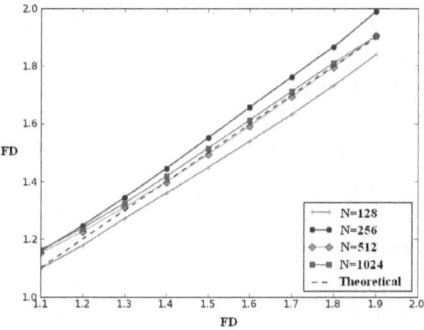

Fig. 1. FD values of the signals generated by the Weierstrass function calculated by the Higuchi algorithm with different window sizes

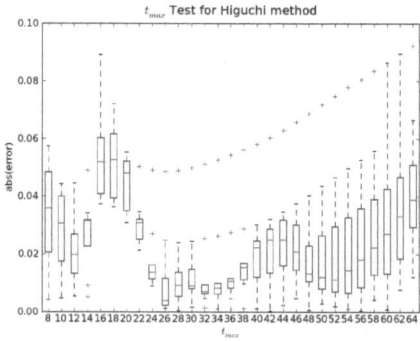

Fig. 2. Abs(error) for different t_{max} with $N = 512$

5.2   Channel Choice

The classical FDR method [34] was applied for the channel selection [7,19,40]. A non-overlapping sliding window with size of 512 samples was used for FD feature calculation. Channel ranking for 32 subjects from the DEAP database was calculated. In DEAP databases, there are 40 experimental trials labelled with arousal, valence and dominance ratings, and in our case (recognition of 8 emotions), for every subject, one trial was selected per emotion. As a result, up to 8 trials EEG data were selected with the corresponding emotions such as PLL, PLH, PHL, PHH, NLL, NLH, NHL, and NHH in the following processing. If the subject has more than one trial that labeled with the same emotions, the trial with extreme rating will be selected. For example, for the state of Arousal>5, Valence>5, Dominance>5, a trial with arousal rating 9, valence rating 8, dominance rating 8 will be used instead of a trial with arousal rating 6, valence rating 6, dominance rating 7. EEG data collected during playing the first 53 seconds of the video were used to calculate FD values in each session. The mean FDR scores for each channel were computed across all the 32 subjects. By using the data provided by the DEAP database, we can have more subjects to get a more general channel rank patterns. The final channel rank is FC5, F4, F7, AF3, CP6, T7, C3, FC6, P4, Fp2, F8, P3, CP5, O1, F3, P8, CP2, CP1, P7, Fp1, PO4, O2, Pz, Oz, T8, FC2, Fz, AF4, PO3, Cz, C4, FC1. The ranking of each channel is visualized in Fig. 3 using EEGLAB [20]. The visualization is based on the mean FDR scores across different subjects for each channel. It is a standard approach to use the channel rank to show spatial pattern. For example, [7] visualizes the weights of the spatial filters obtained from the sparse common spatial pattern (SCSP) algorithm. [40] uses the channel rank score to show the activated brain regions during the motor imagination tasks. The values were scaled for better visualization. From the figure, it can be seen that the frontal lobe is the most active because the most discriminant channels belong to the frontal lobe. Previous research has confirmed that the orbitofrontal cortex, anterior cingulated cortex, amygdala, and insula are highly involved in emotion processing

[69]. For example, it shows that negative emotions increase the amygdale activation [14]. However, the subcortical structures such as amygdala cannot be detected directly by EEG signals which are recorded from the scalp. The amygdale connects and interacts with frontal cortex and emotions are experienced as a result [11,31]. The visualization in Fig. 3 complies with the above-mentioned findings about the importance of frontal lobe in the emotion processing. Then, we followed the final channel rank to calculate the classification accuracy and to choose the number of the channels for our algorithm. The Support Vector Machine classifier described in Section 3.3, implemented by LIBSVM [17] with polynomial kernel for multiclass classification was used to compute the accuracy of emotion recognition using a different number of channels following the rank. 5-fold cross validation of the data was applied: first, the raw data were partitioned into 5 sets without overlapping, and then features were extracted from each set. During the classification phase, 4 sets were used as training sets, and 1 set was used as validation data for testing. The process was run 5 times, and every set was used as the testing data for once. The mean accuracy of the classification in 5 runs was computed as the final estimation of the classification accuracy. The cross-validation can allow us to avoid the problem of over fitting [28]. The parameters of the SVM classifier were set according to [55] where high accuracy of emotion classification was achieved with different feature types as follows: the value of *gamma* in (18) was set to 1, *coef* was set to 1 and order d was set to 5. A grid-search approach was also applied to select the SVM kernel parameters, and the classification accuracy of emotion recognition showed that the above-mentioned parameters were the optimal choice. Fig. 4 shows the mean accuracy of emotion classification over the number of the best channels following the obtained channel rank for subjects who have EEG data labeled with 8, 7, 6 and 5 emotions. Here, FD features were used in the classification, and they were calculated by using a sliding window with size of 512 and moving by 128 new samples (the overlapping rate was 384/512) each time. As it is shown in Fig. 4, in order to minimize the number of channels used, based on the accuracy, the top 4 channels are considered as the optimum choice that can be used for emotion recognition with an adequate accuracy. These 4 channels including FC5, F4, F7, and AF3 electrode positions correspond to the frontal lobe location (Fig. 5). It complies with research results described in [9,30,37,71] where correlation between emotions and the signal activities in the frontal lobe was studied, and the close relationship is confirmed. The frontal lobe is believed to execute processes that require intelligence such as determination and assessment. Human emotions are also associated with the frontal lobe. [9] finds that the damage in prefrontal cortex may cause a weakened or even disabled generation of certain emotions; [37] shows that the prefrontal lobe area plays a role in linking reward to subject's pleasantness; [30] confirms that there is a lateralization pattern in the frontal lobe when processing positive and negative emotions; [71] discovers an asymmetrical pattern in the frontal lobe during the observation of pleasant/unpleasant advertisements.

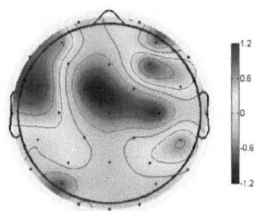

Fig. 3. Visualization of the ranking of 32 channels on the scalp

5.3 Feature Extraction and Classification

We present a subject-dependent algorithm of human emotion recognition from EEG based on the Valence-Arousal- Dominance emotion model. The algorithm consists of two parts: features extraction with a sliding window and data classification with Support Vector Machine (SVM) in order to accomplish efficient emotion recognition. In our work, a 2-42 Hz bandpass filter was applied to the data since it could remove artifacts such as muscle contraction and control [6,33]. We extract features from the entire EEG band from 2-42Hz instead of decomposing it to different frequency bands such as Alpha or Beta waves as it was done in [70] and [74]. As it was shown in Section 5.2, the FC5, F4, F7, and AF3 channels were chosen for the algorithm implementation. The feature vector FV for emotion classification is defined as follows:

$$FV = [FV_1, FV_2, FV_3, FV_4].$$ (19)

where 1 denotes FC5 channel, 2 denotes F4 channel, 3 denotes F7 channel, 4 denotes AF3 channel, and FV_i is the feature vector per channel. Here, the FV_i is composed by the statistical features given in (8), HOC features given in (12), FD features given in (17) or the combinations of different features $FV_{combination_1}$ and $FV_{combination_2}$ as given below in (20) and (21). Normalization is applied to the FD, statistical features and HOC features across the four channels in (19).

$$FV_{combination_1} = [\mu_X, \sigma_X, \delta_X, \overline{\delta_X}, \gamma_X, \overline{\gamma_X}, dim_H].$$ (20)

$$FV_{combination_2} = [D_1, D_2, ..., D_k, \mu_X, \sigma_X, \delta_X, \overline{\delta_X}, \gamma_X, \overline{\gamma_X}, dim_H].$$ (21)

Here, $FV_{combination_1}$ employs 6 statistical and 1 FD features, $FV_{combination_2}$ employs HOC features, 6 statistical and 1 FD features. In (20) and (21), normalization is applied to the statistical features, HOC features, and FD features across the four channels before combining the features. As it was determined in Section 5.1 and 5.2, to obtain training and testing samples for the SVM classifier, a sliding window with the size of 512 with 384 samples overlapping was used to calculate the statistical features (as in (8)), HOC features (as in (12)), and the combined features (as in (20) and (21)). In the DEAP database, the

EEG data collected from 60 seconds when the videos were played were used. As in Experiment 1 only 5 clips were selected in each session, EEG data collected from the first 30 seconds when the sound clips were exposed to the subjects were used. In Experiment 2, EEG data collected from the first 30 seconds when the pictures were shown to the subjects were used. Different HOC orders (k in (12)) were tested using the data labeled with all possible 4 emotions combinations from the 6 subjects who had EEG data with 8 emotions in the DEAP database. The results are shown in Table 4. To save computation time and reduce the size of feature dimension, $k=36$ is the optimal choice. This choice of k is also consistent with the setting in [55], where the optimal choice of HOC order k is set to 36. After feature extraction, the Support Vector Machine classifier with polynomial kernel implemented by LIBSVM [17] (as described in Section 3.3) was used to classify the data. Since in Experiment 1 and 2, the experiments' duration is relatively shorter than in the DEAP database, 4-fold cross validation was applied.

6   Results and Discussion

After the analysis of the questionnaires, in the DEAP database, we have got EEG data labeled with 8 emotions from 6 subjects, namely Subject 7, 8, 10, 16, 19, and 20. For each subject, EEG data from one trial labeled with one of the eight emotions were used in the following processing. In Experiment 1, we have got EEG data labeled with 5 emotions from 1 subject, with 3 emotions from 4 subjects, and with 2 emotions from 6 subjects. In Experiment 2, we have got EEG data labeled with 6 emotions from 2 subjects, with 5 emotions from 1 subject, with 4 emotions from 2 subjects, with 3 emotions from 4 subjects and with 2 emotions from 5 subjects.

Fractal Dimension analysis could be used to quantify the nonlinear property of EEG signals [4]. In this algorithm, we propose to combine FD feature with other best features to improve the classification performance of emotion recognition. Using just 1 FD feature solely has better accuracy than using 6 statistical features or 36 HOC features for some subjects. For example, as it shown in Fig. 6, FD features outperforms the other two types of features in the recognition of NHL and PLL, NHL and NLH, NHL and NLL, PHH and NLH, PLL and NLH for Subject 10; NHL and PHL, NHH and PHH, NHH and PHL for Subject 19 in DEAP database.

In Fig. 7, FD values spatial patterns show that FD values can be used to differentiate 8 emotions. Here, the FD values are calculated from 6 subjects in DEAP database who have 8 emotions' data available. The pattern is obtained as follows. First, the FD values are calculated using the 512 sliding window with 75% overlapping from each channel and subject. Then, the calculated values are averaged across all 57 samples of FD values from each channel per emotion. Secondly, the mean FD values are scaled to -1, 1 across all 32 channels for each subject per emotion. Finally, the scaled mean FD values in step 2 are

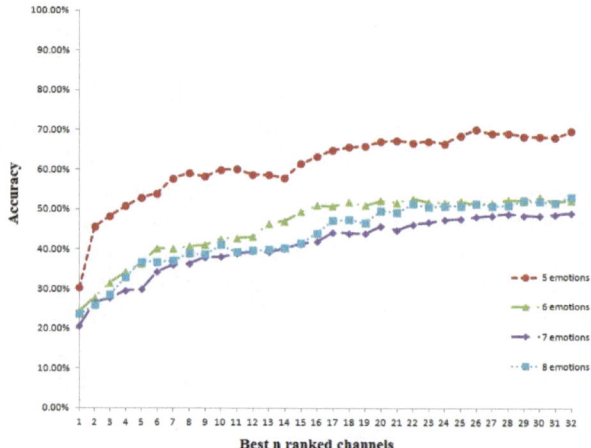

Fig. 4. Mean accuracy of emotions classification of the subjects' data with 5 to 8 emotions

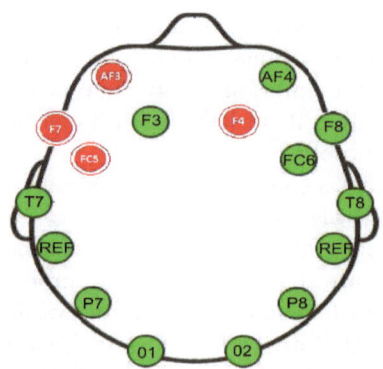

Fig. 5. Positions of the 4 channels (FC5, F4, F7, and AF3)

Table 4. Parameter choice for HOC features

	$k = 10$	$k = 20$	$k = 36$	$k = 50$
Mean Accuracy	49.76%	49.67%	50.13%	50.15%

averaged cross all 6 subjects per emotion and visualized on the brain map. As it can be seen from Fig. 7, different emotions have different spatial patterns, and the frontal lobe is always active (in red or yellow). Higher FD values of EEG reflect higher activity of the brain. FD value can be used for differentiation of valence dimension in the Valence-Arousal-Dominance model [47]. It can be seen from Fig. 7 that in negative emotions such as (a) frightened, (b) angry, (g) unconcerned, (h) sad, the spatial pattern shows that the right hemisphere is more active than the left one, and in (a) frightened, (b) angry, the right hemisphere is more active than the right hemisphere in (g) unconcerned and (h) sad emotions. In positive emotions such as (c) happy, (d) surprise, (e) protected, (f) satisfied, the spatial pattern shows that the left semisphere is more active than the right one, and the left hemisphere is more active in (c) happy, (d) surprise than the left hemisphere in (e) protected, (f) satisfied emotions.

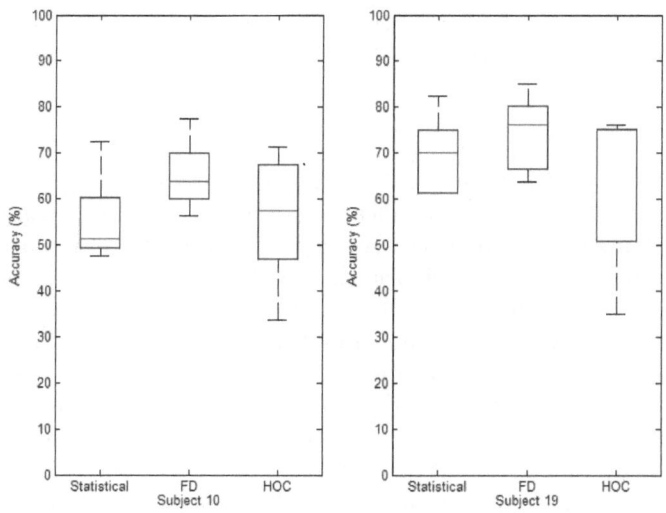

Fig. 6. The comparison of classification accuracies using statistical features, FD, HOC features of Subject 10 and 19

In Table 5, the comparisons of mean accuracy of the emotion classification for 8 emotions using the data from the DEAP database for combination of HOC, 6 statistical and 1 FD features, combination of 6 Statistical and 1 FD feature, 6 statistical features, and HOC features are shown respectively. The accuracy of fewer emotional states was computed as the mean value for all possible combination of emotions in the group across all subjects. For example, the mean accuracy of 2 out of 8 emotions was calculated as follows. Since we have 8 emotions in total, the 2 emotions combinations could be (PHH and PHL), (PLH and NHH), (PLL and NLL), etc. For each subject, there are 28 possible combinations for choosing 2 emotions from 8 emotions. The mean accuracy over 28 combinations

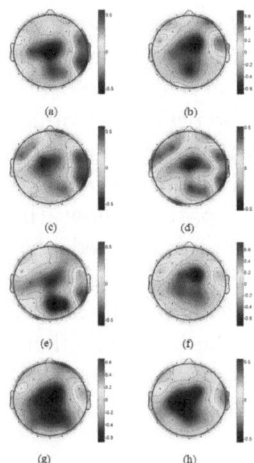

Fig. 7. The visualization of FD pattern for 6 subjects from DEAP with 8 emotions: (a) frightened, (b) angry, (c) happy, (d) surprise, (e) protected, (f) satisfied, (g) unconcerned, and (h) sad

for each subject was calculated, and the mean accuracy over 6 subjects is given in the table. As expected, the classification accuracy increases when the number of emotions recognized is reduced. A one-way ANOVA was performed on the results of the recognition of 4 emotions, and the statistical test was applied to the accuracy by using the combination of HOC, 6 statistical, and FD features and by using other features. As shown in Table 6, the statistical results showed that the proposed combined features when Fractal Dimension feature was included (HOC, 6 statistical and 1 FD) are statistically superior to using solely HOC (p=6.8926e-071) or 6 statistical features (p=0.0056). As can be seen from the Table 5, using the combination of HOC, 6 statistical and 1 FD features has slightly higher accuracy than using the combination of 6 statistical and 1 FD, however, no significant difference is found between these two combined features (p=0.42). Thus, both combinations of features could be used.

Table 5. The classification accuracy computed using the DEAP database

Feature type	Number of emotions recognized						
	8	7	6	5	4	3	2
HOC+6 statistical +FD	53.7	56.24	59.3	63.07	67.9	74.36	83.73
6statistical +FD	52.66	55.28	58.37	62.2	67.08	73.69	83.2
6 statistical	50.36	53.04	56.19	60.07	65.07	71.9	82
HOC	32.6	35.55	39.23	43.92	50.13	58.88	72.66

Table 6. F-values and p-values of the ANOVA tests applied on the accuracy of proposed combined features (HOC, 6 statistical, FD) and the other features

Feature	F-value	p-value
Statistical Features	7.72	<0.01
HOC	385.4	<0.01
6statistical, FD	0.44	0.42

We also validated our algorithm on the data from our own databases (Experiment 1 and 2). The results are presented in Table 7 and 8 correspondingly. The accuracy of fewer emotional states is the mean across all subjects who have the data that are labeled with the corresponding number of emotions. For example, the accuracy for 2 emotions recognition in Table 7 is the average across all 11 subjects in Experiment 1 with their corresponding 2 emotions recognition results. The results in Table 7 and 8 also support our conclusion that the combination of HOC, 6 statistical and 1 FD features or 6 statistical features with 1 FD feature is the optimal choice for real-time applications. The algorithm accuracy improves from 68.85% to 87.02% or 86.17% in Experiment 1 and from 63.71% to 76.53% or 76.09% in Experiment 2 when combinations of HOC, 6 statistical and 1 FD features or 6 statistical features and 1 FD feature were used comparing to HOC features. As it can be seen from Table 5, 7, 8, the classification accuracies for the same number of emotions are comparable among three databases, which gives positive support to the use of the proposed algorithm in real-time EEG-based emotion recognition. The computation time to extract one new sample of the combined feature in Matlab is less than 0.1 second and classifying this sample by SVM takes less than 0.05 seconds. Thus the algorithm can be used in real time.

Since the DEAP dataset has up to 32 channels, we also investigated the relationship between the number of channels and the classification accuracy in Table 9. The increasing of the channels follows the channel rank given in Section 5.2. With 32 channels we can improve the accuracy of our algorithm from 53.7% to 69.53% for recognition of 8 emotions and from 83.73% to 90.35% for recognition of 2 emotions.

When comparing our algorithm with others, it can recognize more emotions, obtain better accuracy with fewer electrodes, and it can be used in real time. For example, 32 channels were used in [42] whereas only 4 channels are needed in our algorithm with an accuracy of 87.02% for recognition of 2 emotions and 53.7% for recognition of 8 emotions. Using the same number of channels, [15] achieved 57.04% accuracy for recognition of 2 emotions, which are lower than ours.

Table 7. The classification accuracy computed using Experiment 1 database

Feature type	Number of emotions recognized			
	5	4	3	2
HOC+6 statistical +FD	61.67	67.08	74.44	87.02
6statistical +FD	55	62.08	75.11	86.17
6 statistical	56.67	61.67	72.72	84.94
HOC	35	42.08	53.17	68.85

Table 8. The classification accuracy computed using Experiment 2 database

Feature type	Number of emotions recognized				
	6	5	4	3	2
HOC+6 statistical +FD	56.6	60.6	58.36	65.52	76.53
6statistical +FD	59.03	62.08	59.86	65.78	76.09
6 statistical	56.94	62.45	55.78	63.73	76.45
HOC	35.42	42.82	42.46	44.43	63.71

Table 9. Investigation of using more channels in the DEAP database

Number of channels	Number of emotions recognized						
	8	7	6	5	4	3	2
1	38.33	41.76	45.82	50.76	57.04	65.5	77.98
2	42.03	45.37	49.26	53.95	59.82	67.6	79.06
3	49.27	52.23	55.79	60.12	65.54	72.57	82.53
4	53.7	56.24	59.3	63.07	67.9	74.36	83.73
16	65.63	67.93	70.53	73.58	77.3	82.09	88.79
32	69.53	71.43	73.73	76.53	80	84.41	90.35

7   Conclusion

In this paper, we proposed a real-time subject-dependent algorithm based on the Valence-Arousal-Dominance emotion model. The algorithm can recognize up to 8 emotions such as happy, surprised, satisfied, protected, angry, frightened, unconcerned, and sad with the best average accuracy of 53.7% using 4 electrodes. 2 emotions can be recognized with the best average accuracy of 87.02% using 4 electrodes. The algorithm consists of two parts: features extraction and classification. The combination of features (HOC, 6 statistical and 1 FD) that gave the best emotion classification accuracy was chosen for the algorithm implementation. The algorithm uses just 4 channels that made it more applicable as less time is needed to mount 4 electrodes. The algorithm was tested using two experimental EEG databases with data collected using the Emotiv EPOC device: one with audio stimuli and the other with visual stimuli. It was also tested on the DEAP benchmark database where video stimuli were used for emotion induction. The accuracy of the proposed algorithm was similar on all databases. By using different databases, it is confirmed that the proposed algorithm is device independent as we get similar accuracy using the EEG data collected by two different devices: 14 EEG channels Emotiv Epoch and 32 EEG channels Biosemi ActiveTwo device. It is also confirmed that our algorithm is stimuli independent since our algorithm is tested on the EEG databases created using audio, visual and video stimuli. The channel selection was performed using the DEAP database as it had 32 subjects and combination of audio and visual stimuli, and FC5, F4, F7, and AF3 channels were chosen for our algorithm implementation. The accuracy of the algorithm was tested on all databases following the fixed channel choice. The proposed algorithm can be used in any EEG-enabled applications such as advertising [45], music therapy [65] and other serious games developments [27]. The combination of EEG and other biosignals should be investigated in the future.

Acknowledgments. This research was done for Fraunhofer IDM@NTU, which is funded by the National Research Foundation (NRF) and managed through the multi-agency Interactive & Digital Media Programme Office (IDMPO) hosted by the Media Development Authority of Singapore (MDA).

References

1. Biosemi, `http://www.biosemi.com`
2. Emotiv, `http://www.emotiv.com`
3. American electroencephalographic society guidelines for standard electrode position nomenclature. Journal of Clinical Neurophysiology 8(2), 200–202 (1991)
4. Accardo, A., Affinito, M., Carrozzi, M., Bouquet, F.: Use of the fractal dimension for the analysis of electroencephalographic time series. Biological Cybernetics 77(5), 339–350 (1997)
5. Aftanas, L.I., Lotova, N.V., Koshkarov, V.I., Popov, S.A.: Non-linear dynamical coupling between different brain areas during evoked emotions: An EEG investigation. Biological Psychology 48(2), 121–138 (1998)
6. Anderson, E.W., Potter, K.C., Matzen, L.E., Shepherd, J.F., Preston, G.A., Silva, C.T.: A user study of visualization effectiveness using EEG and cognitive load. Computer Graphics Forum 30(3), 791–800 (2011)
7. Arvaneh, M., Cuntai, G., Kai Keng, A., Chai, Q.: Optimizing the channel selection and classification accuracy in EEG-Based BCI. IEEE Transactions on Biomedical Engineering 58(6), 1865–1873 (2011)
8. Aspiras, T.H., Asari, V.K.: Log power representation of EEG spectral bands for the recognition of emotional states of mind. In: 8th International Conference on Information, Communications and Signal Processing (ICICS 2011), pp. 1–5 (2011)
9. Bechara, A., Damasio, H., Damasio, A.R.: Emotion, decision making and the orbitofrontal cortex. Cerebral Cortex 10(3), 295–307 (2000)
10. Bolls, P.D., Lang, A., Potter, R.F.: The effects of message valence and listener arousal on attention, memory, and facial muscular responses to radio advertisements. Communication Research 28(5), 627–651 (2001)
11. Bos, D.O.: EEG-based emotion recognition (2006), `http://hmi.ewi.utwente.nl/verslagen/capita-selecta/CS-Oude_Bos-Danny.pdf`

12. Bradley, M.M.: Measuring emotion: The self-assessment manikin and the semantic differential. Journal of Behavior Therapy and Experimental Psychiatry 25(1), 49–59 (1994)
13. Bradley, M.M., Lang, P.J.: The international affective digitized sounds (2nd edn., IADS-2): Affective ratings of sounds and instruction manual. Tech. rep., University of Florida, Gainesville (2007)
14. Burgdorf, J., Panksepp, J.: The neurobiology of positive emotions. Neuroscience & Biobehavioral Reviews 30(2), 173–187 (2006)
15. Cao, M., Fang, G., Ren, F.: EEG-based emotion recognition in Chinese emotional words. In: Proceedings of CCIS 2011, pp. 452–456 (2011)
16. Chanel, G., Rebetez, C., Betrancourt, M., Pun, T.: Emotion assessment from physiological signals for adaptation of game difficulty. IEEE Transactions on Systems, Man, and Cybernetics Part A: Systems and Humans 41(6), 1052–1063 (2011)
17. Chang, C.C., Lin, C.J.: LIBSVM: a library for support vector machines (2001), http://www.csie.ntu.edu.tw/~cjlin/libsvm
18. Cristianini, N., Shawe-Taylor, J.: An introduction to Support Vector Machines: and other kernel-based learning methods. Cambridge University Press, New York (2000)
19. D'Alessandro, M., Esteller, R., Vachtsevanos, G., Hinson, A., Echauz, J., Litt, B.: Epileptic seizure prediction using hybrid feature selection over multiple intracranial EEG electrode contacts: a report of four patients. IEEE Transactions on Biomedical Engineering 50(5), 603–615 (2003)
20. Delorme, A., Makeig, S.: EEGLAB: An open source toolbox for analysis of single-trial EEG dynamics including independent component analysis. Journal of Neuroscience Methods 134(1), 9–21 (2004)
21. Duvinage, M., Castermans, T., Dutoit, T., Petieau, M., Hoellinger, T., Saedeleer, C.D., Seetharaman, K., Cheron, G.: A P300-based quantitative comparison between the emotiv epoc headset and a medical EEG device. In: Proceedings of the 9th IASTED International Conference on Biomedical Engineering, pp. 37–42 (2012)
22. Gao, T., Wu, D., Huang, Y., Yao, D.: Detrended fluctuation analysis of the human EEG during listening to emotional music. J. Elect. Sci. Tech. Chin. 5, 272–277 (2007)
23. Hadjidimitriou, S., Zacharakis, A., Doulgeris, P., Panoulas, K., Hadjileontiadis, L., Panas, S.: Sensorimotor cortical response during motion reflecting audiovisual stimulation: evidence from fractal EEG analysis. Medical and Biological Engineering and Computing 48(6), 561–572 (2010)
24. Hadjidimitriou, S.K., Zacharakis, A.I., Doulgeris, P.C., Panoulas, K.J., Hadjileontiadis, L.J., Panas, S.M.: Revealing action representation processes in audio perception using fractal EEG analysis. IEEE Transactions on Biomedical Engineering 58(4), 1120–1129 (2011)
25. Higuchi, T.: Approach to an irregular time series on the basis of the fractal theory. Physica D: Nonlinear Phenomena 31(2), 277–283 (1988)
26. Hosseini, S.A., Khalilzadeh, M.A.: Emotional stress recognition system using EEG and psychophysiological signals: Using new labelling process of EEG signals in emotional stress state. In: 2010 International Conference on Biomedical Engineering and Computer Science (ICBECS), pp. 1–6. IEEE (2010)
27. Hou, X., Sourina, O.: Emotion-enabled haptic-based serious game for post stroke rehabilitation. In: Proceedings of VRST 2013, pp. 31–34 (2013)
28. Hsu, C.W., Chang, C.C., Lin, C.J.: A practical guide to support vector classification. Tech. rep., National Taiwan University, Taipei (2003)

29. Huang, D., Guan, C., Kai Keng, A., Haihong, Z., Yaozhang, P.: Asymmetric spatial pattern for EEG-based emotion detection. In: The 2012 International Joint Conference on Neural Networks (IJCNN), pp. 1–7 (2012)

30. Jones, N.A., Fox, N.A.: Electroencephalogram asymmetry during emotionally evocative films and its relation to positive and negative affectivity. Brain and Cognition 20(2), 280–299 (1992)

31. Kandel, E.R., Schwartz, J.H., Jessell, T.M., et al.: Principles of neural science, vol. 4. McGraw-Hill, New York (2000)

32. Kedem, B.: Time Series Analysis by Higher Order Crossing. IEEE Press, New York (1994)

33. Khosrowabadi, R., Wahab bin Abdul Rahman, A.: Classification of EEG correlates on emotion using features from gaussian mixtures of EEG spectrogram. In: 2010 International Conference on Information and Communication Technology for the Muslim World (ICT4M), pp. E102–E107. IEEE (2010)

34. Kil, D.H., Shin, F.B.: Pattern recognition and prediction with applications to signal characterization. AIP series in modern acoustics and signal processing. AIP Press, Woodbury (1996)

35. Koelstra, S., Muhl, C., Soleymani, M., Lee, J.S., Yazdani, A., Ebrahimi, T., Pun, T., Nijholt, A., Patras, I.: DEAP: A database for emotion analysis using physiological signals. IEEE Transactions on Affective Computing 3(1), 18–31 (2012)

36. Koelstra, S., Muhl, C., Soleymani, M., Lee, J.S., Yazdani, A., Ebrahimi, T., Pun, T., Nijholt, A., Patras, I.: DEAP dataset (2012), http://www.eecs.qmul.ac.uk/mmv/datasets/deap

37. Kringelbach, M.L.: The human orbitofrontal cortex: Linking reward to hedonic experience. Nature Reviews Neuroscience 6(9), 691–702 (2005)

38. Kulish, V., Sourin, A., Sourina, O.: Analysis and visualization of human electroencephalograms seen as fractal time series. Journal of Mechanics in Medicine and Biology 26(2), 175–188 (2006)

39. Kulish, V., Sourin, A., Sourina, O.: Human electroencephalograms seen as fractal time series: Mathematical analysis and visualization. Computers in Biology and Medicine 36(3), 291–302 (2006)

40. Lal, T.N., Schroder, M., Hinterberger, T., Weston, J., Bogdan, M., Birbaumer, N., Scholkopf, B.: Support vector channel selection in BCI. IEEE Transactions on Biomedical Engineering 51(6), 1003–1010 (2004)

41. Lang, P., Bradley, M., Cuthbert, B.: International affective picture system (IAPS): Affective ratings of pictures and instruction manual. Technical report a-8, University of Florida, Gainesville, FL (2008)

42. Lin, Y.P., Wang, C.H., Jung, T.P., Wu, T.L., Jeng, S.K., Duann, J.R., Chen, J.H.: EEG-based emotion recognition in music listening. IEEE Transactions on Biomedical Engineering 57(7), 1798–1806 (2010)

43. Liu, Y., Sourina, O., Nguyen, M.K.: Real-time EEG-based human emotion recognition and visualization. In: Proc. 2010 Int. Conf. on Cyberworlds, Singapore, pp. 262–269 (2010)

44. Liu, Y., Sourina, O., Nguyen, M.K.: Real-time EEG-based emotion recognition and its applications. In: Gavrilova, M.L., Tan, C.J.K., Sourin, A., Sourina, O. (eds.) Transactions on Computational Science XII. LNCS, vol. 6670, pp. 256–277. Springer, Heidelberg (2011)

45. Liu, Y., Sourina, O.: EEG-based emotion-adaptive advertising. In: Proc. ACII 2013, Geneva, pp. 843–848 (2013)

46. Liu, Y., Sourina, O.: EEG databases for emotion recognition. In: Proc. 2013 Int. Conf. on Cyberworlds, Japan (2013)

47. Liu, Y., Sourina, O.: Real-time fractal-based valence level recognition from EEG. In: Gavrilova, M.L., Tan, C.J.K., Kuijper, A. (eds.) Transactions on Computational Science XVIII. LNCS, vol. 7848, pp. 101–120. Springer, Heidelberg (2013)
48. Lutzenberger, W., Elbert, T., Birbaumer, N., Ray, W.J., Schupp, H.: The scalp distribution of the fractal dimension of the EEG and its variation with mental tasks. Brain Topography 5(1), 27–34 (1992)
49. Maragos, P., Sun, F.K.: Measuring the fractal dimension of signals: morphological covers and iterative optimization. IEEE Transactions on Signal Processing 41(1), 108–121 (1993)
50. Mauss, I.B., Robinson, M.D.: Measures of emotion: A review. Cognition and Emotion 23(2), 209–237 (2009)
51. Mehrabian, A.: Framework for a comprehensive description and measurement of emotional states. Genetic, Social, and General Psychology Monographs 121(3), 339–361 (1995)
52. Mehrabian, A.: Pleasure-arousal-dominance: A general framework for describing and measuring individual differences in temperament. Current Psychology 14(4), 261–292 (1996)
53. Noble, W.S.: What is a support vector machine? Nat. Biotech. 24(12), 1565–1567 (2006)
54. O'Regan, S., Faul, S., Marnane, W.: Automatic detection of EEG artefacts arising from head movements. In: 2010 Annual International Conference of the IEEE Engineering in Medicine and Biology Society (EMBC), pp. 6353–6356 (2010)
55. Petrantonakis, P.C., Hadjileontiadis, L.J.: Emotion recognition from EEG using higher order crossings. IEEE Transactions on Information Technology in Biomedicine 14(2), 186–197 (2010)
56. Petrantonakis, P.C., Hadjileontiadis, L.J.: Adaptive emotional information retrieval from EEG signals in the time-frequency domain. IEEE Transactions on Signal Processing 60(5), 2604–2616 (2012)
57. Picard, R.W., Vyzas, E., Healey, J.: Toward machine emotional intelligence: Analysis of affective physiological state. IEEE Transactions on Pattern Analysis and Machine Intelligence 23(10), 1175–1191 (2001)
58. Pradhan, N., Narayana Dutt, D.: Use of running fractal dimension for the analysis of changing patterns in electroencephalograms. Computers in Biology and Medicine 23(5), 381–388 (1993)
59. Ranky, G.N., Adamovich, S.: Analysis of a commercial EEG device for the control of a robot arm. In: Proceedings of the 2010 IEEE 36th Annual Northeast Bioengineering Conference, pp. 1–2 (2010)
60. Russell, J.A.: Affective space is bipolar. Journal of Personality and Social Psychology 37(3), 345–356 (1979)
61. Schaaff, K., Schultz, T.: Towards emotion recognition from electroencephalographic signals. In: 3rd International Conference on Affective Computing and Intelligent Interaction and Workshops, ACII 2009, pp. 1–6 (2009)
62. Soleymani, M., Pantic, M., Pun, T.: Multimodal emotion recognition in response to videos. IEEE Transactions on Affective Computing 3(2), 211–223 (2012)
63. Sourina, O., Kulish, V.V., Sourin, A.: Novel tools for quantification of brain responses to music stimuli. In: Proc. of 13th International Conference on Biomedical Engineering, ICBME 2008, pp. 411–414 (2008)
64. Sourina, O., Liu, Y.: A fractal-based algorithm of emotion recognition from EEG using arousal-valence model. In: BIOSIGNALS, pp. 209–214 (2011)
65. Sourina, O., Liu, Y., Nguyen, M.K.: Real-time EEG-based emotion recognition for music therapy. Journal on Multimodal User Interfaces 5(1-2), 27–35 (2012)

66. Sourina, O., Sourin, A., Kulish, V.: EEG data driven animation and its application. In: Gagalowicz, A., Philips, W. (eds.) MIRAGE 2009. LNCS, vol. 5496, pp. 380–388. Springer, Heidelberg (2009)
67. Stam, C.J.: Nonlinear dynamical analysis of EEG and MEG: Review of an emerging field. Clinical Neurophysiology 116(10), 2266–2301 (2005)
68. Stytsenko, K., Jablonskis, E., Prahm, C.: Evaluation of consumer EEG device Emotiv EPOC. Poster session presented at MEi: CogSci Conference 2011, Ljubljana (2011)
69. Szily, E., Kéri, S.: Emotion-related brain regions. Ideggyógyászati Szemle 61(3-4), 77 (2008)
70. Takahashi, K.: Remarks on emotion recognition from multi-modal bio-potential signals. In: 2004 IEEE International Conference on Industrial Technology, vol. 3, pp. 1138–1143 (2004)
71. Vecchiato, G., Toppi, J., Astolfi, L., De Vico Fallani, F., Cincotti, F., Mattia, D., Bez, F., Babiloni, F.: Spectral EEG frontal asymmetries correlate with the experienced pleasantness of tv commercial advertisements. Medical and Biological Engineering and Computing 49(5), 579–583 (2011)
72. Wang, Q., Sourina, O., Nguyen, M.K.: EEG-based "serious" games design for medical applications. In: Proc. 2010 Int. Conf. on Cyberworlds, Singapore, pp. 270–276 (2010)
73. Wang, Q., Sourina, O., Nguyen, M.: Fractal dimension based neurofeedback in serious games. The Visual Computer 27(4), 299–309 (2011)
74. Zhang, Q., Lee, M.: Analysis of positive and negative emotions in natural scene using brain activity and gist. Neurocomputing 72(4-6), 1302–1306 (2009)

Author Index